Studies in Celtic History XXVIII

THE CULT OF SAINTS AND THE VIRGIN MARY IN MEDIEVAL SCOTLAND

This volume examines the phenomena of the cult of saints and Marian devotion as they were manifested in Scotland, ranging from the early medieval period to the sixteenth century. It combines general surveys of the development of the study of saints in the early and later middle ages with more focused articles on particular subjects, including St Waltheof of Melrose, the obscure early medieval origins of the cult of St Munnu, the short-lived martyr cult of David, duke of Rothsay, and the Scottish saints included in the greatest liturgical compendium produced in late medieval Scotland, the Aberdeen breviary. The way in which Marian devotion permeated late medieval Scottish society is discussed in terms of the church dedications of the twelfth and thirteenth-century aristocracy, the ecclesiastical landscape of Perth, the depiction of Mary in Gaelic poetry, and the pervasive influence of the familial bond between holy mother and son in representations of the Scottish royal family.

STUDIES IN CELTIC HISTORY

ISSN 0261–9865

General editors
Dauvit Broun
Máire Ní Mhaonaigh
Huw Pryce

Studies in Celtic History aims to provide a forum for new research into all aspects of the history of Celtic-speaking peoples throughout the whole of the medieval period. The term 'history' is understood broadly: any study, regardless of discipline, which advances our knowledge and understanding of the history of Celtic-speaking peoples will be considered. Studies of primary sources, and of new methods of exploiting such sources, are encouraged.

Founded by Professor David Dumville, the series was relaunched under new editorship in 1997. Proposals or queries may be sent directly to the editors at the addresses given below; all submissions will receive prompt and informed consideration before being sent to expert readers.

Professor Dauvit Broun, Department of History (Scottish), University of Glasgow, 9 University Gardens, Glasgow G12 8QH

Dr Máire Ní Mhaonaigh, St John's College, Cambridge, CB2 1TP

Professor Huw Pryce, School of History, Welsh History and Archaeology, Bangor University, Gwynedd LL57 2DG

For titles already published in this series
see the end of this volume

THE CULT OF SAINTS
AND THE VIRGIN MARY
IN MEDIEVAL SCOTLAND

Edited by

STEVE BOARDMAN
EILA WILLIAMSON

THE BOYDELL PRESS

First published 2010
The Boydell Press, Woodbridge

ISBN 978–1–84383–562–2

The Boydell Press is an imprint of Boydell & Brewer Ltd
PO Box 9, Woodbridge, Suffolk IP12 3DF, UK
and of Boydell & Brewer Inc.
668 Mt Hope Avenue, Rochester, NY 14620, USA
website: www.boydellandbrewer.com

A catalogue record of this publication is available
from the British Library

The publisher has no responsibility for the continued existence or
accuracy of URLs for external or third-party internet websites referred to
in this book, and does not guarantee that any content on such websites
is, or will remain, accurate or appropriate

This publication is printed on acid-free paper

Printed and bound in Great Britain by
CPI Antony Rowe, Chippenham and Eastbourne

CONTENTS

ILLUSTRATIONS AND TABLES

CONTRIBUTORS

HELEN BIRKETT is a Mellon Fellow at the Pontifical Institute of Mediaeval Studies in Toronto

STEVE BOARDMAN is a Reader in Scottish History, School of History, Classics and Archaeology, University of Edinburgh

RACHEL BUTTER is an Honorary Research Associate, Department of Celtic and Gaelic, University of Glasgow

THOMAS OWEN CLANCY is Professor of Celtic, Department of Celtic and Gaelic, University of Glasgow

DAVID DITCHBURN is a Senior Lecturer in Medieval History, Trinity College Dublin

The late AUDREY-BETH FITCH was Associate Professor of History, California University of Pennsylvania, Pittsburgh, USA

MARK A. HALL is History Officer, Perth Museum & Art Gallery

MATTHEW H. HAMMOND is a Lecturer in Scottish History, School of History, Classics and Archaeology, University of Edinburgh

SÌM R. INNES is a postgraduate student in the Department of Celtic and Gaelic, University of Glasgow

ALAN MACQUARRIE is a Research Associate in History, University of Strathclyde

ABBREVIATIONS

Abdn. Reg.	*Registrum Episcopatus Aberdonensis*, ed. Cosmo Innes, Spalding and Maitland Clubs, 2 vols (Edinburgh, 1845)
Aberdeen Breviarium	*Breviarium Aberdonense*, facsimile edition, ed. William Blew, 2 vols, Bannatyne, Maitland and Spalding Clubs (London, 1854)
AHRC	Arts and Humanities Research Council
APS	*The Acts of the Parliaments of Scotland*, eds Thomas Thomson and Cosmo Innes, 12 vols (Edinburgh, 1814–75)
BA	*Breviarium Aberdonense* (Edinburgh, 1509/10)
BL	London, British Library
CDS	*Calendar of Documents relating to Scotland preserved in Her Majesty's Public Record Office, London*, ed. Joseph Bain, 4 vols (Edinburgh, 1881–8); *Calendar of Documents relating to Scotland preserved in the Public Record Office and the British Library*, vol. v, eds Grant G. Simpson and James D. Galbraith ([Edinburgh], n.d.)
Chron. Bower	Walter Bower, *Scotichronicon*, ed. D. E. R. Watt et al., 9 vols (Aberdeen and Edinburgh, 1987–98)
CSSR	*Calendar of Scottish Supplications to Rome*
Dunf. Reg.	*Registrum de Dunfermelyn*, ed. Cosmo Innes, Bannatyne Club (Edinburgh, 1842)
EETS	Early English Text Society
ER	*The Exchequer Rolls of Scotland*, eds John Stuart et al., 23 vols (Edinburgh, 1878–1908)
Forbes, *Kalendars*	Alexander Penrose Forbes, *Kalendars of Scottish Saints* (Edinburgh, 1872)
Glas. Reg.	*Registrum Episcopatus Glasguensis*, ed. Cosmo Innes, Maitland and Bannatyne Clubs, 2 vols (Glasgow and Edinburgh, 1843)
Inchaff. Chrs	*Charters, bulls and other documents relating to the abbey of Inchaffray*, ed. William Alexander Lindsay et al., Scottish History Society (Edinburgh, 1908)
IR	*Innes Review*
James IV Letters	*The Letters of James the Fourth 1505–13*, eds Robert Kerr Hannay and R. L. Mackie, Scottish History Society (Edinburgh, 1953)
James V Letters	*The Letters of James V*, eds Robert Kerr Hannay and Denys Hay (Edinburgh, 1954)
JMH	*Journal of Medieval History*
MRHS	Ian B. Cowan and David E. Easson, *Medieval Religious Houses: Scotland* (London, 1976)
NAS	Edinburgh, National Archives of Scotland

NLS	Edinburgh, National Library of Scotland
NMS	National Museums Scotland
ODNB	*Oxford Dictionary of National Biography*, eds H. C. G. Matthew and Brian Harrison, 60 vols (Oxford, 2004); also online at http://www.oxforddnb.com/
Pais. Reg.	*Registrum Monasterii de Passelet*, ed. Cosmo Innes, Maitland Club (Edinburgh, 1832)
PL	*Patrologiae cursus completes ... series Latina*, ed. J.-P. Migne, 221 vols (Paris, 1844–64)
PSAS	*Proceedings of the Society of Antiquaries of Scotland*
RCAHMS	The Royal Commission on the Ancient and Historical Monuments of Scotland
RMS	*Registrum Magni Sigilli Regum Scotorum. The Register of the Great Seal of Scotland*, eds John Maitland Thomson et al., Scottish Record Society, 11 vols (Edinburgh, 1882–1914; reprinted 1984)
RRS	*Regesta Regum Scottorum*, eds G. W. S. Barrow et al. (Edinburgh, 1960–)
RS	Rolls Series
RSS	*Registrum Secreti Sigilli Regum Scotorum*, eds M. Livingstone et al. (Edinburgh, 1908–)
St A. Lib.	*Liber Cartarum Prioratus Sancti Andree in Scotia*, ed. Thomas Thomson, Bannatyne Club (Edinburgh, 1841)
SHR	*Scottish Historical Review*
SHS	Scottish History Society
STS	Scottish Text Society
TA	*Accounts of the Lord High Treasurer of Scotland*, eds Thomas Dickson et al., 13 vols (1877–1978)
TNA	London, The National Archives

INTRODUCTION

This volume arises from a conference held in Edinburgh in September 2007 to mark the conclusion of an AHRC-funded project, *The Survey of Dedications to Saints in Medieval Scotland*. The publication includes chapters based on papers delivered at that conference, supplemented by a number of invited contributions. This is the second edited volume arising from the 'Dedications to Saints' project, the first, *Saints' Cults in the Celtic World*, having been published by Boydell and Brewer in 2009. The database compiled by the project team can be consulted at http://www.shca.ed.ac.uk/Research/saints/. The main aim of the project is to stimulate and facilitate research into the cult of saints and the associated themes of piety and religious enthusiasm in medieval Scotland.

The present volume contributes to this endeavour in two discrete, but interlinked, ways. First, the contributions of Clancy and Ditchburn have been designed as wide-ranging reviews, providing general comment on, and challenges to, the paradigms governing the scholarly study of saints and their cults in the early and late middle ages. Clancy's article concentrates on the various ways in which place-name evidence has been used to trace or analyse the development of saints' cults in early medieval Celtic societies. Clancy suggests that the investigation of place-names, church dedications, and hagiographical material relating to saints has too often been moulded to fit established scholarly paradigms, particularly through the tendency of earlier historians to treat these sources as useful guides to the 'real' lives and achievements of early medieval missionary saints in northern Britain or by the privileging, in both the surviving evidence and modern scholarship based on it, of those cults adopted and propagated by powerful ecclesiastical figures or institutions. While not dismissing the potential usefulness of these interpretative models in particular contexts, Clancy argues that historians should be aware of the limitations of these dominant paradigms and lays out a number of models which might provide alternative explanations for specific patterns in place-names and church dedications relating to early medieval saints. Clancy's chapter, then, proposes a more nuanced and rounded reading of the evidence, one that might recover richer and more complex historical processes, in which cults actually, or supposedly, based on early medieval figures could grow in popularity for a variety of reasons, or decline and disappear altogether, or be rediscovered (or invented) in subsequent ages.

Ditchburn's chapter, meanwhile, interrogates what he characterises as the 'McRoberts thesis', laid out in Monsignor David McRoberts's influential *Innes Review* article from 1968.[1] Ditchburn takes issue with McRoberts's argument that the emergence, development and celebration of 'native' saints' cults in fifteenth-century Scotland reflected and reinforced a growing 'national', and specifically anti-English, sentiment in religious observance. Instead, Ditchburn suggests that the devotional culture of late medieval Scotland seems largely to have mirrored wider trends in Western European piety, with an increased emphasis on cosmopolitan christocentric, biblical and, especially, Marian cults developing alongside, not in opposition to, a new (or renewed) interest in the veneration of local and regional figures. For Ditchburn, enthusiasm for local, regional or 'national' cults should not be viewed as something that precluded wider attachments, but as part of a continuum of religious feeling that might embrace a saint venerated in a single parish alongside devotion to the great universal cults of late medieval Europe.[2] Ditchburn's analysis of ship- and peasant-naming patterns in Scotland also raises fundamental questions about how far the concerns and interests of the clerical elite, obviously heavily represented in the surviving sources, were reflected in the devotional practices and behaviour of other social groups.

The reviews provided by Clancy and Ditchburn sit alongside a number of more focused studies covering a variety of topics. In some instances these chapters reinforce, or relate to, points raised by the general surveys. Rachel Butter's study of the cult of St Munnu, for example, touches on the issues mentioned by Clancy in terms of the difficulty of understanding and interpreting the appearance of early medieval saints as the foci for late medieval cults. The importance of treating the veneration of a particular saint as a malleable and mutable social phenomenon, subject to changing economic, political and ecclesiastical conditions, but also capable of displaying considerable continuity, is made obvious in Butter's examination of St Munnu's cult in medieval Argyll. Four chapters, meanwhile, highlight aspects of devotion to the Virgin Mary in late medieval Scotland and certainly tend to confirm Ditchburn's observations on the importance of Scottish engagement with the various manifestations of the Marian cult. Matthew Hammond examines how the twelfth- and thirteenth-century monarchs and aristocrats of Scotland displayed an increasing interest in Mary, Christ and the Holy Trinity as formal dedicatees for the religious houses and churches they founded or came to be associated with. The enthusiasm for Mary, which was shared by both 'native' and 'immigrant' families (insofar as those labels were still relevant), may have partly excluded or obscured established 'insular' saints and their cults, but Hammond suggests that this disengagement was by no

---

[1] David McRoberts, 'The Scottish Church and nationalism in the fifteenth century', *IR* 19 (1968), 3–14.

[2] Here Eamon Duffy's work on the proliferation and diversity of devotions to be found in late medieval England would seem to offer a useful comparison. Eamon Duffy, *The Stripping of the Altars: Traditional Religion in England 1450–1580* (London, 1992).

means universal and that many of these earlier cults continued to thrive and prosper into the fourteenth and fifteenth centuries. The late Audrey-Beth Fitch explores the portrayal of Mary's relationship to Jesus and the way in which it both reflected and shaped changing social expectations of the bond between mothers and their sons, with a particular emphasis on the significance of the Marian model as an exemplar for the conduct of Scottish queens. The chapter also traces the emergence of Mary as a source of salvation whose favour and support would be especially critical and effective on the day of judgement. The wide recognition of Mary as a type of 'super intercessor' does much to explain the intense and widespread veneration of the Virgin in Perth, highlighted in Mark Hall's survey of the religious houses founded in and around the medieval burgh. Sìm Innes's sensitive exploration of the depictions of the various personas of the Virgin within the Gaidhealtachd, particularly in Gaelic poetry, similarly reinforces the powerful contemporary appeal of Mary's unparalleled intercessory powers, most evocatively as the 'Empress of Hell', capable of descending into Satan's own realm to wrest the souls of her devotees from damnation.

The remaining chapters are less obviously grouped around discrete themes, although the contributions of Birkett and Boardman both concentrate on the contentious issues surrounding the recognition and promotion of sanctity. Birkett's careful examination of the debates within the Melrose community over the posthumous standing of St Waltheof reveals the various dilemmas faced by the monks of his house and the wider Cistercian order in deciding whether to support or suppress his claims to sanctity. While Birkett's work treats of a clerical figure whose personal piety and holiness were clearly the basis of his saintly reputation, Boardman's assessment of the shadowy martyr cult that grew up around David, duke of Rothesay (*ob.* 1402) deals with a very different kind of man. Rothesay's apparently degenerate life made him an unlikely focus for veneration, but the circumstances of his death encouraged both popular piety and devotion. The emergence of the Waltheof and Rothesay cults emphasises the uncertainty and contingency that could surround the development of any particular saintly devotion in the medieval period. In contrast, Alan Macquarrie's appraisal of the importance of the *Breviarium Aberdonense* as a source for the study of Scottish saints' cults, gives an insight into a clerical venture to direct popular veneration through the production of a national liturgy. Although Ditchburn provides some important caveats about the usefulness of the Breviary as a guide to the trends in popular piety within the kingdom at the close of the middle ages, the work remains the most significant and wide-ranging liturgical project undertaken by the medieval Scottish ecclesiastical hierarchy. At the least, then, the Breviary offers an invaluable insight into the thinking of senior figures within the Scottish church as they sought to create an official cycle of worship deemed to be appropriate for the subjects of James IV. As

Macquarrie emphasises, the Breviary is also valuable because it incorporates a range of earlier hagiographical material which is otherwise unknown and which might, with careful analysis, tell us much about the development of saints' cults long before the opening decade of the sixteenth century. The appearance of a full-scale modern edition of the Breviary, a project in which Macquarrie is currently engaged, is clearly at the top of the list of desiderata for scholars working on saints' cults in Scotland

THE BIG MAN, THE FOOTSTEPS, AND THE FISSILE SAINT: PARADIGMS AND PROBLEMS IN STUDIES OF INSULAR SAINTS' CULTS

Thomas Owen Clancy

In this chapter, the focus is primarily on the problems that beset investigating saints' cults in the early medieval period, something approached also in Rachel Butter's incisive case-study of St Munnu.[1] *The Survey of Dedications to Saints in Medieval Scotland*[2] is one of the most welcome developments in such investigations. First, it will help us understand the dynamism and evolution of saints' cults during the later medieval period, a period for which there remains a great deal of work to do, and much headway to be gained in refining and opening out our understanding of medieval Scottish piety and the nexus between society and religion. Second, and more importantly for this contribution, it will help to clarify for us what we do and do not know about the later medieval position of the cult of those saints already present in the Scottish landscape in the period before the twelfth century. It has become increasingly apparent in recent studies that no real progress can be made in our understanding of early medieval saints' cults without a firm grasp of the nature of the later medieval evidence for those cults. This is especially so, given the paucity of clear documentation cited for the likes of church dedications or fair days by key secondary sources like Mackinlay's *Ancient Church Dedications* and Watson's *Celtic Place-Names of Scotland*.[3] This chapter primarily addresses the evidence provided by one source which has had to remain largely outwith the remit of the Survey: place-name evidence.

Although my title promises to tackle approaches to the cults of saints in a wider insular context, factors of time and space have led me to focus on a number of problems particular to the use of saints' cults in the understanding

---

[1]   Rachel Butter, 'St Munnu in Ireland and Scotland: an exploration of his cult', in this volume.

[2]   Web address: http://www.shca.ed.ac.uk/Research/saints/; for a brief account of the survey, see Steve Boardman, 'The survey of dedications to saints in medieval Scotland', *IR* 59 (2008), 189–91.

[3]   James Murray Mackinlay, *Ancient Church Dedications in Scotland, vol. II: Non-Scriptural Dedications* (Edinburgh, 1914); W. J. Watson, *The History of the Celtic Place-Names of Scotland* (Edinburgh, 1926).

of the earlier middle ages in Scotland. The chapter has a wider insular, indeed Celtic, background, however, and it is hoped that the observations made will be helpful in other contexts as well. The problems and paradigms examined here have also been invoked and discussed in the context of studies of saints' cults in Ireland, Wales, Cornwall and Brittany. These Celtic regions have, and have been seen to have since medieval times, an unusually abundant crop of local or localised saints' cults.[4] This phenomenon – if it is one phenomenon and not several different ones – is capable of numerous explanations, but in every case a number of observations can be made fairly straightforwardly. First, this abundance of local or localised cults derives in the main from the period before the twelfth century, though as Rachel Butter discusses elsewhere in this volume, one cannot exclude the possibilities of introduction and dissemination of such cults in the later middle ages. That this is so is demonstrable because these cults appear to be present, in many cases enshrined, in place-names preserved in charters and related records, sometimes already by the twelfth century showing signs of misunderstanding and corrupt forms as the names crossed linguistic boundaries.[5] Second, then, this abundance of cults relates in some way to the ecclesiastical history of each region in the earlier middle ages. This is not to say that, as has sometimes been understood, the 'Celtic church' had a particular approach to sanctity or to church organisation that lent itself to such proliferation and localisation of cults (though, saving any sense that the 'Celtic church' is a valid concept,[6] it may be so), but rather it is to say that in each region, factors have been at work that have caused this phenomenon, and discovering the roots of it may allow us to catch some glimpse of the church history of each region.

It is this second hope that has tempted scholars over the years to employ the cults of saints as narrative tools for telling the ecclesiastical history of their regions. It should be said that this is least the case in the region for which there is the greatest abundance of evidence: Ireland. That historians of the Irish church have largely eschewed narratives derived from hagiography and other signs of the cults of saints, may tell us something about the extent

---

4   See in particular the observations in Oliver J. Padel, 'Local saints and place-names in Cornwall', in *Local Saints and Local Churches in the Early Medieval West*, eds Alan Thacker and Richard Sharpe (Oxford, 2002), 303–60; Karen Jankulak, 'Adjacent saints' dedications and early Celtic history', in *Saints' Cults in the Celtic World*, eds Steve Boardman, John Reuben Davies and Eila Williamson (Woodbridge, 2009), 91–118.

5   For example, Kilduncan and Kilconquhar in Fife, dedicated most probably to Dúnchad, abbot of Iona. The latter is first found in the form *Kilconcat* (1165×1169), with subsequent variant forms. See Simon Taylor with Gilbert Márkus, *The Place-Names of Fife, Volume 3: St Andrews and the East Neuk* (Donington, 2009), s.n., noting that Kilconquhar could instead be for an unknown saint Conchad; Simon Taylor, 'Place-names and the early church in eastern Scotland', in *Scotland in Dark-Age Britain*, ed. Barbara E. Crawford (St Andrews, 1995), 93–110, at 100 for discussion.

6   On this problem, see Kathleen Hughes, 'The Celtic Church: is this a valid concept?', *Cambridge Medieval Celtic Studies* 1 (1981), 1–20; Wendy Davies, 'The myth of the Celtic Church', in *The Early Church in Wales and the West*, eds Nancy Edwards and Alan Lane (Oxford, 1992), 12–21; Gilbert Márkus, 'Pelagianism and the "Common Celtic Church"', *IR* 56 (2005), 165–213.

to which these are useful historical tools, if there are other options available.[7] In Scotland, however, it has been a particularly unavoidable tool, given the paucity of early historical texts, and the proportion of those we have that are hagiographical in nature.[8]

On the other hand, Scotland's linguistic and cultural evolution has seemed to hold out greater hope of gaining some purchase on the chronology of saints' cults. Because regions have shifted their main language during the course of the early middle ages, and because place-names often preserve the names of saints, it has been thought that names might act as, essentially, fossil records of cult and church development. For instance, the preservation of the name of a saint in a linguistically Pictish context in eastern Scotland might be seen to point to the origins of that cult in the period before that language lost ground in the east.[9] In such a context it has been an understandable temptation to augment what we might seem to know about a saint such as Columba or Ninian by a consideration of the distribution of dedications to that saint. Taken as a study of the afterlife of such an individual (that is,

---

[7] It should be noted that this is not because Ireland lacks for hagiographical evidence. On the contrary, it has a very considerable corpus not just of saints' Lives, but also of a diverse array of other material relating to saints' dossiers: anecdota, martyrologies, genealogies, litanies, etc. Irish scholars have been at the forefront of more rigorous approaches to the construction and therefore historical usefulness of saints' Lives in the early medieval insular world: see especially the work of Máire Herbert, for example, *Iona, Kells and Derry: The History and Hagiography of the Monastic Familia of Columba* (Oxford, 1988; repr. Dublin, 1996). They have also pioneered approaches to the very complex ancillary material, such as saints' genealogies: see especially the work of Pádraig Ó Riain, for references to whose work see below, n. 12; Edel Bhreathnach, 'The genealogies of Leinster as a source for local cults', in *Studies in Irish Hagiography: Saints and Scholars*, eds John Carey, Máire Herbert and Pádraig Ó Riain (Dublin, 2001), 250–67; and also Thomas M. Charles-Edwards, 'Early Irish saints' cults and their constituencies', *Ériu* 54 (2004), 79–102. Scholars such as Ailbhe Mac Shamhráin have attempted to use these more refined approaches to hagiographical material to construct very different kinds of historical narrative; see, for example, his *Church and Polity in Pre-Norman Ireland: The Case of Glendalough* (Maynooth, 1996). For reviews of Irish hagiographical literature, see Máire Herbert, 'Hagiography', in *Progress in Medieval Irish Studies*, eds Kim McCone and Katharine Simms (Maynooth, 1996), 79–90; 'Latin and vernacular hagiography of Ireland from the origins to the sixteenth century', in *Hagiographies* III, ed. Guy Philippart (Brussels, 2001), 326–60.

[8] I am thinking of texts like Adomnán's Life of Columba, a key text for our understanding of the sixth and seventh centuries; or the Life of St Margaret, crucial for our understanding of the late eleventh century. For an intelligent approach to using this material as a historical source, see the work of Alan Macquarrie, *The Saints of Scotland: Essays in Scottish Church History, AD 450–1093* (Edinburgh, 1997); and for cautionary comments on the general approach, see Dauvit Broun, 'The literary record of St Nynia: fact and fiction?', *IR* 42 (1991), 143–50; Thomas Owen Clancy, 'The real St Ninian', *IR* 52 (2001), 1–29, esp. 1–2.

[9] An example might be that of Exmagirdle (*Eglesmagril*, 1211×1214), derived from the putatively Brittonic (here Pictish?) element *eclēs (< Latin *ecclesia*) with the name of a saint, probably Grillán, preceded by the first-person possessive pronoun *mo* often used in the formation of hypocoristic names for saints. It should be noted that although the place-name may be a Pictish one, the saint is probably Irish, one of the companions of St Columba. See G. W. S. Barrow, 'The childhood of Scottish Christianity: a note on some place-name evidence', *Scottish Studies* 27 (1983), 1–15, at 12, 7; Watson, *Celtic Place-Names of Scotland*, 519; Alan O. and Marjorie O. Anderson, *Adomnán's Life of Columba* (Edinburgh, 1961), 546–7.

as a study of cult proper), this is entirely valid as an approach. Scholars have over the years, however, been tempted to go the extra distance and make connections between historical activity and saints' dedications. These are the 'Footsteps' of my title, the notion that the distribution of dedications to a saint record, in some way, the activities of that saint.[10] Even where that has been at an early date seen as an inappropriate explanation of certain kinds of distribution, recourse has been had to the secondary notion that a saint through his followers, or through an expanding federation of churches looking to that saint as a patron, was somehow involved in the distribution of cult. This in a sense is the 'Big Man' paradigm referred to in my title, a paradigm that refers the cults of saints back to the activities of a very small group of original historical individuals who are seen as marking the main turning points in ecclesiastical history. A different way to view this, both from the point of view of modern scholarship and of the evolution of saints' cults, would be to think of the way in which those saints with effective hagiographical dossiers, particularly Latin Lives, based at effective centres of promotion, are to be seen in a dominant position within the dedicatory hierarchy of saints in Scotland.[11]

Since the 1970s, the researches of Professor Pádraig Ó Riain have provided yet another paradigm for understanding some of the proliferation of local and localised cults in Celtic regions.[12] Ó Riain's work has demonstrated the disturbing phenomenon of the 'Fissile Saint', the propensity for the cult of an original individual to divide over time into many separate local and localised cults as a result of a number of cogent pressures which may have been more important in a Celtic, and particularly in a Gaelic, context than elsewhere. These include, first, the tendency towards the formation of multiple hypocoristic names for saints along the lines of those demonstrable for the name lying behind St Columba: Columb, Mo Cholm, Colmán, Mo

---

[10] An example may be found in the work of W. Douglas Simpson, *The Historical Saint Columba* (Aberdeen, 1927); E. G. Bowen pursued this line of enquiry from a slightly different theoretical angle, but with many of the same presumptions: see especially his *Saints, Seaways and Settlements in the Celtic Lands* (Cardiff, 1969). For recent reviews of these paradigms as applied to other Celtic regions, see John Reuben Davies, 'The saints of south Wales and the Welsh church', in *Local Saints and Local Churches*, eds Thacker and Sharpe, 361–95, at 361–5; Susan Pearce, 'Saintly cults in south-western Britain: a review', in *Saints of Europe: Studies towards a Survey of Cults and Culture*, ed. Graham Jones (Donington, 2003), 261–79; Jankulak, 'Adjacent saints' cults'.

[11] I have commented on this issue in Clancy, 'Scottish saints and national identities in the early middle ages', in *Local Saints and Local Churches*, eds Thacker and Sharpe, 397–422.

[12] His main works on this subject include: 'Towards a methodology in early Irish hagiography', *Peritia* 1 (1981), 146–59; 'Cainnech alias Colum Cille, patron of Ossory', in *Folia Gadelica*, eds Pádraig de Brún, Seán Ó Coileáin and Pádraig Ó Riain (Cork, 1983), 20–35. 'Finnio and Winniau: a return to the subject', in *Ildánach Ildírech: A Festschrift for Proinsias Mac Cana*, eds John Carey, John T. Koch and Pierre-Yves Lambert (Andover and Aberystwyth, 1999), 187–202, restates his arguments regarding the complex of saints relating to these names and gives necessary previous bibliography.

Cholmóc, Mo Chonna, Do Chonna, Mo Chummai, etc.[13] Second, we can witness the localising tendencies of kindred interests and proprietorial attitudes towards churches and saints, which also gave rise to the extraordinary abundance of genealogies of saints in Ireland.[14] One might add to Ó Riain's researches the observation that in Celtic regions it may be that the very fact that Celtic toponymy created place-names along the order of {ecclesiastical toponymic element + saint's name}, whether that be Kilmacolm in Scotland, Donaghpatrick in Ireland, Llanbadarn in Wales, Constantine in Cornwall, or Locronan in Brittany, contributed both to the preservation of the memory of cult – even often the faintest traces – where elsewhere it might have been lost, and also to the propensity for division, reanalysis, and localisation. In other words, that a place has acquired the name *Cill Mo Choluim* at some stage in the early middle ages has preserved the memory of that church's dedication to a saint called Mo Cholum longer than might have happened had the church been called something else, and thereby also set in train a demand for local faithful to know, or discover, who their particular Mo Cholum was.

My main purpose in what follows is to suggest that a better understanding of the implications of saints' cults would be achieved by a greater openness about the fact that we interpret the available evidence of these cults using a number of different paradigms. No one paradigm provides the answer for the entirety of the evidence we have, in any of the Celtic regions, and a fuller appreciation of this will also help our growing appreciation of the dynamic nature of saints' cults, and the different ways in which churches, places, times and objects came to commemorate saints.

One example may help to ground this abstract observation in the concrete before we move on. This relates to the cult of St Ninian, a topic on which I have been controversially involved in recent years.[15] A number of critics of my 2001 article on St Ninian have pointed to the large and important medieval parish of Eccles, now St Ninians, Stirling, as one place where evidence of an early, probably pre-Northumbrian British church intersects with the cult of St Ninian.[16] This has long been a suggestive intersection. *Eccles* names

---

[13] The key review of this issue is Paul Russell, 'Patterns of hypocorism in early Irish hagiography', in *Saints and Scholars. Studies in Irish Hagiography*, eds John Carey, Máire Herbert, Pádraig Ó Riain (Dublin, 2001), 237–49; see also Ó Riain, 'Cainnech alias Colum Cille'.

[14] See Pádraig Ó Riain, 'Irish saints' genealogies', *Nomina* 7 (1983), 23–30; *idem*, 'Irish saints' cults and ecclesiastical families', in *Local Saints and Local Churches*, eds Thacker and Sharpe, 291–302; Thomas M. Charles-Edwards, '*Érlam*: the patron-saint of an Irish church', in *ibid.*, 267–90.

[15] Especially in 'The real St Ninian', *IR* 52 (2001), 1–28; see also Clancy, 'Scottish saints and national identities', 399–404.

[16] For criticism in general, see G. W. S. Barrow, *St Ninian and Pictomania* (Whithorn, 2004); John MacQueen, *St Nynia*, new edn (Edinburgh, 2005), 152–4. I am guessing that the absence of any reference to or engagement with either my article or that of James Fraser in Prof. MacQueen's 2006 Whithorn Lecture *Ninian and the Picts* (Whithorn, 2007) is an implicit form of criticism, or at least tantamount to a summary dismissal. The recently published papers from the 2007 Whithorn Study Day, *St Ninian and the Earliest Christianity in Scotland*, ed. Jane Murray

have been held to relate in some way to the early and British phase of the church in southern and central Scotland, as in parts of England;[17] the dedication to St Ninian is, aside from Whithorn, perhaps the earliest attested – it was certainly dedicated to him by 1242.[18] It seems to me that we stand our best chance of evaluating these two pieces of evidence dispassionately if we acknowledge the different paradigms through which we might interpret their intersection, and acknowledge also the difficulty of objectively choosing from among them the correct paradigm.

One paradigm would interpret the dedication as a record of the personal activity of the person commemorated. In this analysis, St Ninian's British background, the key location and seeming ancient connection with Stirling (which may or may not be the British fortress of Iudeu/Bede's *urbs Giudi*),[19] and the simplex name Eccles, all may combine to suggest that this is one of the many monasteries held to be founded by Ninian in the two eighth-century texts relating to his life.[20] In other words, this is a church founded by the saint to whom it is dedicated. A related, but less historically charged view would be to see the Eccles place-name here as fundamentally related to a British phase of Scottish church history, and to place the Ninian dedication as also a relic of this: that is, the continuation of a British commemoration of a British saint, at a site with a Brittonic ecclesiastical place-name. This more nuanced view would acknowledge the British background to both the saint and the place-name, but not necessarily view both as of equal antiquity.

My view of the Ninian question in 2001, while it has been somewhat altered or muted by the subsequent responses to it of both critics and supporters,[21]

(Oxford, 2009) make for an important new contribution. Jonathan Wooding's article addresses the 2001 proposal most directly, and finds judiciously against it, and I find some of his reasons persuasive: 'Archaeology and the dossier of a saint: Whithorn excavations 1984–2001', in *ibid.*, 9–18. I would, however, maintain that Bede's descriptions of Ninian, while not of course implausible (I have never argued they were), are too conveniently aligned with Northumbrian ecclesiastical agenda to be taken at face value.

17 Barrow, 'Childhood of Scottish Christianity'; see also K. Cameron, 'Eccles in English place-names', in *Christianity in Britain, 300–700*, eds M. W. Barley and R. P. C. Hanson (Leicester, 1968), 87–92.

18 On Eccles/St Ninians, see Alan Macquarrie, 'St Ninians by Stirling: a fragment of an early Scottish minster kirk', *Records of the Scottish Church History Society* 28 (1998), 39–54; A. A. M. Duncan's description of this as 'the one dedication to St Ninian most likely to be ancient' is quoted by Macquarrie, 42 (see Duncan, *Scotland: The Making of the Kingdom* (Edinburgh, 1975), 39–40). For the date of the dedication to Ninian, see Barrow, *Saint Ninian and Pictomania*, 11.

19 See on this most recently James E. Fraser, 'Bede, the Firth of Forth and the location of *Urbs Iudeu*', *SHR* 87 (2008), 1–25.

20 Bede, *Historia Ecclesiastica Gentis Anglorum* book III, ch. 4: *Bede's Ecclesiastical History of the English People*, eds Bertram Colgrave and R. A. B. Mynors (Oxford, 1969), 220–3; Winifred W. MacQueen, 'Miracula Nynie Episcopi', *Transactions of the Dumfriesshire and Galloway Natural History and Antiquarian Society* 38 (1960), 21–57. Of course a stumbling block here is that St Ninians by Stirling was not, according to most reckoning, in what would have been considered the kingdom of the Picts in Bede's day.

21 This is not the place to discuss some of the criticisms levelled at the article, some of which are entirely justified, but many of which cannot be easily sustained (MacQueen's contribution in

has not changed in one regard. Whatever we think of the historical person behind St Ninian, the *cult* of St Ninian is as we have it initially a Northumbrian phenomenon, and secondarily one belonging to the twelfth-century and later reforming church. The evidence we have provides no clear evidence of a pre-Northumbrian cult of Ninian. In this context it is important that recent studies are increasingly inclined to see the simplex Eccles names mainly in conjunction with those found in southern Scotland and northern England where *eclēs* has been incorporated as a specific within English place-names (Eccleshall, Eaglesham).[22] In other words, *eclēs*, although a term of British derivation, is in many cases in southern Scotland and northern England a linguistically English place-name element. If this is so in the case of Eccles/ St Ninians, then we should perhaps look to the evidence we have for Northumbrian interest in the Stirlingshire region from the mid-seventh to the eighth centuries – precisely the time when St Ninian's cult was being first propagated in Northumbrian circles.[23] Both the Eccles name and the dedication to St Ninian could, therefore, be seen as fundamentally part of the Northumbrian history of this region. Given the politicised nature of the eighth-century descriptions of Ninian's activities, he could easily be seen as a 'Northumbrian saint', despite his British background, and a dedication could therefore be seen as part of a Northumbrian statement about their control of the region.

---

particular suggests some wilful misreading). Nor do I wish to give the impression that my views on the issue are unaltered. However, both supporters and detractors have had a tendency to describe the argument advanced there as suggesting that 'St Ninian never existed' (see MacQueen, *St Nynia* (2005 edn), 152). This was not, of course, what I did suggest (rather, I suggested that his name as we have it may have been the victim of scribal error and its preservation in a largely literary environment until the twelfth century). The main point of the article – that all we know of the pre-twelfth-century cult of Ninian is channelled narrowly through texts produced in the polemicised environment of the eighth-century Northumbrian church – has unfortunately largely been passed over for the more controversial suggestions of the second and third part of the article. I accept a large part of the blame for this over-emphasis, and consequent skewing of the article's reception. For an inflected, though not uncritical building on the core case made in the article, see James E. Fraser, 'Northumbrian Whithorn and the making of St Ninian', *IR* 53 (2002), 40–59.

22 See Alan James, '*Eglēs/Eclēs* and the formation of Northumbria', in *The Church in Place-Names*, ed. Eleanor Quinton (Nottingham, 2009), 125–50; see also Carole Hough, 'Eccles in English and Scottish place-names', in *ibid.*, 109–24. Note the brief but cogent comments of Richard Sharpe on this issue, resulting in his conclusion: 'The survival of Eccles as a place-name element is therefore almost certain to depend on some other factor, such as its becoming a loan-word in Anglo-Saxon and being (however briefly) productive of place-names in English rather than Brittonic.' Sharpe, 'Martyrs and local saints in late antique Britain', in *Local Saints and Local Churches*, eds Thacker and Sharpe, 75–154, at 147. It should be cautioned that this issue is distinct from the situation in Scotland north of the Forth, and to a lesser extent south of it, where names in *eclēs* + a saint's name suggest a different and Celtic (Brittonic or Gaelic) context for coinage of these names. See Simon Taylor, 'Place-names and the early church in Scotland', *Records of the Scottish Church History Society* 28 (1998), 1–22, esp. 3–7. Neither Barrow, *Saint Ninian and Pictomania*, nor MacQueen, *Ninian and the Picts*, seem to have sufficiently taken on board the importance of Taylor's distinguishing these two different sets of *eclēs* place-names within the Scottish corpus.

23 The evidence is best reviewed in Peter Hunter Blair, 'The Bernicians and their northern frontier', in *Studies in Early British History*, ed. Nora Chadwick (Cambridge, 1939), 137–72.

Here our paradigm is one in which saints' cults relate to the values placed on particular saints by political or ecclesiastical groups. It may in this case be significant that among those *eclēs* place-names north of the Forth containing affixed saints' names, there are significant dedications to universal saints such as Peter, John and Martin.

Finally, although the dedication by 1242 may well suggest to some that it is an ancient church dedication, nonetheless the cult of St Ninian in Eccles/ St Ninians cannot be shown to antedate the thirteenth century, and we know there to have been interest in St Ninian during this period, including by one twelfth-century reformer who was intimately involved with the royal dynasty, Aelred of Rievaulx. This being so, there is nothing that would entirely militate against a new twelfth- or even thirteenth-century dedication to Ninian here, though the channels through which it happened would remain uncertain. I suspect the growth in the cult is not solely prompted by Aelred's Life – one must also remember that among the Scottish clergy in the twelfth century there was a much increased access to Bede and later historians using Bede. I have suggested, following Watson and others, that many, perhaps most medieval church dedications to St Ninian date from this later period, and correspond to the evolution of Ninian into a type of national saint, and I suspect that a detailed study of all the attested medieval Ninian dedications in their full context would help underpin this suspicion.[24]

There are two further points of interest here. One is that *all* of these phenomena may have some role to play in the dedication of this important medieval church to St Ninian. For the preservation of saints' cults, as crucial as the cause of the initial dedication is what ensures their continuity. As Matthew Hammond's contribution to this collection indicates, replacement and augmentation of saints' cults was a common feature, certainly of the central middle ages. In the case of St Ninians/Eccles, British, Northumbrian *and* twelfth-century Scottish church contexts may all have contributed to the reaffirmation of this church site's importance and association with the saint called Ninian – the last phase certainly contributing the form of his name as we first find it there.

The second point of interest relates to the proposed intersection between early church name and early saint. A point I did not sufficiently consider – indeed, a point which I think has not, in a Scottish context at least, been sufficiently considered – is the chronological horizon for the dedication of churches to saints by name, and the incorporation of those names into place-names. That this was already happening in a Gaelic context by *ca* 700 can be shown by the work of Adomnán,[25] but it is difficult to be so certain in

---

24 Watson, *Celtic Place-Names of Scotland*, 293–4; Clancy, 'Real St Ninian', 10.
25 Adomnán, *Vita Columbae*, i.31; Anderson and Anderson, *Adomnán's Life of Columba*, 268–9. See also the comments of Davies, 'Saints of south Wales', 392.

a British, especially a northern British context.[26] If in 2001 I made a great deal of the absence of place-names incorporating the name of St Nynia, I was wrong not to point out the virtual absence of linguistically Brittonic names from southern Scotland incorporating saints' names in this way at all.[27] Those securely Brittonic names we can associate with churches are not so constructed. That said, the paucity of any kind of non-literary evidence of Ninian's pre-twelfth-century cult remains striking, in relative terms, in contrast especially to prominent Northumbrian saints like Oswald and Cuthbert.

Paradigms

I would like to review in what follows some different kinds of paradigm I see as having been invoked to explain the introduction or spread of saints' cults in early medieval Scotland, and one or two which have been underplayed, and to suggest one or two instances where each of these may be the appropriate paradigms through which to view particular dedications or clusters of dedications.

'Foundational'

We would do well not to abandon completely the notion that some churches bear the dedication of the saint that founded them. There is no particular reason, for instance, to detach the Pictish St Drostan from the two important medieval churches in the northeast that bear his name: Aberdour and Deer.[28] Iona, Lismore, Applecross all bear dedications to those saints who are well attested historically as founders of these monasteries.[29] What all these share, however, is the nature of their names: none (with the exception of Iona in its modern Gaelic designation) incorporate the dedication in the name, and none at all use an ecclesiastical place-name generic. More complicated are instances such as Kingarth, on Bute, and its relationship with the medieval

---

[26] John Reuben Davies considers this strangely overlooked issue with considerable caution in 'Saints of south Wales', 361–95, esp. 391–4.

[27] A possible exception may be a few names employing the element *loc* 'church site' (<L. *locus*). I hope to examine these names in the future. On one prospective such name, see Andrew Breeze, 'St Kentigern and Loquhariot, Lothian', *IR* 54 (2003), 103–7. As noted above, the names in {*eclēs* + saint's name} seem to constitute a different subset, not certainly Brittonic in the context of their naming, given the prevalence of Gaelic saints as their specifics, and largely Pictish in their distribution. Taylor's work (see above, n. 22) would associate them with a date range of the late seventh and early eighth century, rather than anything earlier.

[28] On these see Mackinlay, *Ancient Church Dedications*, 214–19; Thomas Owen Clancy, 'Deer and the early church in north-eastern Scotland', in *Studies on the Book of Deer*, ed. Katherine Forsyth (Dublin, 2008), 363–97.

[29] Respectively Columba, Moluag (earlier Mo Luóc) and Mael-Ruba.

parish church of St Blane's – and the evidence for a Gaelic name *Kilblain* corresponding to it. This has recently been explored with considerable nuance by Rachel Butter in her doctoral thesis.[30] While the name *Kilblain* (which seems to have been an ephemeral name, and is presumably now St Blane's Church) clearly came about because of St Bláán's role in founding or ruling the monastery at Kingarth, it is not at all certain that the dedication as such of a church to a saint called Bláán is part of the same moment – that dedication may belong to a later phase in the evolution of the site and of Bute itself. We may say something similar, perhaps about the relationship of the place-name Kildonnan on Eigg to wherever St Donnan's original foundation was. That Donnan founded a monastery on Eigg is not in doubt. When a church dedicated to him, named Cill Donnáin, now Kildonnan, was founded and so named is less clear, and could be separated by some centuries from Donnan's time. I should note that John Davies has suggested similar things about certain sites in Wales.[31] What I am trying to say is that the foundational role of a saint in relation to a given church is not quite the same as the process by which a church becomes associated with him or her as its patron. This may be especially the case in those instances where originally monastic foundations later became primarily parish churches or similar; or where a monastic community has given rise to a related local church.

'Proprietary'

It may be well to mention one type of place-name 'dedication' that is little discussed or considered, but which may lie behind some, at least, of our place-names. Oliver Padel has discussed the real probability that in some ecclesiastical place-names incorporating personal names, those names are not those of saints as such, but rather those of individuals associated with the churches in a different way, either as secular donors of estate churches, or as the ecclesiastical personnel attached to or ruling the church at a key phase of its existence (for instance, when questions of property rights have arisen).[32] Equally, the person named may have been a founder, but not in the first instance regarded as a saint, so that the name, while it commemorates the individual, may not mark a saint's cult as such. In such an instance 'Colmán's church' for instance, might describe a church either founded by a man called Colmán as a patron (rather than as a religious founder) or currently managed by a clergyman called Colmán, or one of a number of variations on this theme. He might, of course, later be understood as a saint, or conflated with

---

[30] Rachel Butter, 'Cill- names and saints in Argyll : a way towards understanding the early church in Dál Riata?' (University of Glasgow, unpublished PhD thesis, 2007), 186–90.

[31] Davies, 'Saints of south Wales'.

[32] Padel, 'Local saints', 312–13.

one of the many saints called Colmán. We may think in this context of the church described by Adomnán as lying on the shores of Loch Awe, called by him *cella Diuni*, and as he says named after a man who was the brother of the church's *praepositus* during Columba's time.[33] There is no implication in anything Adomnán says that Diún was regarded as a saint, or a holy man; he may or may not have been the founder of the church. Indeed, Adomnán may be taken as implying that Columba was its founder and certainly its ultimate line manager. It is simply that in Adomnán's time his name had become attached to the church as a way of naming. Now it may be that this man came to be regarded as a saint, that his tomb was treated as containing the relics of a holy dead man. But this need not be the case. We must I think leave the door open for such a phenomenon lying behind some dedications. I should caution, though, that on the whole the majority of Scottish dedications should probably best be referred to the context of the cult of saints.

'Missionary'

Just as influential in its way as a model for explaining the dedication of places to particular saints has been a missionary model.[34] This sees the spread of cult as fundamentally related to the initial phases of the spread of christianity into particular areas. This is of course what has been long envisaged by those seeing an early date for Ninian dedications in Pictland, and is, indeed, the role that Bede envisaged for that saint. More profitable, one might think, would be to approach the dedications to St Columba as a marker of the known activities of Iona personnel in the conversion of the Picts, theoretically bearing the cult of their founder with them as their sphere of work expanded. Yet in fact studies of the spread of dedications to Columba by both Nollaig Ó Muraíle and Simon Taylor have shown remarkably little of promise in this area.[35] More persuasive has been Taylor's investigation of dedications to 'minor' Iona abbots of the seventh century, by no means all of whom were considered saints in any real sense, as well as two individuals dying in the early eighth century, Adomnán and Cóeti, whose cults are to be found well attested in Atholl, at Dull and Logierait among other sites.[36] Equally persuasive is Taylor's suggestion that major Columba dedications on Inch-

---

[33] Adomnán, *Vita Columbae* i.31; see Thomas Owen Clancy, 'Annat in Scotland and the origins of the parish', *IR* 46 (1995), 91–115, at 112–13.

[34] On the mission context in early medieval Europe generally, see Ian Wood, *The Missionary Life: Saints and the Evangelisation of Europe, 400–1050* (London, 2001).

[35] Nollaig Ó Muraíle, 'The Columban onomastic legacy', in *Studies in the Cult of Saint Columba*, ed. Cormac Bourke (Dublin, 1997), 193–228; Simon Taylor, 'Seventh-century Iona abbots in Scottish place-names', in *Spes Scotorum, Hope of Scots. Saint Columba, Iona and Scotland*, eds Dauvit Broun and Thomas Owen Clancy (Edinburgh, 1999), 35–70, esp. 36–40.

[36] Taylor, 'Seventh-century Iona abbots', 57–60.

mahome and Inchcolm reflect early routeways through to Lindisfarne.[37] Just as we cannot dismiss the foundational paradigm out of hand, so too there are some instances in which dedications may indeed reflect the real spread of the influence of certain churches, and the activities of individual churchmen like Bishop Cóeti or Abbot Dúnchad of Iona. Whether 'missionary' is precisely the right word for such activity, given the considerable baggage it carries, is a subsidiary question: the label will do for the moment.

'Reliquary'

Of course, discussion of cults of Iona saints in Atholl must come up abruptly against the fact that in 849 the church at Dunkeld became home to at least some of St Columba's relics,[38] and however long they stayed (some at least of his relics were taken in flight from Vikings to Ireland in 878), this Columban dimension to Dunkeld may have had some effect on the dedications of churches in the region to Iona personnel of the previous two centuries – we cannot demonstrate which came first. At the very least (bearing in mind a point I made above), this presence may have helped to stabilise some of those minor Iona cults putatively established earlier in the locale. Certainly, though, the evidence is there – in the Life of Cathroe among other places – to show that the royal dynasty of Alba had devotion not just to the cult of Columba, but also was able to 'call up' his relics for service in their battles.[39]

The development of this sort of relic cult has good parallels in Carolingian Europe, especially in royal contexts, but this case does highlight how little we know about the involvement of relics in the creation of saints' dedications in early medieval Scotland (or other Celtic regions for that matter). Although the presence of the bodies of saints at their foundations may be assumed, and the distribution of relics – primary or secondary – would also be expected, the evidence is mixed on this front, especially when it comes to bodily relics.[40] I think what is problematic here is the way in which Celtic hagiography tended to work: on the whole, instead of adopting a strategy of incorporating churches within the authority of a saint's hegemony by discussing relics and their power (as may be seen copiously elsewhere), hagiographers preferred

---

[37] *Ibid.*, 43–52, esp. 48.

[38] Marjorie O. Anderson, *Kings and Kingship in Early Scotland* (Edinburgh, 1980), 250; see John Bannerman, 'The Scottish takeover of Pictland', in *Spes Scotorum*, eds Broun and Clancy, 71–94; Thomas Owen Clancy, 'Iona, Scotland and the *céli Dé*', in *Scotland in Dark-Age Britain*, ed. Barbara E. Crawford (St Andrews, 1996), 111–30, at 114–15.

[39] Thomas Owen Clancy, 'Columba, Adomnán and the cult of saints in Scotland', in *Spes Scotorum*, eds Broun and Clancy, 3–34, at 26–30; Alan O. Anderson, *Early Sources of Scottish History* (Edinburgh, 1922), 440.

[40] See, for instance, discussion in Clancy, 'Columba, Adomnán and the cult of saints', 5–10.

to create narratives of the live activity of the saints themselves – much in the way of nineteenth-century scholars.

And yet some churches surely derive their dedications from relic cults. St Andrews is a prime example. Even if scholars have not been able to settle on a consensus view of when the cult of St Andrew reached Cennrígmonaid, the underlying story of its foundation legend, that relics of Andrew were at its basis, is thoroughly believable.[41] Equally, the cult of St Lawrence in Lawrencekirk is, I have suggested, perhaps traceable to the distribution of relics of Lawrence from Armagh, known to have them and to have been distributing them to subject churches, from the seventh century.[42]

'Organisational'

Another way of looking at patterns of dedications has been to think in terms of their reflecting organisational patterns of certain centres. John Davies has recently confirmed the extent to which dedications to St Teilo in south Wales probably do to some extent reflect early medieval allegiances to Llandeilo itself as a monastic centre, but has cautioned that similar spreads of dedications to other saints do not suggest this as a template to be employed consistently in our interpretations.[43] Here it should be said that in thinking about dedications as reflecting the organisation of church centres, we may still be talking about some of the earlier paradigms I have discussed – actual foundations, 'missionary' activity, the distribution of relics. A paradigm emphasising the role of church organisation in the presence of dedications to saints needs further models to explain the mechanisms involved in creating the dedications.

One of the most tempting clusters of dedications to approach from this point of view are those around the Sound of Raasay area – on the mainland, on Raasay, and on Skye – to St Maelrubha.[44] This cluster has an epicentre at Maelrubha's own monastic foundation, dating from the late seventh century, at Applecross in Wester Ross.[45] While of course dedications to Maelrubha as the pre-eminent local saint could have sprung up at any time during the middle ages (most of the Maelrubha dedications are not attested very early at all, in common with much of the rest of the West Highlands), it is tempting

41 J. E. Fraser, 'Rochester, Hexham and Cennrígmonaid: the movements of St Andrew in Britain, 604–747', in *Saints' Cults*, eds Boardman, Davies and Williamson, 1–17; Taylor, *Place-Names of Fife, vol. 3*, appendix 1.

42 Thomas Owen Clancy, 'The foundation legend of Laurencekirk revisited', *IR* 50 (1999), 83–8.

43 Davies, 'Saints of south Wales', 365–8, but see also the article in its entirety for his cautionary comments regarding employing this as a default explanation for dedications, for example, in the case of St Dyfrig.

44 See Bowen, *Saints, Seaways and Settlements*, 101, for a flawed but still useful distribution map of the cult.

45 See Watson, *Celtic Place-Names of Scotland*, 287–9.

to think of this area as in some sense the early medieval 'diocese'[46] of Apple-cross, and churches bearing his name, at least, bearing witness to this.

Perhaps the most sustained attempt to view dedications in this way in a Scottish context has been Raymond Lamb's discussion of the distribution of Peterkirks in Orkney, and his suggestion that these stem from an early eighth-century attempt at church reform and reorganisation there.[47] The nature of the evidence from Orkney is too fragile to either confirm or refute this hypothesis, though on the whole my inclination would be for a twelfth-century context for the bulk of these *dedications* (without wanting to suggest that some of the churches themselves were not constructed on earlier sites). That said, the cult of Peter in early medieval Scotland would repay a study in its own right. Too often it is aligned to Roman or Northumbrian interests, perhaps through an overly deterministic reading of Bede's use of church dedications to Peter. And yet, the inscribed stone from near Whithorn called the Peter stone reveals that there devotion to Peter the Apostle seems to have predated Northumbrian intervention – and it is far from alone in this, if we think in terms of Ireland, for instance.[48]

'Political'

That said, there is no doubt that Bede saw dedications to certain saints as a way of demarcating political allegiance, or more specifically ecclesiastical or doctrinal allegiance. When King Naiton of the Picts brought his kingdom and its churches over to the Roman dating of Easter, Bede tells us, he placed his kingdom under Peter's patronage and built a church in stone dedicated to him.[49] Whether or not this church is related to the lost Egglespether in Angus, the point is significant. Dedications could be public statements of political allegiance, rather than simply ecclesiastical genealogies or organisation.[50] This is how I have tended to understand the pattern of dedications to two saints found commemorated at two of the River Clyde's premiere churches: Kilpatrick, whose cult of St Patrick must date back at the very least to the eighth century, and Govan, with its less easily datable cult of the elusive

---

46 Some term that avoids the contentious term *paruchia* is demanded here.
47 Raymond Lamb, 'Carolingian Orkney and its transformation', in *The Viking Age in Caithness, Orkney and the North Atlantic*, eds Colleen E. Batey, Judith Jesch and Christopher D. Morris (Edinburgh, 1993), 260–71; idem, 'Pictland, Northumbria and the Carolingian Empire', in *Conversion and Christianity in the North Sea World*, ed. Barbara E. Crawford (St Andrews, 1998), 41–56.
48 See Katherine Forsyth, '*Hic Memoria Perpetua*: the early inscribed stones of southern Scotland in context', in *Able Minds and Practised Hands: Scotland's Early Medieval Sculpture in the 21st Century*, eds Sally M. Foster and Morag Cross (Leeds, 2005), 113–34, at 127–30.
49 Bede, *Historia Ecclesiastica*, v.21.
50 On this in the context of the twelfth and thirteenth centuries, see Matthew Hammond's contribution *infra*.

St Constantine.[51] Both saints have dedications of churches or church land on the upper Clyde (Constantine's church at Crawford is the southernmost in Lanarkshire and includes much of the uppermost reaches of the Clyde after its descent from the watershed); and in Dumfriesshire, including some significant Patrick dedications in Annandale. Fiona Edmonds has recently cautioned that these and other Patrick dedications in the southwest could reflect the Dublin origins of the Gaelic-Scandinavian settlers of the area in the tenth century and later, for which patterns of dedications to other, more obscure Leinster saints bear witness.[52] Nonetheless, I currently prefer to understand the Patrick and Constantine dedications within the context of the expansion of the kingdom of Cumbria during this same period, with these two saints standing essentially as emblematic saints for the Strathclyde dynasty. One could perhaps less readily incorporate the cult of Kentigern into this scenario, especially the prime site of Hoddom.[53]

'National/ethnic'

If we allow for these more political uses of saints and their cults to have lain behind some of our dedications, it may be difficult to distinguish between the politics of 'kingdoms' and of 'peoples' or nations. Were, we may ask, the cults of Northumbrian saints like Oswald and Cuthbert as found in southwest Scotland at sites like Kirkoswald and Kirkcudbright, particularly emblematic of English/Northumbrian ethnicity? In Galloway and Ayrshire, certainly, we might well wish to view the significant churches of Kirkcudbright, Ballantrae, and Kirkoswald, as mother churches dating from the time of the Northumbrian rule of this area. Did the introduction, whenever it may have been, of the cults of Argyll saints like Mo Luag and Maelrubha into eastern Scotland represent an intentional 'Gaelicisation' of cult in these areas? This is the view that Alex Woolf and I have put, via different formulations of the process involved, in recent work.[54]

51 Thomas Owen Clancy, 'The cults of Saints Patrick and Palladius in early medieval Scotland', in *Saints' Cults*, eds Boardman, Davies and Williamson, 18–40.

52 Fiona Edmonds, 'Personal names and the cult of Patrick in eleventh-century Strathclyde and Northumbria', in *Saints' Cults*, eds Boardman, Davies and Williamson, 42–65.

53 See John Reuben Davies, 'Bishop Kentigern among the Britons', in *Saints' Cults*, eds Boardman, Davies and Williamson, 66–90.

54 I suggested these approaches in 'Scottish saints and national identities', 409–16, but I am conscious that other paradigms may be applied to this evidence. See also Clancy, 'Deer and the early church', 387–9; Alex Woolf, 'The cult of Moluag, the See of Mortlach and church organisation in northern Scotland in the eleventh and twelfth centuries', in *Fil Súil nGlais. A Grey Eye Looks Back. Festschrift in Honour of Colm Ó Baoill*, eds Sharon Arbuthnot and Kaarina Hollo (Ceann Drochaid, 2007), 299–310.

'Emigratory'

It has long been recognised that there are a number of clusters of 'mirror' or parallel cults in Scotland. Two that have been most commented on are the mirrored dedications of Kintyre and western Ayrshire, with parallel dedications to, for example, Colmán Ela, Michael, Coinneach, Ciaran, etc.; and the sporadic appearance of Cowal and Bute saints in central Scotland (for example, Kessoc, Blane, Cattan).[55] Less well discussed are the interesting clusters of dedications in Caithness to saints with a northeast provenance for their cult, for instance, Drostan.[56] One way to understand some of these patterns might be in terms of larger population movements, whereby cults of the 'homeland' may be replicated elsewhere. I should note though that at least in terms of the Cowal and Bute saints, Alex Woolf has preferred to understand them in terms of movements of relics, and to see a largely Viking age context for such movements, something which may also lie behind the eastern dedications to Maelrubha and Mo Luag, for instance.[57] This does not seem to me to be a satisfactory solution for the run of mirrored church dedications in Kintyre and Ayrshire, however. Here, some process that allows for a considerable period of cross-firth contact and organisation, and a considerable commonality of population, at least at the level of those in control of estates and churches, seems to me by far the best way to understand this arrangement. For Caithness, there are good, albeit thirteenth-century, contexts for the relationship between northeastern Scotland and Caithness.[58]

'Fragmentation and localisation'

Of course, it cannot be certain whether the disruptions, dynastic changes, assaults on churches, and popular settlements of the Viking age served in some cases to disrupt continuity and memory of saints' cults or otherwise. Certainly we can point to cases where saints who may have once been understood as the same individual have become localised and transformed, though it is less easy to suggest how this has occurred. My own prime example of this is the cluster of dedications along the straths of the White Cart and the Garnock to saints who must ultimately go back to one cult. The dedications,

---

[55] I have commented on both of these sets in different contexts. See Thomas Owen Clancy, 'The Gall-Ghàidheil and Galloway', *Journal of Scottish Name Studies* 2 (2008), 19–50, at 44; 'Philosopher-King: Nechtan mac Der-Ilei', *SHR* 73 (2004), 125–49, at 140. The phenomenon was noted by Watson in the case of the Kintyre/Carrick names, *Celtic Place-Names of Scotland*, 173.

[56] See Simpson, *The Celtic Church in Scotland* (Aberdeen, 1935), 73–89, and see fig. 10 opposite p. 73; Clancy, 'Deer and the early church', 387–9.

[57] Alex Woolf, *From Pictland to Alba 789–1070* (Edinburgh, 2007), 102; *idem*, 'The cult of Moluag'.

[58] Barbara E. Crawford, 'The Earldom of Caithness and the Kingdom of Scotland, 1150–1266', in *Essays on the Nobility of Medieval Scotland*, ed. Keith Stringer (Edinburgh, 1985), 25–43.

at Inchinnan, Lochwinnoch, Beith, Kilwinning take a variety of names for the saint: Innan, Winnoc, Winnin, etc., but given their comparative contiguity, they should best be understood as relating to a single cult, that of a saint modern scholarship would call Uinniau, perhaps ultimately to be understood as St Finnian of Moville.[59] And yet each of these parishes seem to have had different understandings of their own saint, different names, feast days. What lies behind such fragmentation and localisation? This is particularly hard to explain given the strong influence of the monastery of Kilwinning in the local area, the cult of whose saint might have been expected to dominate these local realisations, but seems not to have, even in a parish like Beith which was early appropriated by Kilwinning.[60] This certainly suggests that the phenomenon is a pre-1100 one. Was there some sort of disruption to an originally coherent diocese or ecclesiastical unit, leading to its replacement by smaller units in which localisation was seen as beneficial?

'Kindred'

In an Irish context one of the factors that has been seen as lying behind some of the instances of 'fissile' saints has been the urge to domesticate saints, that is, to bring them into the kindred network of local families by making them saints 'of' those kin-groups – often by means of invented or elaborated genealogies.[61] My Colmán thereby becomes distinguishable from yours by attaching him to my family tree, or to that of the local ruling dynasty. There is much work to be done – and for the later middle ages the Survey's dedications database provides us with some ammunition in doing so – in tracing kindred allegiances to particular saints. Rachel Butter has elsewhere in this volume pointed in the direction of the Campbells as one potential source of the cult of St Mun in Argyll, while Steve Boardman has noted Stewart involvement in the cult of St Brendan.[62] It would be useful to push this paradigm consider-ably further than has been done to date. It is notable however that where this has been achieved in Scotland, it has been in a later medieval context, where the evidence for connections between families and cults becomes available. Only very occasionally, as in the connections between the ruling dynasty of Scotland and St Columba, or between the rulers of Bamburgh and St Patrick, can we make such connections during the early medieval period.[63]

---

59 Clancy, 'Scottish saints and national identities', 411–13.
60 See Ian Cowan, *The Parishes of Medieval Scotland* (Edinburgh, 1967), 16.
61 See nn. 12, 13 and 14 above.
62 Butter, 'St Munnu', *infra*; Steve Boardman, 'The Gaelic world and the early Stewart court', in *Mìorun Mòr nan Gall, 'The Great Ill-Will of the Lowlander'? Lowland Perceptions of the Highlands, Medieval and Modern*, eds Dauvit Broun and Martin MacGregor (Glasgow, 2007), 83–109, at 86–100. This book may be found at http://www.arts.gla.ac.uk/scottishstudies/ebooks/miorunmor.htm.
63 See Clancy, 'Columba, Adomnán and the cult of saints'; Edmonds, 'Personal names'.

'Personal'

If kindreds may be involved as patrons in spreading or localising cult, we must of course make room for the individual. It may be that many of our church dedications derive from the decisions of individual patrons, whose foundations of churches dedicated to certain saints may stem from such circumstances as a belief that a saint has saved them from mortal danger, or a battle has been won on a particular saint's feast day. For the early middle ages in Scotland, this is virtually unrecoverable data, but Simon Taylor's demonstration that just such phenomena have been at work during the later middle ages in the spread of the cult of St Fillan into eastern Scotland must I think give us pause.[64] Were such activities also a feature of the earlier middle ages? Certainly writers thought they might be. The foundation legend of Abernethy traces its origins to the exile of a Pictish king in Ireland – ostensibly at Kildare – and the gratitude of that king upon his return, leading to its dedication to St Brigit.[65] This legend is at least as old as the eleventh century, and if we distrust the particular king's reign to which it is dated, the basic events it describes are plausible, and indeed well-paralleled in the circumstances of the founding of Lindisfarne by Oswald in 635. I find myself drawn to this sort of explanation, more than any other, to explain one of the most obscure of Scottish dedications: that of Kinnethmont in Aberdeenshire to one of the two Northumbrian saints called Alchmund, most probably the one commemorated in St Alkmund's in Derby, enshrined in a sarcophagus that provides a famous parallel for those of St Andrews and Govan.[66] The best explanation available to me is one which would see some sort of close connection between a Pictish king and a Mercian one, at a time that allows for this very specialised cult to have been established in the northeastern Pictish landscape. We know of significant traffic between Pictland and various English kingdoms in the eighth and ninth centuries, so perhaps this gives us a way forward.

'Devotional'

Finally, lest we forget, the paradigm underlying perhaps all of these dedications, and certainly the overt paradigm of some, should be that of devotion. At our peril we reduce the cult of saints to the mere naming of churches or distribution of relics, to political expediency or ethnic dress. Without a

---

[64] Simon Taylor, 'The cult of St Fillan in Scotland', in *The North Sea World in the Middle Ages: Studies in the Cultural History of North-western Europe*, eds Thomas R. Liszka and Lorna E. Walker (Dublin, 2001), 175–210.

[65] Anderson, *Kings and Kingship*, 247, 262.

[66] Steven Plunkett, 'The Mercian perspective', in *The St Andrews Sarcophagus. A Pictish Masterpiece and its International Connections*, ed. Sally M. Foster (Dublin, 1998), 202–26, at 222–3.

belief in the efficacy of the saints as patrons, without some sense that their help and advocacy was of benefit to the individual, there would be no cult of saints. It is in such a context that we should be prepared to view the expansion of the cults of universal saints, not just in Europeanising terms. When the noblemen and women of Buchan dedicated a new church to Christ and St Peter, rather than to a local saint like Drostan,[67] it was not purely to show their European credentials, like so much hagiographical bling. It was also because the patronage of saints like Peter, and a renewed intensity of devotion to the person of Christ, was part of the religious mentality of the early twelfth century in northeastern Scotland.[68] I have wondered for some time if this is the best paradigm for understanding the many dedications to St Brigit in Scotland and further afield – not as a specifically Leinster saint, but as a saint whose devotional base was very widespread. Thomas Charles-Edwards has recently suggested that one of Brigit's main 'constituencies' was not a kindred or church, but 'the weak and oppressed'.[69]

Conclusions

I have rehearsed such a variety of paradigms – there are, no doubt, more I could have brought forward – not in order to see which are most convincing, but to emphasise that each of these in particular contexts may be the most appropriate paradigm through which to seek an explanation for the dedication of a particular church to a particular saint. This confronts us not with an explanatory template for understanding the spread of cults and of the church in the early middle ages, but a stark warning sign that we use such templates at our peril. More positively, we can say that there *are* instances in which we can feel some confidence in one or another explanation of the roots of a particular dedication, and that reasonably secure evidence, not just hypothesising, shows us the variety of explanations we need to allow for.

All of this relates only to one kind of aspect of saints' cults and church dedications. It is increasingly clear to me that despite the multiple paradigms available to us for understanding how dedications of churches come about, they do little justice to the dynamism and activity of these cults – or indeed the breaks in continuity and episodes of reinvention – during the middle ages. Returning to the example of St Ninian, whatever we may think of the saint himself, his historicity, or his association with Whithorn, we can be reasonably confident that he was turned to by the Northumbrian paralytic and

---

[67] Forsyth, Broun and Clancy, 'Property records', 138–9.
[68] See Hammond, *infra*.
[69] Charles-Edwards, 'Early Irish saints' cults', 83–4.

later monk of Whithorn, Pechtgils in the eighth century, and by the Gallovidian nobleman Fergus MacDowell in the fourteenth century, and that his power was seen as the source of their respective freedoms from illness and ambush.[70] This is a different history of church dedications and saints' cults: the production *by* such dedications of associations, convictions and relationships; the bonds of society and the solace of individuals.[71]

---

[70] MacQueen, *St Nynia* (2005 edn), 96–7; W. M. Metcalfe, *Legends of the Saints*, STS, 3 vols (Edinburgh, 1896), II.304–45, at 327–31; C. E. Palmer, trans., *The Life & Miracles of St Ninian* (Whithorn, n.d.), 10–11.

[71] This chapter was originally given as a talk to the RICHES Seminar Series in the Department of Celtic and Scottish Studies, University of Edinburgh, in January 2004; and then subsequently as part of the conference which formed the foundation of this essay collection. I am extremely grateful to Professor Donald Meek for the initial invitation to address the RICHES Seminar, and to Dr Steve Boardman for the invitation to revisit this material for the conference.

2

ST MUNNU IN IRELAND AND SCOTLAND:
AN EXPLORATION OF HIS CULT

Rachel Butter

Munnu, or Fintan Munnu, as he is sometimes called in Scotland, is an apparently straightforward saint, with an eighth-century *vita*, an obit in the Annals of Ulster,[1] an appearance in Adomnán's *Vita Columbae*,[2] and a name – Mun or Mund – which appears in a distinctive form in place-names in Scotland: four Kilmuns in Argyll, and an Eilean Munde near Ballachulish in Lochaber. He is intriguing too in the survival of traces of his cult in fifteenth-century references to a keeper of his crozier,[3] and in the surname Mac Gille Mund, evident in Argyll at least into the seventeenth century.[4]

This cheerful opening may sound like a prelude to the cruel news that in fact Munnu is not straightforward at all – that his obit is unreliable, that the person in *Vita Columbae* is someone else altogether, and that Kilmun may commemorate another saint. I will indeed flag up some potential problems towards the end of this chapter but for now I am going to treat Munnu as if he were a nice simple saint, uncontaminated by overlap or confusion with other saints. And I treat his strange double name – Fintan Munnu – as a helpful aid in our attempts to track his cult. This name derives from the common name

---

[1] '635.5 Quies Fintain m. Telcháin & Ernani m. Creseni'. *The Annals of Ulster (to AD 1131)*, eds Seán Mac Airt and Gearóid Mac Niocaill (Dublin, 1983), 118. Henceforth all entries from the Annals of Ulster will be taken from this edition and indicated *AU* + year + numerical position of the entry in that year.

[2] Adomnán's *Vita Columbae* i.2. Henceforth references to this work will be indicated *VC* + book and chapter number. Latin texts are from *The Life of St Columba*, ed. William Reeves (Dublin, 1857). Translations are from *Life of Columba by Adomnan of Iona*, ed. Richard Sharpe (Harmondsworth, 1995).

[3] At Inverchapel, 5km north-north-east of Kilmun in Cowal, a half mark of land called 'Pordewry' is said in 1497 to be occupied by an official called a dewar who held the crozier of St Munnu. *RMS*, II.no. 2385.

[4] George F. Black, *The Surnames of Scotland* (New York, 1946), 545. 'Members of this old sept of unknown origin are often found mentioned in writs connected with Cowal.' There are examples in sixteenth-century Bute and seventeenth-century Loch Aweside. The name MacPhun may also come from Mac Gille Mhund. Holders of the name are found in seventeenth-century Argyll.

Fintan, of which there were many bearers,[5] followed by an affectionate form
of the same name, arrived at thus: Fintan > *Mo Finn ('my Finn' where the
f is lenited and therefore silent) > Mun > Munnu.[6]

There are many interesting aspects to Munnu's story: his depiction, for
instance, as a supporter of the old Easter, perhaps even the *paries dealbatus*,
'the whited wall', said in Cummian's letter to Abbot Ségéne of Iona to be
standing in the way of agreement,[7] and the strange insistence, even – up to
a point – in his own Lives, on his harshness, jealousy and arrogance, linked,
in some sources, with his traditional role as leper.[8] The fact that Munnu's is
one of the longest entries in the ninth-century *Martyrology of Tallaght* and
includes the names of 219 of his monks[9] is worthy of investigation, as is the
possibility that his father Tulchán, called a druid in a commentary on *Félire
Oengusso*, may have been the subject of stories in his own right.[10]

Any of these aspects of Munnu would make an interesting discussion but
here I will concentrate on the ways in which he is most frequently characterised: as a Leinster saint and as a saint with particularly close connections with Iona. Are these the most helpful ways to explore his cult, and do

---

5   There are over fifty Fintans listed in *Corpus Genealogiarum Sanctorum Hiberniae*, ed. Pádraig
    Ó Riain (Dublin, 1985), though only five have genealogies. In the possibly eighth-century Life
    of Ailbe we are told that there are many Irishmen in Rome, many with the same name 'id est
    duodecim Comani et .xii Domongenii et .xii Fintani'. *Vita S. Albei* ch. 14, in *Vitae Sanctorum
    Hiberniae e Codice olim Salmanticensi nunc Bruxellensi*, ed. W. W. Heist (Brussels, 1965), 121.
    In an Irish litany of saints the monks of Fintan mac Uí Echach are mentioned, 'eight Fintans
    among them' (*Irish Litanies: Text and Translation*, ed. Charles Plummer, Henry Bradshaw Society
    (London, 1925), 61), and commentary on *Félire Oengusso* in Rawlinson B 512 on 21 February
    adds to the evident confusion about the identity of Fintan Corach the comment that at Cluain
    Eidnech there are four Fintans, *i Cluain ednech atat na .iiii. Finntain* (*Félire Óengusso Céli Dé:
    Martyrology of Oengus the Culdee*, ed. Whitley Stokes, Henry Bradshaw Society (London, 1905),
    79).
6   Paul Russell, 'Patterns of Hypocorisms in Early Irish Hagiography', in *Saints and Scholars*, eds
    John Carey, Máire Herbert and Pádraig Ó Riain (Dublin, 2001), 237–49, at 242.
7   *Cummian's Letter De Controversia Paschali together with a Related Irish Computistical Tract De
    Ratione Conputandi*, eds Maura Walsh and Dáibhí Ó Cróinín (Toronto, 1988), 93–5.
8   In *VC* i.2 'natura enim illius viri aspera est'. In the Life of Mochue m. Lonáin, Munnu is
    'superbus'; Mochua cures Munnu of leprosy which Munnu had asked for in penance for his
    arrogance. *Vita Mochua* chs 5–7, in *Vitae Sanctorum Hiberniae*, ed. Charles Plummer, 2 vols
    (Oxford, 1910), II.184–9.
9   *Martyrology of Tallaght* [henceforth *MT*], 21 October, in *The Martyrology of Tallaght, from the
    Book of Leinster and MS. 5100–4 in the Royal Library, Brussels*, eds Richard Irvine Best and
    Hugh Jackson Lawlor, Henry Bradshaw Society (London, 1931), 82.
10 Columb Cille tells Munnu's father Tulchán that he (Tulchán) will be famous because of his son.
    Vita prior S. Fintani seu Munnu abbatis de Tech Munnu [henceforth *vita prior*] ch. 2, in *Vitae
    Sanctorum*, ed. Heist, 198. In *Vita altera S. Fintani seu Munnu abbatis de Tech Munnu* [henceforth
    vita altera] ch. 3, in *Vitae Sanctorum*, ed. Heist, 248, and the Aberdeen Breviary ([*BA*], 2 vols
    (Edinburgh, 1510; reprinted, Spalding and Maitland Clubs, 1854), 21 October lesson 2, Tulchán
    becomes a monk. In the commentary to *Félire Oengusso* in Oxford, Bodleian Library MS Laud
    610, Tulchán is described as a druid – 'Munna mac Telchain druad' (*Félire*, ed. Stokes, 226) – and
    Tulchán is as important as his son in the story about them in the Life of Cainnech. *Vita Cainnechi*
    ch. 26, in *Vitae Sanctorum*, ed. Heist, 188. There is no-one of this name in the martyrologies,
    however, except one in the list of Munnu's monks under 21 October in *MT*.

they help to determine when and by what means Munnu's cult might have reached Scotland? Evidence for his following in Ireland will be examined first, followed by a look at his cult in Scotland. I will end by touching on a few problems.

Munnu's earliest appearance in literature is in Adomnán's *Vita Columbae*. It is his depiction there that is responsible for the abiding view of him as being closely associated with Iona, and Leinster. Here he is given considerable importance, heading the first narrative chapter in the work:

> St Fintan, by God's help, kept himself chaste in body and soul from his boyhood and devoted himself to the pursuit of godly wisdom, and in due course he came to enjoy renown among all the churches of the *Scotti* [*per universas Scotorum ecclesias*].[11]

It is notable that a life of Columba should start off by singing the praises of a saint other than Columba; Munnu might be regarded as a minor saint now but in Adomnán's view he was of sufficient renown that Munnu's devotion to Columba could be used to magnify Columba's own glory. We are told that our saint was 'by race (*gente*) Moccu Moie' which refers to a group, unattested outside *Vita Columbae*, based somewhere near Derry (a more precise location will be suggested below). He wished to become a monk under Columba (as indeed another man described as *Moccu Moie* already was),[12] but on his arrival Baithéne, Columba's successor, turned him away saying that Columba had prophesied his coming. Columba's instructions were that he should be sent back to Ireland, to Leinster in particular, where he would build a monastery.

Here Adomnán is both giving Munnu the ultimate praise – the approval of Columba himself – and perhaps claiming him as a kind of Iona plant in Leinster. Munnu's own monks were also promoting their founder as a would-be pupil at Iona, it seems. Adomnán reports that he was told the story by an old man who had been a monk under Munnu. If true (and we do not have reason to doubt it) then the implication is that the monks of Taghmon, Munnu's principal monastery, in Leinster,[13] were, at the time Adomnán wrote, allying themselves, through stories of how their monastery had been founded, with Iona. Munnu may not have been trained on Iona, they seem to be saying, but he had Columba's sanction.

The earliest of Munnu's own lives (henceforth *vita prior*), probably dating from the eighth century,[14] seems to take the connection with Columba further.

---

11 *VC* i.2. Sharpe translates 'of Ireland', but this does not give room for his renown in the parts of Scotland which the term *Scotti* would allow.

12 *VC* i.18. The monk was called Lasrén.

13 It is possible that the informant, Oisséne moccu Néth Corb, came from another of Munnu's monasteries (of which more below), though given the location of Oisséne's people on the boundary of Leinster and Munster (*Life of Columba*, ed. Sharpe, 259), it is reasonable to suppose he came from the Leinster monastery of Tech Munnu.

14 The life may have been written before 769 when Cennselach of the Síl Máeluidir, killed the reigning king, Dubcalgach, to become king of Uí Chenselaig. Alfred P. Smyth, *Celtic Leinster*

Here Munnu's greatness is predicted by Columba who meets and admires him as a young boy. Columba is one of his teachers in Ireland, they voyage together (with Cainnech and Brendan) to the Land of Promise,[15] and Munnu is assigned to Columba's kin, the Cenél Conaill.[16]

Columba is far from the only important saint depicted in *vita prior* as having good relations with Munnu, however: Comgall is another of Munnu's teachers in Ireland,[17] and Munnu is prior of one of Comgall's Leinster monasteries;[18] it is stressed that relations with Molaisse remained cordial, despite their disagreement over the date of Easter;[19] and Cainnech is not just Munnu's companion to the Land of Promise, as mentioned above, but in Cainnech's own Life Cainnech is heralded as Munnu's saviour when none other than Columba attempts to dispose of the baby Munnu by tossing him into the sea.[20] Finally, the saint who is described in the *vita prior* as 'the wisest man in all Ireland and Britain' is not Columba, but a nameless abbot on Devenish in Loch Erne.[21]

(Blackrock, Co. Dublin, 1982), 65. Munnu made a prophecy in *vita prior*, ch. 16, which implied that no king of the Síl Máeluidir branch would reach such a position. The prominence of the Easter debate in the life might suggest an earlier date. The tone of the exchange suggests that by the time of writing the judgement on the matter had gone against Munnu's position, but that the issue was still sufficiently live, and Munnu's position in the debate still sufficiently well known, for it to appear evasive not to mention it.

[15] *vita prior*, chs 2, 5, 31. Could there be a lost Voyage Tale involving these saints? It is interesting that all those on board had cults in Argyll.

[16] *vita prior*, ch. 1.

[17] It is, however, possible that the Comgall section was originally about Columba. It begins by referring to Comgall as *Mochoma*, a hypocoristic form not usually of Comgall, but of Colum. This Mochoma comes from Connacht. Immediately following the Comgall episode, Munnu is found in Cell Mor Dithrib (in Connacht) with Columba. But even if this section is about Columba there still remains an important connection between Munnu and Comgall (or his monastery) in the *vita prior*.

[18] *vita prior*, ch. 15. The relationship between Comgall's monks and Munnu's is not simple, as depicted in Munnu's lives; a disagreement of some kind (it varies between versions of the life) results in Munnu predicting misfortune for Comgall's monastery when Munnu leaves. *vita prior*, ch. 17.

[19] Lethglenn, Molaisse's main foundation, may have been in the hands of a minor branch of the Uí Bairrche, a group whose main land-holdings were around Tech Munnu in Leinster. Thomas Charles-Edwards, *Early Christian Ireland* (Cambridge, 2000), 428.

[20] *Vita Cainnechi*, ch. 26, in *Vitae Sanctorum*, ed. Heist, 188.

[21] The most famous saint of Devenish is Molaisse who is one of the twelve apostles of Ireland (*Corpus*, ed. Ó Riain, no. 402) and is assigned to the Dál nAraide (*ibid.*, no. 117). *AU* records Molaisse's death in either 564 or 571 which would make an association with Munnu difficult given Adomnán's statement that Munnu was 'a young man' in 597 (*VC* i.2). The other versions of Munnu's life call Munnu's teacher *Silell* (or *Filell*) *filius Miannaidh* (vita altera, ch. 6, *Vita Sancti Munnu sive Fintani abbatis de Tech Munnu*, ch. 6 in *Vitae Sanctorum*, ed. Plummer, 228) who seems to correspond to a pupil of Finnian of Clonard ('Sinellus filius Maenachi' in *Vita S. Finniani abbatis de Cluain Iraird*, ch. 19, in *Vitae Sanctorum*, ed. Heist, 101). No such person is visible in the martyrologies or the genealogies. The Aberdeen Breviary calls Munnu's teacher 'Sillenus' (*BA* 21 October, lesson 3), and there are various persons of this name who might correspond. On 21 October, that is, the same day as Munnu (but not among his monks), appears *Sillán magister* in *MT*, with a longer entry in the Martyrology of Cashel: *Sillanus Hua Gairbh, cognomento Magister, Abbas Magbilensis*. This abbot of Mag Bile would appear to correspond

The saintly collaborations in *vita prior*, exemplified by the voyage tale, might be seen as part of a general trend observed by Thomas Charles-Edwards to be present in the O'Donohue Lives[22] (of which *vita prior* is one) in which a particular effort is made to show alliances between monasteries. This is often manifested in pacts made between saints, and occurs also in *Vita Columbae* (pacts between Columba, Comgall, Brendan and Cormac). The O'Donohue Lives are particularly concerned with saints of the Irish midlands, where most of the main monasteries were located and where this kind of pact building would be particularly important.[23] Munnu is usually associated with Leinster, as we have observed, but perhaps he too had a more significant presence in the midlands than is at first apparent.

The most obvious clue to this is the presence of another monastery called Taghmon (< Tech Munnu, as we have seen) in Westmeath, but the earliest remains there are fifteenth-century. A reference in the commentary to *Félire Oengusso*[24] to a cult of Munnu in Meath may perhaps be pointing to this other Taghmon, but even if not it still is evidence for a cult of Munnu somewhere in Meath by perhaps the late twelfth century. Around the same time, or perhaps a bit earlier, a genealogy is constructed which places him among the Corco Roíde,[25] a group whose territories centred in Westmeath. It seems, then, that there was a cult of Munnu here at least by the eleventh century. To push it back earlier we can look at *vita prior*. Here his origins are said to be among the Uí Néill; on his father's side he is assigned to the northern Uí Néill, but on his mother's side he is among a side branch of the southern Uí Néill, based in Co. Longford[26] (neighbouring Co. Westmeath). He is alleged to have been born near Uisnech,[27] where the stone on which he was born was honoured 'up to today', he sets up a monastery in Tech Taille, identified as Tihilly,[28]

---

to the one mentioned in *AU* at 619.2. An obit of Sillan of Devenish (a bishop) appears in the Clonmacnois group of annals at 659. Thomas Charles-Edwards, *The Chronicle of Ireland*, 2 vols (Liverpool, 2006), I.151. He is assigned to 17 May in the *Martyrology of Donegal*, but in a later hand. *The Martyrology of Donegal*, ed. James Henthorn Todd (Dublin, 1864). It is possible that this Sillan corresponds to *Scellanus*, one of the recipients of the pascal letter of Pope John elect (*ca* 640) according to Bede. *Historia Ecclesiastica* ii.19, in *Bede: A History of the English Church and People*, ed. Leo Sherley-Price (Harmondsworth, 1968), 136, 342.

22 A group of nine or ten Lives, all printed in *Vitae Sanctorum*, ed. Heist, whose composition Sharpe dates to 'earlier than about 800'. Richard Sharpe, *Medieval Irish Saints' Lives: An Introduction to Vitae Sanctorum Hiberniae* (Oxford, 1991), 334.

23 Partly perhaps because of the constant danger of hostilities, for example, *AU* 760.8 Clonmacnois v. Birr, *AU* 764.6 Clonmacnoise v. Durrow, *AU* 817.5 Tech Munnu v. Ferns.

24 '.i. Munnu mac Techlán (sic) o Thig Munnu in Huib Censelaig & hi Mide'. MS Rawlinson B 486, *Félire*, ed. Stokes, 226.

25 *Corpus*, ed. Ó Riain, no. 155.

26 He is 'de genere Maini, filii Neill'. *vita prior* ch. 1. The descendents of Maine – the Cenél Maine – were (or thought they were) a branch of the southern Uí Neill who ruled the area of southern Tethbae, now roughly Co. Longford, and possibly part of Co. Offaly. Francis Byrne, *Irish Kings and High Kings* (Dublin, 1973), 87, 89; Charles-Edwards, *Early Christian Ireland*, 16.

27 *vita prior*, ch. 4.

28 *vita prior*, ch. 11.

1. Sites associated with St Munnu in Ireland

in the parish of Durrow, and performs a miracle at Kilbixy which may be in Co. Westmeath.[29] All these indicate cult presence by, say, the eighth century.

In *vita prior* he goes to several places to study: Cell Mór Dithrib, probably in Co. Roscommon,[30] Devenish in Co. Fermanagh (as mentioned) and (perhaps) a monastery headed by Comgall, possibly also in Connacht.[31] These mentions may imply the presence of his cult in these places, but more compelling is an intriguing hint in the annals at a connection between Munnu

---

[29] *Corpus*, ed. Ó Riain, 314, suggests that this is in the barony of Moygoish, Co. Westmeath. But Smyth, *Celtic Leinster*, 65 notes (via Hogan) a Cell Bicsige in the Idrone area of Carlow, and another in Uí Garrchon, around Arklow, Co. Wicklow. Both of these are in Leinster.

[30] Cell Mór Díthruib is equated with Kilmore parish in the barony of Ballintober North, Co. Roscommon. *Corpus*, ed. Ó Riain, 316; *Life of Columba*, ed. Sharpe, 317.

[31] He 'read with Comgall and learnt his rule' (*vita prior*, ch. 4), but see n. 17.

and northern Ireland: *AU* 784.2 '… Ciaran abb Ratho Maighe Oenaigh & Tighe Mo-Finnu …'

Here we see a connection between what is likely to be Munnu's monastery of Taghmon – either the one in Wexford or the one in Meath – and Ráith Maige Oenaig, identified either as Raymoghy in Rye parish, Raphoe North Barony in eastern Co. Donegal or Rateen, near the Swillyburn, also in eastern Co. Donegal.[32] There is much uncertainty here, but both places identified as Ráith Maige Oenaig lie within or near what may have been Munnu's homeland, which might suggest that the factor which connects these two far-flung places is that both have Munnu as patron. There is a parallel in the case of St Colmán Ela. His main church is Lann Ela (Lynally) in Co. Offaly in the midlands, and there is an eighth-century annal entry which records the death of an abbot of both Lann Ela and Connor.[33] Connor is in Co. Antrim in the northeast of Ireland, and is where Colmán Ela's family, the Dál Sailni are from.[34]

The basis on which it is thought reasonable to suggest that the group referred to by the name Moccu Moie, might be from this area is the implication in *Vita Columbae* that they lived within a day's journey from Derry. Further refinement is, however, given by Francis John Byrne who has suggested that the Cenél Moain or Moen of Mag nÍtha of the eleventh and twelfth centuries may have their origins in the group to which Fintan Munnu belonged.[35] Mag nÍtha, in the lower reaches of the River Foyle, between the Swillyburn and the River Finn, is border territory. Its lands are in what is now eastern Donegal, it borders Tyrone to the south and east, and the parishes which best represent the ancient territory of Mag nÍtha lie in the diocese of Derry.[36] This area, dominated by the Croaghan Hill ridge, was of considerable strategic importance, as is suggested by its rich concentration of archaeological monuments as well as its visibility in history, mythology and legend: 'In all, this cultural concentration highlights the social, political and ritual significance of the area throughout ancient times.'[37] The Cenél Moain were said to be a minor branch of the Cenél nÉogáin, and Mag nÍtha is placed, in the *Tripartite Life*, in Cenél nÉogáin territory. It is argued by Brian Lacey, however, that Mag

---

[32] The first identification is made in various places including Charles-Edwards, *Chronicle of Ireland*, I.167. Lacey rounds up the evidence and suggests Rateen. Brian Lacey, *Cenél Conaill and the Donegal Kingdoms, AD 500–800* (Dublin, 2006), 124–6. There is an Adamnán bishop of Ráith Maige Oenaig who dies in *AU* 731.8, and, in the *Tripartite Life*, a bishop Brucach of Ráith Maige Oenaig. *The Tripartite Life of Patrick*, ed. Whitley Stokes, 2 vols (London, 1887), I.166.

[33] *AU* 778.6 'Dormitorio Ainfchellaigh abbatis Conndire & Lainne Ela.'

[34] And in the case of both saints their specific northern origins are revealed in *Vita Columbae*, but in most later material they are broadly assigned to the Uí Néill.

[35] Francis Byrne, 'Ireland and her neighbours, c1014–c1072', in *A New History of Ireland Vol. 1: Prehistoric and Early Ireland*, ed. D. Ó Cróinín (Oxford, 2005), 862–98, at 881, as cited in Lacey, *Cenél Conaill*, 141.

[36] Lacey, *Cenél Conaill*, 133.

[37] *Ibid.*, 132 (map), 135–6.

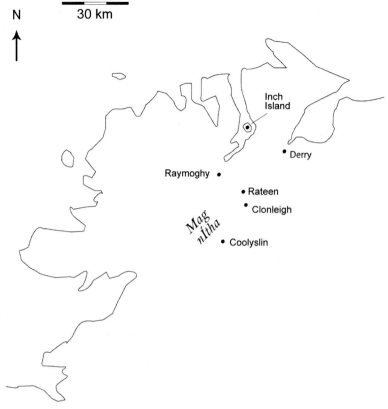

N

30 km

2. Sites associated with St Munnu in north-west Ireland

nĺtha was the homeland not of the Cenél nÉogáin but of the Cenél Conaill. It was not until the seventh century that it came under pressure from the Cenél nÉogáin, and 'would be entirely conquered by them in the first half of the eighth century'.[38] It is thus possible that Munnu came from a territory which pertained, at the time of his birth, to the Cenél Conaill, but which, by the time the *vita prior* was written, was controlled by the Cenél nÉogáin. The relevance of all this will become apparent in due course.

Both the sites suggested for Ráith Maige Oenaig are just to the north of Mag nĺtha in territory which the Cenél Conaill took towards the end of

[38] *Ibid.*, 137. This is part of Lacey's argument that the northern Uí Néill did not come into Donegal from outside, as is traditionally thought to be the case, but that instead they emerged within Donegal from existing peoples. Further, the Cenél Conaill and the Cenél nÉogáin, both of the Uí Néill, probably had no connection with the eponymous Niall Noígíallach, but later (during the eighth century, suggests Lacey, *ibid.*, 155) were 'attached to the Uí Néill by fictional genealogical links – as it were, re-invented, with fresh (false) identities, as part of a newly-constructed, "national" ruling elite'. *Ibid.*, 33.

the sixth century, conquering the Cenél nÉnnai.[39] In Mag nÍtha itself, on its northern boundary, is the ancient church site of Cluain Laogh. It is highly speculative, but Lacey's suggestion that the Tech Munnu mentioned in the 784 annal above may have been on this site rather than representing either of Munnu's better-known monasteries is interesting, not least for the associated observation of a site nearby called Muhine (from Mo-Fhinniu?) Bridge.[40]

Whatever one believes about the exact location of the group referred to by the name Moccu Moie and its political make-up, and regardless of which of the two identifications is chosen for Ráith Maige Oenaig, the evidence for some kind of cult of Munnu in the north, at least by the eighth century, is at least encouraging and this may be backed up by evidence from *vita prior*. After his dispatch from Iona Munnu lived, according to *vita prior*, 'in insula Cuinrigi'. Hogan did not find a satisfactory identification for this place, suggesting, probably on the basis of Munnu's well known connection with the area, 'in Ui Cennselaig(?)', that is, in Co. Wexford. I would like to suggest that the place intended was Inch Island on Lough Swilly, an island which belonged to the Cuirenrige or Culenrig.[41] This identification fits well with the reading given in *vita altera* – 'insula Cuirmrigi or Cuirinrigi'.[42] It is close to Derry and thus to Munnu's homeland, and makes sense of Munnu's itinerary which places Munnu, two chapters later, *ubi natus est*. While on the island Munnu 'hears the shout of the men of Hell on the day on which the battle of Slemain [*bellum Slenne*] was carried out'. Hogan links this with the battle of Slemain of Mide in *AU* 499, a place whose trace Charles-Edwards notes as surviving in the modern townlands of Slanemore and Slanebeg near Mullingar.[43] Another possibility, and one which fits both place and date better, is that the battle referred to was the one recorded in *AU* in 601 and 602: *bellum slenne*. In the Annals of Tigernach the place is given as *Cúl Slemna*,[44] and is suggested by Lacey, following Díarmuid Ó Murchadha, to correspond to Coolyslin in Co. Tyrone.[45] This, again, fits with what I believe to be the northern focus of this section of *vita prior*, and possibly also with Munnu's own concerns, given his family connections. I will come back to this. Raymoghy, Rateen and Clonleigh, all mentioned above as having possible connections with Munnu, are at a distance from Coolyslin of 18km, 13km and 9km respectively.

Turning now to his Leinster profile, we cannot deny that his monastery in Wexford was of considerable importance. It is acknowledged in *Vita*

---

[39] *Ibid.*, 134. The Tripartite Life places Ráith Maige Oenaig 'i crich Conaill'. *The Tripartite Life*, ed. Stokes, I.166.
[40] Lacey, *Cenél Conaill*, 142.
[41] *Ibid.*, 135.
[42] *vita altera*, ch. 8, in *Vitae Sanctorum*, ed. Heist, 249.
[43] Charles-Edwards, *Early Christian Ireland*, 450.
[44] Charles-Edwards, *The Chronicle of Ireland*, I.122.
[45] Lacey, *Cenél Conaill*, 132 (map), 137.

Columbae, as we have seen; it is the most significant foundation in his own Lives, and it is still visible in the annals in the eleventh century.[46] Traces of his cult are still visible in the area today, with several place-names (Aughermon < Eachar Munnu, Munnu's field, for example)[47] and at least three wells. One of the wells (in Browncastle) was, in the nineteenth century, visited by as many as a hundred people a day, and several cures reported in the local press. A shale outcrop nearby, known as 'St Mun's Bed', was famous for cures of the back. Ritual activity was prohibited there in 1800.[48]

Aside from the location of his main monastery, Munnu is not, however, a Leinster saint in any straightforward way. If we look at the dynamics in the *vita prior*, his independence from the struggles of the main Leinster dynasties is striking. He does not usually have a Leinster genealogy (not from one of the four *prímslointe*),[49] he is given land for his monastery not by a member of one of the Leinster dynasties but by a king of the Fothairt (one of the *fortuatha*, or outsiders), and in every struggle described the Leinster leader comes off badly. Munnu neither helps, nor is helped by, any of the Uí Chennselaig, the dominant group in south Leinster from at least the eighth century, nor the Uí Bairrche, who were struggling with the Uí Chennselaig for power in the Taghmon region from the late sixth century.[50] Comparison with a saint like Maedoc of Ferns is revealing. Maedoc, whose monastery was the chief centre of the Uí Chennselaig from the mid-eighth century, is depicted as one of the group's most powerful allies, uncompromisingly giving support to Brandub, the scourge of the Uí Néill, and eventual killer of Columba's kinsman, Áed mac Ainmirech.[51]

For the writer of the *vita prior*, then, it is not his identity as a Leinster saint that is most important. What is revealed, rather, is the instability of all the Leinster groups, the faction fighting, the constant struggle for power between and within the different dynasties, and Munnu's disapproval of all that. Of course, any portrayal of a saint, and by implication his monastery, as being detached from such civil strife is a reflection of an ideal rather than

---

[46] *Annals of Inisfallen* 1060.5. 'Domnall Déssech, cenn crabuid & dérce na nGoedel, & is he ro imthig do neoch imdeochaid Crist i talmain, quieuit in Domino hi Tich Munnu'. *The Annals of Inisfallen*, ed. Seán Mac Airt (Dublin, 1988), 218. It cannot be certain, of course, that this is the Tech Munnu in Wexford.

[47] Edward Culleton, 'St. Munna of Taghmon', *Journal of the Taghmon Historical Society* 2 (1997), available at http://taghmon.com/.

[48] Nuala Carroll, 'The Holy Wells of the parish', *Journal of the Taghmon Historical Society* 2 (1997), available at http://taghmon.com/.

[49] There is an attempt in one MS of the *Corpus Genealogiorum Sancti Hiberniae* to link him with the Uí Dega. *Corpus*, ed. Ó Riain, no. 155.

[50] Smyth, *Celtic Leinster*, 65. The Uí Bairrche 'ceased to count as a great people in Leinster by AD 700'. *Ibid.*, 81.

[51] Máedóc, however, like Munnu, does not have a Leinster genealogy; he is assigned to the Airgialla. *Corpus*, ed. Ó Riain, no. 63. Smyth, *Celtic Leinster*, 19 notes how few 'Leinster' saints belong to the Uí Chenselaig or Uí Dunlainge, suggesting that though these groups were the predominant ones in later centuries, it was other groups, such as the Uí Bairrche, who earlier had power.

of reality, and this is manifested in an annal entry of 817 which records a battle involving the *familia* of Tech Munnu against the community of Ferns, in which 400 people died.[52] Ironically, the group whom the monks of Tech Munnu helped to victory are the very group about whom Munnu, in *vita prior*, prophesied a future lack of power.[53]

The aim, in the *vita prior*, to give Munnu an air of neutrality, extends even to his relations with his own family,[54] to whom he shows only grudging favour. He will not allow his mother to come closer than 'Lugmath', probably in Louth, to greet him, and his parting message is scarcely encouraging: 'if you come to me another time, I will go away from whatever province I am in, across the sea to Britain'.[55] Further, the battle which he hears from 'Insula Cuinrigi' is one which may have been of some interest to Munnu, given its proximity – if the identifications are right – to his people; this is one of the many battles between the Cenél Conaill and Cenél nEogáin in the area, in this case a victory for the latter.[56] But Munnu is made to express no support either way: 'I will not live in a place where I have heard the shout of the men of Hell.'[57]

So, to round up the foregoing, Munnu has a complex profile, probably reflecting a reasonably dispersed cult. He has several different genealogies, and several *foci* of his cult. His main monastery was in Wexford, but it is possible that other ecclesiastical sites, especially in Meath, and probably in eastern Co. Donegal in northern Ireland, may have been important too. His Leinster profile is complex, and his relationship with Iona was important, but perhaps the usual reliance on the testimony of Adomnán has made it seem *the most important*, when his relationship with others such as Comgall and Bangor are as significant. I have not had space to explore the Easter question but this too has been viewed in the context of Munnu's relationship with Iona, when here too his relationship with Bangor (another late supporter of the old Easter) – or rather the relationship between Munnu's followers and Comgall's – may be as important when looking at the development of his cult.

In turning now to Scotland we find that any hopes we might have of being

---

[52] *AU* 817.6. 'A battle won by Cathal son of Dunlang and by the community of Tech Munnu against the community of Ferna, where 400 were slain.'

[53] This prediction concerned Guare mac Eogain, father of Máel Odar, who gave his name to the Síl Maeluidir. *vita prior*, ch. 16.

[54] 'And Fintan came to his people, where he was born, but he did not see that land, except only the road on which his feet were walking, nor did he greet anyone there, not father, not mother, not brothers, not sisters, who were all alive there'. *vita prior*, ch. 10 (translation my own). A saint's severing of family ties is a common hagiographical motif.

[55] *vita prior*, ch. 11.

[56] For a map showing some of the battles, see Lacey, *Cenél Conaill*, 279. Byrne also notes the contentious nature of the area: 'Mag nítha was to be for a thousand years the crucial battleground between the Cenél nEogáin and the Cenél Conaill . . . Thus it comes about that the term 'Fir Maige Ítha is exasperatingly ambiguous, varying as it does according to the actual power in the land.' Byrne, 'Ireland and her neighbours'.

[57] *vita prior*, ch. 9.

1. The ruined fifteenth-century bell-tower of the collegiate church of Kilmun, centre of the late medieval veneration of St Munnu. © and courtesy of Alasdair Ross

able to find a context in which to explain the arrival of his cult there are frustrated by Munnu's complex and multiple identities. A simple Leinster solution is not good enough, nor is invocation of his alliance with Iona.

First, how far back in time can we push the cult in Scotland? *Vita Columbae* could be read either as supporting or throwing doubt on the early existence of a cult there. Adomnán implies that the cult's centre is in Leinster. He makes no mention of a cult in Scotland, though states, as we have seen, that Munnu 'postea per universas Scotorum ecclesias valde noscibilis [later came to enjoy renown among all the churches of the *Scotti*]', which could include Argyll.[58] It could be that Munnu's prominence in *Vita Columbae* might partly be explained by Adomnán's need to claim a potentially rival cult in Argyll as being a sub-Iona one. A parallel can again be found in Colmán Ela, who gave his name to a parish in Kintyre, Argyll, and who has two appearances in *Vita Columbae*.[59] It might tentatively be suggested that Ernéne mac Craséni, who appears immediately after the chapter in *Vita Columbae* about Munnu, and who Adomnán says was 'postea per omnes Scotiae ecclesias famosus et valde notissimus [later famous through all the churches of *Scotia* and very highly regarded]' had a cult in Argyll (and elsewhere in Scotland) too. There are problems here, however, both in determining the identity of the Marnock (from Mo-Ernóc, an affectionate form of the name Ernán) in Scotland and, in all three cases, in dating the origins of the cults.[60]

To return to Munnu, his cult must certainly have been active and well known by the late thirteenth century, when the Life of Molaisse has Munnu in Scotland as Molaisse's teacher.[61] From a little earlier come the first documentary references to one of the Kilmuns: Kilmun on Holy Loch in Dunoon, Cowal.[62]

Of the four Kilmuns this is the only one to become a parish church. There is evidence of early christian activity here in the form of a cross-incised stone. It is very plain – similar to ones from Ardnadam (Cowal), Cladh a' Bhile (Knapdale), Dunans (Knapdale), Kilkenneth (Tiree), Calgary (Mull), Kirkapoll (Tiree), and Iona.[63] There is evidence of other early christian activity in the immediate area in the form of a chapel a few miles away at Ardnadam, and long-cists at Innellan.[64] The name of the loch on which the

58 *VC* i.2.
59 *VC* i.5, ii.15.
60 *VC*, i.3. See also n. 82 and Rachel Butter, 'Inchmarnock and Kildavanan: the place-name evidence', in Christopher Lowe, *Inchmarnock: An Early Historic Island Monastery and its Archaeological Landscape* (Edinburgh, 2008), 53–4.
61 Molaisse is 'instructed by his doctrine and ruled by the example of his life', which is interesting given their opposite positions in the Easter debate, at least according to Munnu's *vita prior*. *Vita S. Lasriani seu Molaisse abbatis de Lethglenn*, ch. 4, in *Vitae Sanctorum*, ed. Heist, 341.
62 1230×46 in *Pais. Reg.*, 132–3.
63 Ian Fisher, *Early Medieval Sculpture in the West Highlands and Islands* (Edinburgh, 2001), 31.
64 RCAHMS, *Argyll: An Inventory of the Monuments*, 7 vols (Edinburgh, 1971–92), VII.no. 4 and 135.

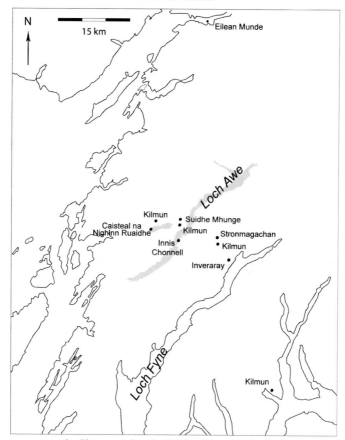

3. Sites associated with St Munnu in Scotland

site is situated is itself suggestive: Holy Loch on modern maps, Loch Aint on Pont,[65] and Loch Shiant in the Statistical Account of the 1790s indicating an original Gaelic *seunta*, 'sacred'.[66]

The surviving church is fifteenth-century but the site became the main burial place of the Loch Awe Campbells perhaps from as early as the mid-fourteenth century when they first acquired the land.[67] In 1442 a collegiate

---

[65] MS of maps by Timothy Pont published on the NLS website at: www.nls.uk/pont; Jeffrey C. Stone, *The Pont Manuscript Maps of Scotland* (Tring, 1989), 103.

[66] Malcolm MacLennan, *A Pronouncing and Etymological Dictionary of the Gaelic Language* (Edinburgh, 1925), 554. N. D. Campbell, 'The Origin of the Holy Loch in Cowall, Argyll', *SHR* 10 (1913), 29–34.

[67] Sometime between 1347 and 1361 Mary, countess of Menteith, gave over all her lands in Cowal 'held directly from the Steward [i.e. Robert, future Robert II – overlord of Cowal]' to Gill-easbuig Campbell; this included the lands of Kilmun with the patronage of the kirk of St Mun. Stephen I. Boardman, '"Pillars of the Community": Clan Campbell and architectural patronage in the fifteenth century', in *Lordship and Architecture in Medieval and Renaissance Scotland*, eds

church was established on the site by Duncan Campbell of Loch Awe, first Lord Campbell, and by at least the early sixteenth century Kilmun in Cowal was promoted as the main monastery of St Munnu in Scotland; in the Aberdeen Breviary it is said that he founded a monastery here, and that this is where he was buried. Near Kilmun, a half mark of land is said in 1497 to be occupied by an official who held the crozier of St Munnu, as we have seen.[68] The whereabouts of this crozier is now unknown.

Another Kilmun with possible early christian remains is a site in Glen Aray. The layout of the site, with a chapel within a sub-circular enclosure of about 17m diameter, is suggestive of an early date and is comparable to chapel sites on Islay. It is, in fact, the only chapel site on mainland Argyll – apart from Ardnadam – which the Royal Commission on the Ancient and Historical Monuments of Scotland considers to be early in form on the basis of surviving architecture alone.[69] No carvings have been found here and the earliest reference to the name is 1631, but there is an interesting name in the immediate vicinity, possibly suggestive of early ecclesiastical activity: Bile Garbh, which may include reference to a sacred tree – *bile* – often associated with royal inaugural sites but sometimes also with early ecclesiastical sites.[70]

The final two Kilmuns are within a few kilometres of each other near Loch Awe. One, near Dalavich, consists of the scanty remains of a rectangular building, 'presumably a chapel', within an enclosure of irregular shape.[71] There is a tradition that the site was used for burial during the Campbell occupation of the castle on Innis Chonnell (and presumably before they buried their dead at Kilmun in Cowal), less than 3km SSE on Loch Awe, but there are no tombstones visible at the site now. The other Kilmun, 400m N of Loch Avich, comprises a circular wall enclosing a rectangular structure. It may occupy the site of an early medieval chapel or burial, but the surviving remains are of eighteenth-century character and the physical evidence does not support the identification of the inner structure as a chapel.[72] It is first

---

Richard D. Oram and Geoffrey P. Stell (Edinburgh, 2005), 123–60, at 126. Sir Duncan was the first Campbell unquestionably to have been buried at Kilmun, though there may have been one or two beforehand. *Ibid.*, 136. See also Stephen Boardman, *The Campbells, 1250–1513* (Edinburgh, 2006), 141–3.

68 This piece of ground is included in a charter confirming the sale of certain lands by John Colquhoun to Archibald, earl of Argyll. *RMS*, II.no. 2385. These lands, including *Kilmone*, had been given to John Colquhoun of Luss in 1474, on their resignation by James Scrimgeour (*Jac. Scrimgeour de Dudup*). *Ibid.*, II.no. 1185.

69 RCAHMS, *Argyll*, VII.no. 79.

70 Cf. Cladh a' Bhile in Knapdale. *Ibid.*, no. 20. Gondek discusses the role of this important early christian burial ground as part of a wider ritual landscape. Meggen Gondek, 'Early Historic Sculpture and Landscape: a case study of Cladh a' Bhile, Ellary, Mid-Argyll', *PSAS* 136 (2006), 237–58. For discussion of Cell Bile in Meath, see Thomas Charles-Edwards, *Early Christian Ireland* (Cambridge, 2000), 24.

71 RCAHMS, *Argyll*, II.no. 265.

72 *Ibid.*, II.no. 226.

mentioned in 1414 and is described in the Ordnance Survey Name Book as a private burial-ground of the MacDougalls.[73]

A notable feature of all these Kilmuns is their proximity to centres of power chosen by the Campbells of Argyll from perhaps the thirteenth century: the Kilmun on Loch Avich is close to Caisteal na Nighinn Ruaidhe;[74] Kilmun on Loch Awe is close to Innis Chonnell,[75] possibly occupied by the Campbells from the first half of the thirteenth century, certainly by early in the fourteenth; Kilmun in Glen Aray is near both to Inveraray, where a new seat of administrative power was built by the Campbells in the mid-fifteenth century, and to an earlier Campbell site, Stronmagachan;[76] Kilmun in Cowal is in the area where the Campbells' power grew in the fourteenth century. It is the site chosen by them for the burial of their dead from perhaps the mid-fourteenth century, and was elevated by Duncan Campbell of Loch Awe into a collegiate church in 1442.

It is tempting to suppose that the Campbells themselves introduced the cult of Munnu to Argyll. Close inquiry reveals, however, that all these sites were taken over from local kindreds, all with Irish ancestry, or so they claimed. Their alleged common ancestor was a member of the Cenél nÉogáin of the eleventh century, a claim which David Sellar considers reasonably plausible.[77] Might there have been a cult of Munnu in the Irish territories of these people which they brought with them when they moved to Scotland? This seems quite possible. We have seen that Munnu's origins were around Derry, in territory which may have been inhabited, in Munnu's lifetime, by the Cenél Conaill but which, by the eighth century was under Cenél nÉogáin control. These kindreds – the Lamonts, the MacGilchrists and the MacSweens – or rather the people ancestral to all of them, may have brought the cult of Munnu to Argyll, or they may have embraced and perpetuated it on arrival, recognising it from their home territories.

---

[73] Name-books of the Ordnance Survey, County of Argyll (unpublished notebooks available at *National Monuments Record*) no. 53, 137 via RCAHMS, *Argyll*, II.no. 226.

[74] RCAHMS, *Argyll*, II.no. 281. Possibly of thirteenth-century origin.

[75] *Ibid.*, II.no. 292. Built in the early thirteenth century. A MacDougall refers in 1308 to his '3 castles upon a lake' or '3 castles as well as a lake' (depending on translation). If the former is correct Innis Chonnell, Fraoch Eilean and Fincharn might be meant, possibly even if the latter is the correct reading. Perhaps the MacDougalls built Innis Chonnell and it was not in Campbell hands until the early fourteenth century. Fincharn previously belonged to the MacGilchrists. Alasdair Campbell of Airds, *A History of Clan Campbell, vol. I: From Origins to Flodden* (Edinburgh, 2000), 33, 73.

[76] The castle or manor of Inveraray appears to have been a residence of the lords of Lochawe. It was 'built or rebuilt' by Sir Colin Campbell, first Laird of Glenorchy, who died in 1480. RCAHMS, *Argyll*, VII.no. 132. A house at Stronmagachan (NN 082141) is alleged to have been occupied by the Campbells before they moved to Inveraray. Campbell, *History of Clan Campbell*, 124.

[77] The MacSweens, Lamonts and MacGilchrists all claimed descent from Niall Noígiallach via the Cenél nÉogáin kings of Ailech in Northern Ireland. The sixteenth-century *Leabhar Chlainne Suibhne* claims that Ánrothán son of Aodh Athlamhan was the first to come to Scotland (Aodh died in 1033). W. D. H. Sellar, 'Family Origins in Cowal and Knapdale', *Scottish Studies* 15 (1971), 21–37, at 24.

A context for its earlier arrival might also be suggested but there is much uncertainty and some danger of building a house of cards. If we look, for instance, to the years quite soon after Munnu's death in 635 by which time Columba's prophecy that he would come to 'enjoy renown among all the churches of the *Scotti*' would, we might assume, be fulfilled, we might quite easily envisage the transmission of a cult which was flourishing in territory that at that time was controlled by the Cenél Conaill (Mag nÍtha and the area to the north) under a powerful Cenél Conaill overking (Domnall mac Aedo, the first to be described in the Chronicle of Iona as King of Ireland[78]) into an Argyll whose chief monastery of Iona (which almost certainly had land-holdings in various parts of Argyll, including on Loch Awe where two of the Kilmuns are located) was in the hands of Ségéne, a relative of Colum Cille and therefore also of the Cenél Conaill.[79] To add to this there was supposed to be a co-operative relationship between the Dál Riata of Argyll and the Cenél Conaill, and there is copious evidence of physical contact between Argyll and the Irish north.[80] Of course, there is a danger of oversimplification here, and there are some doubts about almost every element of this picture: Mag nÍtha seems always to have been a contested area so its links with one group rather than another might be considered insecure, and its links to Munnu are in any case tentative;[81] Munnu's cult might have greater affiliation with Cenél nEógáin;[82] Iona's role may be exaggerated because of Adomnan's skill as propagandist and Ségéne may not have been of the Cenél Conaill at all;[83] and finally, the link between Dál Riata and Cenél Conaill seems to have been strained at this time, and there may have been other inter-group relationships which were equally if not more significant. In sum certainties are impossible when there are so many variables, when specific affinities are so difficult to determine and when individual decisions regarding which saint to honour,

---

[78] *AU* 642.1 'Mors Domnaill m. Aedo regis Hibernie in fine Ianuari'.

[79] *Life of Columba*, ed. Sharpe, table 1.

[80] An example, though later, is that the island in Lough Swilly on which Munnu is placed in *vita prior* was subject to attack by a king of the Argyll Cenél Loairn in 733: *AU* 733.1 'Dungal m. Selbaich dehonorauit Toraich cum traxit Brudeum ex ea & eadem uice Insola Cuilenrigi inuassit'.

[81] For a map of the battles fought in the area, see Lacey, *Cenél Conaill*, 279. The identification of the Cenél Moan with the group referred to by the name Moccu Moie is far from certain, and their location in Mag nÍtha is recorded hundreds of years after Munnu's *floruit*. Note also the possible confusion with the Cenél Moen in the Mag nÍtha in Leinster (among the Fothairt). *Corpus Genealogiarum Hiberniae*, ed. M. A. O'Brien (Dublin, 1962), 126 a 33.

[82] The Cenél Moan are said to be part of the Cenél nEógáin in, for example, the genealogy of Ernán of Tory. *Corpus*, ed. Ó Riain, no. 16. The possibility that there was a genealogical relationship between this Ernán and Munnu is interesting given the proximity of Munnu and Ernéne mac Craséni both in *Vita Columbae* (*VC* i.2, i.3) and in *AU* (their obits are in the same entry in 635). There is some evidence to suggest that Ernán of Tory and Ernéne m. Craséni might be the same person, but this requires further exploration.

[83] Lacey suggests that Ségéne and several other Iona abbots were members of the Cenél Duach. Lacey, *Cenél Conaill*, 98–9.

and where, might be subject to whim. Perhaps the most one can say is that this context is at least as plausible as a Leinster one.

Other suggestions for the cult's origins in Argyll can be made,[84] but whichever (if any) is right it seems that the Campbells in Argyll, as their power grew in areas formerly controlled by the Lamonts, MacGilchrists and MacSweens, may have found it expedient to appropriate the cults of their local saints. Munnu was a saint with a powerful cult in Argyll possibly from the seventh century. The sites bearing his dedications were in strategic positions (all near routeways and waterways, well spaced within Argyll), and may have been near early secular centres, now gone. The Campbells may have taken advantage of the proximity of dedications to Munnu as a way of reinforcing their ancient rights, their rootedness in the ancient landscape, and what better way of asserting authority and ownership over significant pieces of land than by burial there of the family's dead?[85] It is possible too that by appropriating a cult that had previously belonged to a local kindred that might have been a rival, they neutralised the power of that cult, diminishing its usefulness as a badge of identity for their rivals and their rivals' followers.

The prominence of the Campbells has meant that Kilmun in Cowal, latterly their most important ecclesiastical site, has assumed a greater significance in comparison to the other Kilmuns than perhaps it had in the early medieval period. Thus Mackinlay reports a tradition that Munnu was buried near Kilmun in Cowal, at a place called *Sith-Mun*,[86] a name which would appear to come from the Gaelic *suidhe* meaning seat and often applied to prominent landscape features associated with saints.[87] There is no such place now known near Kilmun in Cowal, but there is a Suidhe Mhunge[88] beside Kilmun on Loch Awe. 'Tradition', it seems, has relocated the site to the place which latterly had more importance. It is possible that the Kilmun on Loch Awe, perhaps near the Columban foundation *Cella Diuni*, was originally the more

---

84 Could it be something to do with the Vikings' exodus from Ireland in the early tenth century? Dáibhí Ó Cróinín, *Early Medieval Ireland, 400–1200* (London, 1995), 255. Lamont is a Norse name and Wexford, near Munnu's foundation of Tech Munnu, was a Norse settlement. There is some evidence that Irish saints' cults travelled with the Norse to Cumberland at this time (Fiona Edmonds, 'Saints' Cults and Gaelic-Scandinavian Influence around the Cumberland Coast and North of the Solway Firth' in the forthcoming proceedings of a conference entitled *Celtic/Scandinavian Interaction by the Irish Sea*, eds Timothy Bolton et al. (Leiden)), and it is possible they reached Argyll too.

85 It is possible that a site near the Kilmun in Glen Aray was used for Campbell burial. Near the early christian site there is Creag a'Chaibeil, where *caibeal, -eil* means chapel or family burial ground. Edward Dwelly, *The Illustrated Gaelic-English Dictionary*, 11th edn (Edinburgh, 1993), 140. Tom na Cuirte, 2km NNE, is from *cùairt*, circle, circuit (*ibid.*, 284) or court, palace (MacLennan, *Gaelic Dictionary*, 114), which is suggestive of assertions of power of a different kind.

86 James Murray Mackinlay, *Ancient Church Dedications in Scotland, vol. II: Non-Scriptural Dedications* (Edinburgh, 1914), 71 (no source given, other than 'tradition').

87 Examples include Suidhe Blaan and Suidhe Cattan on Bute. Further examples are in W. J. Watson, *The History of the Celtic Place-Names of Scotland* (Edinburgh, 1926) (see index).

88 Suidhe Mhunge is at NM 9714 (OS pathfinder 355).

important site commemorating Munnu. It is intriguing, in this connection, that around the west end of Loch Awe a cluster of the Mac Gille Muns are to be found in records from the seventeenth century.[89]

Apart from the sites mentioned in Argyll there is a commemoration of the saint at Eilean Munde on Loch Leven, near Ballachulish, where there is an old parish church and burial-ground containing three medieval monuments. The burial enclosure is said to be that of MacDonald of Glencoe.[90] This is outside the area of Campbell control and has led some commentators to propose that a different Munnu is being commemorated here.[91] This attempt to split Munnu into two is also prompted by the evidence of feast day. Munnu's usual commemoration in all Irish Calendars is 21 October (and it is the one used by the Campbells)[92] but those of Adam King, Dempster and Camerarius (none very reliable, and there is some interdependence between them) record a date of 15 April.[93] This is a good way into the problems I noted at the beginning of this chapter.

First, his name. In most of his earliest mentions – *vita prior*, *Vita Columbae*, Annals of Ulster, *Martyrology of Tallaght* and *Félire Oengusso* – he is called Fintan rather than Munnu. We know that the form Munnu was used too, as *Domus Mundu* (the Latinisation of Tech Munnu) appears in *vita prior*, but the fact that Fintan seems early to have been the preferred form opens up the possibility that his name appears in place-names other than those containing 'Mun': for example, Killundine/Cill Fhionntáin and Kilintag[94] in Ardnamur-

---

89 Joanne mcDonche VcIlmund, sasine witness Glasver and Arnfad in barony of Glasrie, 1608 (Black, *Surnames of Scotland*, 545); Angus M'Illmund, Fincharne Nedder, 1672 (*Highland Papers*, ed. J. R. N. MacPhail, SHS, 4 vols (Edinburgh, 1914–34), II.208); several men called Mc Illmun in Glassary parish, 1692 (Duncan C. MacTavish, *The Commons of Argyll* (Lochgilphead, 1935), 38–9).

90 'This church served the former parish of Elanmunde which comprised, on the north side of Loch Leven, the districts of Mamore and Onich, lying in Invernessshire and, on the S side of Loch Leven, Glencoe and part of Appin, lying in Argyll.' RCAHMS, *Argyll*, II.no. 245. There also may be a commemoration in Forfar, where there was a *Forum S. Moindi*. RMS, IV.no. 1442.

91 Campbell, *A History of Clan Campbell*, 124. Campbell's source is 'Angus McLean, unpublished manuscript', a source used also by the Clan Campbell Society of North America who distinguish Fintan Munnu from a St Mund who was 'a 10th century saint who was abbot of Glenorchy with his seat at Clachandysart' (see under the name MACPHUN at www.ccsna.org/septs.htm). This looks like a conflation of data from the Aberdeen Breviary and *Adam King*, but without seeing the manuscript it is impossible to comment further.

92 In 1490 Earl Colin Campbell had Kilmun recognised as a burgh, and a fair established on 21 October. As Boardman notes, the fair conveniently coincided with the time when merchants from Spain, France and Brittany were most likely to be in the Firth of Clyde. Boardman, '"Pillars of the Community"', 299. 21 October is also the date in the Aberdeen Breviary, the Martyrology of Aberdeen ('Scottish Entries in the Martyrology of Aberdeen', in Forbes, *Kalendars*, 125–37), the Perth psalter (Francis C. Eeles, 'The Perth Psalter', *PSAS* 66 (1931–2), 426–41), the Paris psalter (Oxford, Bodleian Library, MS Douce 50), and the Glenorchy psalter (BL, Egerton 2899).

93 Dempster: *In Orcadibus Mundi abbatis sanctitate mirabilis*. Adam King: *S. Munde abbot and confess. in argyl vnder king kennede 2. 962.* Camerarius: *Sanctus Mundus Abbas, sanctitate vitae & miraculis celebris ad haec nostra tempora in prouincia Argathelia.* These works are all printed in Forbes, *Kalendars*, 196, 150, 236.

94 Watson, *Celtic Place-names*, 304.

chan. Crossfintan in Wexford is proposed as a possible commemoration of the saint, and, interestingly a site such as *Lathreg inden* in *Vita Columbae*, a place which seems to be near Derry, thus close to Munnu's origins, is another possibility.[95] It is also possible that a name like Kilfinan, a parish in Cowal, might commemorate Munnu. This is usually said to contain the name Fínán, which has a completely different derivation, but the course of place-name development is scarcely predictable, making it unwise to rule out this possibility altogether.

Second, his possible overlap with other saints. A story to explain Munnu's dual name is given in *Félire Oengusso* notes in Laud 610 which declares that it is the simple result of a name swap with Fintan of Cluain Eidnech (Fintan m. Garbáin).[96] Perhaps interaction between the two Fintans went deeper simply than a name swap however, as a gloss on the Martyrology of Gorman and the entry in the Martyrology of Donegal say Munnu is abbot of Cluain Eidnech.[97] A look at the genealogy of Fintan of Cluain Eidnech and at his Life in the *Codex Salmanticensis* reveals several similarities with the profile of Munnu: both are connected with the Fothairt, Munnu as their supporter, Fintan m. Garbáin as a relative;[98] significant stones are associated with both saints, Munnu's being the one on which he was born, Fintan's being the stone on which he was baptised;[99] both are associated with Dímma of the Fothairt,[100] and with a saint called Mochuma;[101] both are depicted as very strict or harsh and both are visited by angels; there are seven churches at Cluain Eidnech, and seven *loca* at Taghmon.[102] Many of these points are common hagiographical motifs and on their own amount to little. Together they are at least suggestive of some overlap of tradition between the two

---

95   *VC* i.20.

96   Commentary on *Félire Oengusso* in Oxford, Bodleian Library MS Laud 610, 21 October (*Félire*, ed. Stokes, 226): 'Fintan .i. Mundu .i. Fintan .i. Munna mac Telchain druad ideo hic Fintan dicitur .i. aenta doroine 7 Fintan Chluana hEidnech i Láigis, co tartad ainm cechtair de for araile in commemoraitione (sic) societatis.' It is interesting that the Fintan on the day before (20 October) also has a name swap with Fintan of Clonenagh – this is Fintan Maeldub (who is made into two separate saints in the Martyrology of Donegal). There may be a dedication to Maeldub at Inveraray.

97   *Martyrology of Donegal*, ed. Todd, 280; *The Martyrology of Gorman*, ed. Whitley Stokes, Henry Bradshaw Society (London, 1895).

98   *Corpus*, ed. Ó Riain, no. 3.

99   *vita prior*, ch. 1; commentary to *Félire Oengusso* in Rawlinson B 512 (*Félire*, ed. Stokes, 77).

100   In the case of Fintan of Cluain Eidnech this connection is through Berchán (*Félire*, ed. Stokes, 77), said elsewhere to be son of Dímma of the Fothairt.

101   In *vita prior*, ch. 4 this seems to be an alternative name for Comgall. In the life of Fintan of Cluain Eidnech, Mochuimi (in *Codex Salmanticensis*)/Mochummin (in the Dublin manuscript tradition: Primate Marsh's Library MS Z3.1.5 and Trinity College MS 175)/Mocumma (in the Oxford manuscript tradition: Bodleian Library MS Rawlinson B 485 and Rawlinson B 505) is a fellow disciple under Columba of Terryglass. *Vitae Sanctorum*, ed. Heist, ch. 3, 146; *Vitae Sanctorum*, ed. Plummer, II.97.

102   *vita prior*, ch. 19, 203. The 'seven churches of Clonenagh' are part of local tradition. John O'Hanlon, *Lives of the Irish Saints*, 9 vols (Dublin and London, 1875–1905), II.578.

saints.[103] It is interesting too that Fintan of Cluain Eidnech's feast day – 17 February in *Félire Oengusso* and the *Martyrology of Tallaght*, etc. – is one which was observed in Scotland, at least according to the somewhat unreliable testimony of Adam King.[104]

Munnu is more straightforward than many Gaelic saints, but he is not so clear-cut as he has sometimes been portrayed: his simple characterisation as a Leinster saint and a saint with important connections with Iona, may not be the most helpful way in which to approach his cult; if we admit place-names commemorating saints called Fintan, it is possible that his cult in Scotland is more widespread, and less easy to define; it is possible that there is some overlap with at least one other saint called Fintan, and, at the same time it is just possible (though I think unlikely) that there was a completely separate saint in Scotland called Munde.

He is interesting nonetheless, not least because of the evidence of the apparent appropriation of the cult by a late medieval expansionist force, giving testament to the enduring authority of the saint both at popular level and as an instrument of power among lords and bishops. And the persistence of personal names associated with a saint in places whose link with the saint is very ancient shows how deeply embedded into everyday life was devotion to saints.

---

[103] Both have obits in *AU*, however. Munnu's is in 635, as we have seen, and Fintan of Cluain Ednech appears at 603: 'Quies Finntain filii nepotis Ecdach'.

[104] 'S. Fintane pryor in scotland. 973.' Calendar of Adam King, in Forbes, *Kalendars*, 141–71. 'In Scotia Fintani prioris. ML. qui postea episcopatum gessit'. Calendar of Saints by Thomas Dempster, in *ibid.*, 177–229. This is also the day of Finan of Lindisfarne, successor of Aidan who is commemorated in several Scottish Calendars. Both *Fintane* and *Finnane* appear in Adam King's calendar.

3

THE STRUGGLE FOR SANCTITY:
ST WALTHEOF OF MELROSE, CISTERCIAN IN-HOUSE
CULTS AND CANONISATION PROCEDURE AT THE TURN
OF THE THIRTEENTH CENTURY[1]

Helen Birkett

In mid-1206, a group of six inquisitive lay brothers at the Cistercian house of Melrose made an exciting discovery. The brethren had been preparing a tomb for the recently deceased Abbot William II, who was to be buried alongside the tomb of his saintly predecessor, Abbot Waltheof. Waltheof's most famous attribute was the miraculous preservation of his body, a state that had last been witnessed over thirty years previously in 1171. Overcome by the desire to witness this miracle for themselves, the brothers urged the abbey's mason, Brother Robert, to raise the marble cover of St Waltheof's tomb and peer in.[2]

This second discovery of Waltheof's incorruption was an event that must have both re-awakened interest in the saint's cult and re-opened older questions surrounding its promotion. The immediate response of the house appears to have been to commission the well known Cistercian hagiographer, Jocelin of Furness, to write an official account of Waltheof's life and deeds, a work that was begun during the brief abbacy of William's successor, Abbot Patrick (*ob.* 1207).[3] The *Vita*'s main intention was to raise the profile of Waltheof's

---

[1] I am grateful to the AHRC for funding this research and to Professor Christopher Norton, Professor Jocelyn Wogan-Browne and Dr Bronach Kane for their comments on earlier versions of this chapter.

[2] The *Vita S. Waldevi* actually dates this event to 1207 but the context makes it clear that 1206 is the intended date. All citations of the *Vita* refer to the edition produced by George McFadden, which is based on the *Acta Sanctorum* version of the text. Many of the translations quoted in this chapter come from McFadden's edition; however, in a number of instances I have found my own translations preferable. A manuscript copy of the *Vita* (Madrid, Biblioteca del Palacio Real, MS II 2097) has also recently been rediscovered – where necessary, differences between the two extant versions of the text are noted in the footnotes. George Joseph McFadden, 'An Edition and Translation of the Life of Waldef, Abbot of Melrose by Jocelin of Furness' (Columbia University, unpublished PhD thesis, 1952), 197–8, 352–4 (henceforth referred to as *Vita Waldevi*).

[3] *Vita Waldevi*, 94, 204–5; *The Chronicle of Melrose, from the Cottonian Manuscript, Faustina B.IX in the British Museum*, eds Alan Orr Anderson, Marjorie Ogilvie Anderson and William Croft Dickinson (London, 1936), 52–3; 'The Chronicle of Melrose', in *The Church Historians of England*, trans. Joseph Stevenson, 5 vols in 8 (London, 1854–6), IV pt i.79–242, at 149.

2. A view of Melrose Abbey, centre of the contested cult of St Waltheof.
© and courtesy of Richard Fawcett

cult. The possession of an incorrupt corpse was, as the *Vita* makes clear, no common claim. Waltheof joined a select group of only six English saints, the shrines of whom were major sites of pilgrimage in the religious landscape of Britain: Canterbury, Bury St Edmunds, Durham, Ely, and London.[4] Yet despite the possession of such a rare gift, the *Vita* indicates that Melrose had yet to make a significant impact on the wider pilgrimage circuit. Although the text records the journeys of two English pilgrims to the shrine, that this marked the extent of outside interest in the period of half a century following the saint's death indicates the cult's rather limited appeal.[5]

Analysis of the text reveals that one of the most significant factors to constrain the success of the cult was the mixed feelings towards Waltheof's sanctity within Melrose itself. As the *Vita* shows, the first decade of the cult was dominated by divisions within the house over how to accommodate Waltheof's growing cult with the isolationist ethos of the Cistercian order. Yet even when the decision had been made fully to sanction the cult, the changing requirements of canonisation procedure meant that by the time of the discovery in 1206, earlier attempts to authorise Waltheof's sanctity were deemed insufficient. Jocelin's *Vita* played a crucial role in the early thirteenth-century campaign to canonise formally Waltheof. Responding to

---

4   *Vita Waldevi*, 198–9, 355–6.
5   *Ibid.*, 185–6, 195–7, 339–40, 350–2.

the new requirements demanded by the papal *curia*, the text included the now obligatory eyewitness accounts that attested to the saint's powers and indicates that the *Vita* was intended to form part of an initial application for papal canonisation. This chapter will trace the development of Waltheof's cult during its first fifty years, exploring the changing attitudes towards the cult and the continued efforts made by members of the Melrose community officially to authorise Waltheof's sanctity.

The early development of the cult

Evidence within the *Vita* reveals that Jocelin's text was the latest in a number of attempts to achieve formal recognition of Waltheof's sanctity, the earliest of which had begun immediately after the saint's death in 1159. The first signs that certain members of the community wished to accord Waltheof special status are found in the treatment of the abbot's corpse during the preparation for its burial. Although the body had been washed and clothed in a monastic habit, 'it seemed to some that he ought to be clothed in his vestments, as they had read of Blessed Bernard'.[6] Further debate seems to have produced a compromise measure: the body remained in the tunic and cowl of the order but was wrapped in an additional waxed cloth.[7] This attempt to imitate Bernard of Clairvaux reflects an explicit desire within the Melrose community to venerate Waltheof as a figure of comparable sanctity.[8] As further contention over the location of Waltheof's tomb implies, it was a desire also felt by some outside the order. By this point, news of Waltheof's death had brought a number of other prominent religious and ecclesiastical figures to the monastery. Several of those gathered, including Bishop Herbert of Glasgow, argued that Waltheof should be buried in the church, a measure that would have allowed easier access to his tomb for any prospective pilgrims and indicates the expectation that a cult would develop around his memory. However, others, including Eanfrith, abbot of the Cistercian house of Newbattle, urged otherwise and eventually Waltheof was laid to rest in the chapterhouse in the very place he had indicated during

---

6   As recorded in the *Vita Prima Bernardi* – although it is also possible that the Melrose monks received this information via word of mouth or from a Cistercian newsletter on the subject. *Vita Waldevi*, 162, 311; *S. Bernardi Opera Omnia IV, PL*, CLXXXV.360.

7   The *Vita* is careful to record that this sheet, a contravention of Cistercian statutes, had disintegrated by the time of the first discovery of Waltheof's incorruption in 1171. *Vita Waldevi*, 162, 189, 311, 343.

8   Although Bernard was not formally canonised until 1174, those within the order regarded him as a saint. In 1159, the General Chapter decreed that houses of the Clairvaux filiation, of which Melrose was a member, were to celebrate the Office of the Dead in Bernard's honour. *Twelfth-Century Statutes from the Cistercian General Chapter*, ed. Chrysogonus Waddell, Studia et Documenta 12 (Citeaux, 2002), 71; Adriaan H. Bredero, *Bernard of Clairvaux: Between Cult and History* (Edinburgh, 1996), 33.

his lifetime.[9] Although still a prestigious location and the customary burial place for an abbot, as an area restricted to monastic personnel it seems likely that the choice of this site also represented a deliberate attempt to limit the growth of the cult.[10] The opposition of Eanfrith, the abbot of one of Melrose's daughterhouses, was to prefigure a deep political division within the Melrose community itself and one which would eventually force a change of leadership at the house.

The growth of Waltheof's cult during the 1160s seems to have been directly linked to increasing discontent with the rule of Waltheof's successor, Abbot William I.[11] William was, perhaps, unlucky to have stepped into Waltheof's shoes. Apparently a much-loved abbot, Waltheof provided an exemplar of abbatial rule to which his successor could be compared.[12] The primary virtue valued by the pro-Waltheof faction within the monastery – and one emphasised by the order as a whole – was the saint's humility.[13] Although Waltheof was a man with intimate links to the Scottish and English royal houses, he had chosen to shun both riches and status, not only by becoming a Cistercian, but in his general modes of social interaction.[14] According to the *Vita*, the saint made careful efforts to ensure that he was not set apart from the rest of the community. He insisted on being subjected to exactly the same rules of discipline and bound other members of the house to punish him should he commit any wrongdoing.[15] He also seems to have enjoyed a close relationship with the lay brothers. The *Vita* tells us that on one occasion when Waltheof was preaching to them, he inadvertently disclosed that it was he, not an anonymous third party, who had experienced a vision of Christ in the heavens.[16] Such intimacy was evidently valued by the lay brother community

---

[9] *Vita Waldevi*, 154, 163, 300, 311–12.

[10] Although lay brothers were members of the community, even their presence in the chapterhouse was restricted to certain feast days. Megan Cassidy-Welch, *Monastic Spaces and their Meanings: Thirteenth-Century English Cistercian Monasteries*, Medieval Church Studies 1 (Turnhout, 2001), 105, 171.

[11] Although both Derek Baker and A. A. M. Duncan have previously commented on this conflict, neither analysed it in depth. Derek Baker, 'Legend and reality: the case of Waldef of Melrose', in *Church Society and Politics: Papers Read at the Thirteenth Summer Meeting and the Fourteenth Winter Meeting of the Ecclesiastical History Society*, ed. Derek Baker, Studies in Church History 12 (Oxford, 1975), 59–82, at 67–8, n. 36; A. A. M. Duncan, 'Sources and uses of the Chronicle of Melrose, 1165–1297', in *Kings, Clerics and Chronicles in Scotland 500–1297: Essays in Honour of Marjorie Ogilvie Anderson on the Occasion of her Ninetieth Birthday*, ed. Simon Taylor (Dublin, 2000), 146–85, at 149–50.

[12] Elizabeth Freeman provides a more general discussion of Waltheof's representation as an exemplary abbot: Elizabeth Freeman, 'Models for Cistercian life in Jocelin of Furness's *Vita Waldevi*', *Cistercian Studies Quarterly* 37 (2002), 107–21, at 112–14.

[13] Martha G. Newman, *The Boundaries of Charity: Cistercian Culture and Ecclesiastical Reform, 1098–1180*, Figurae: Reading Medieval Culture (Stanford, 1996), 162–3.

[14] *Vita Waldevi*, 102–3, 126, 128, 218–20, 254–5, 257–8.

[15] *Ibid.*, 123–5, 127, 249–51, 256.

[16] *Ibid.*, 149–50, 293–4.

– their devotion is shown by the amount of testimony in the *Vita* provided by lay brother sources.[17]

In contrast, William's abbacy is presented as a perversion of the *Benedictine Rule*. Whereas Waltheof closely followed Benedict's instructions and strove to be more loved than feared, William is explicitly stated to have done the opposite.[18] A hint of William's harsh rule is provided by the *Vita*'s statement that Prior Jocelin was a man whom William 'had oppressed in many matters before'.[19] If we can presume that William chose to exercise his power in the chapterhouse, one of the major sites of monastic confession and punishment, any sense of injustice experienced by Jocelin can only have been enhanced by the presence of Waltheof's grave in the same space.[20] In the chapterhouse, the juxtaposition of the two abbots provided not just a spiritual but also a physical contrast.

Analysis of the posthumous *miracula* in the *Vita Waldevi* attests to the rising tensions that centred on the memory of the former abbot. The sequence of healing miracles that precede William's eventual departure in the text records the growing unease surrounding access to Waltheof's tomb. The first miraculous cure followed the apparently spontaneous action of the lay brother, Gillesperda. Having being diagnosed with an incurable form of dropsy, Gillesperda successfully sought Waltheof's intercession during a night of prayer at the abbot's tomb.[21] The report of this miracle persuaded a layman suffering from the same illness to request permission for a similar overnight vigil – permission was granted and the desired cure swiftly followed.[22] The third miracle provides evidence of increasing concern over this access: another layman suffering from dropsy was admitted to the

---

[17] Waltheof's cult had a significant lay brother following; however, I think that this has been over-emphasised by McFadden and Baker. Although the *Vita* cites more lay brother witnesses than monastic ones, the amount of monastic testimony is not inconsiderable. It should also be noted that in a number of cases the direct source of Jocelin's narratives is unclear – the references below include the implied sources for narratives (that is, the individuals mentioned within the narrative). In addition, the *Vita*'s use of 'monachi' and 'conversi' as interchangeable in the account of the discovery in 1206 means that the sole use of the word 'monachus' cannot be taken to imply choir monk status – only those whose status can be confirmed by other information in the text are noted in the references that follow. Lay brother testimony can be found in the *Vita Waldevi*, 138–40, 148–51, 156, 157–9, 167–77, 178–80, 181–2, 194–5, 197–8, 272–6, 291–6, 302, 304–6, 318–30, 331–3, 334–5, 349–50, 353–4. Monastic testimony can be found in *ibid.*, 110, 124, 134–5, 142, 144, 145, 156, 193, 228, 250–1, 267–9, 280, 285, 288, 302, 348. See also *ibid.*, 65, 354 n. 3; George McFadden, 'The Life of Waldef and its author, Jocelin of Furness', *IR* 6 (1955), 5–13, at 7; Baker, 'Legend and reality', 70 and n. 49.

[18] *Vita Waldevi*, 121, 187, 245, 341; *RB1980: The Rule of St Benedict in Latin and English with Notes*, eds Timothy Fry et al. (Collegeville, 1981), 282, 283.

[19] 'quem ipse in multis ante gravaverat'. This may well refer to excess during punitive beatings, which would continue until the abbot decreed that the sinner had suffered enough. Cassidy-Welch, *Monastic Spaces*, 125–6; *Vita Waldevi*, 187.

[20] Cassidy-Welch, *Monastic Spaces*, 120, 124, 125.

[21] *Vita Waldevi*, 181–2, 334–5.

[22] *Ibid.*, 182–3, 336.

tomb only after he 'most urgently requested' entry.[23] In the fourth miracle, the appearance at the abbey gate of a sick householder, accompanied by a sizeable procession of family and friends, must have done little to ease fears about the growth of the cult. Again, there is notable reluctance to grant the sick man access: it was only after 'repeated and devout petition' that he was allowed to observe an overnight vigil at the tomb.[24] Strictures placed on access to the abbot's tomb also affected those inside the monastery. The fifth healing miracle concerns a Melrose monk, Benedict, who suffered from an almost complete loss of sight and hearing. Jocelin describes how, in 'pious and wholesome stealth', he secretly crept to the tomb one night to pray for a cure.[25] The sixth miracle provides some evidence of unchallenged access to the tomb, but only for those considered beyond all earthly help: an anonymous monk 'filled onlookers with commiseration and despair of his life … He was led, therefore, to the saint's tomb'.[26] The recipient of the seventh miracle was met with a less accommodating attitude. The appearance of a clerk from a distant part of England 'drawn by the holy reputation of Abbot St Waltheof' seemed to prove that despite any attempts to stall its development, the cult continued to gain in fame.[27] It was only 'by begging, wailing, [and] imploring' that the clerk was able to overcome the reluctance to grant him entry.[28] If the chronology of the miracles is correct, Abbot William's reaction to the clerk's visit was to announce a complete prohibition on access of the sick to the holy man's tomb. That this suppression of the cult was characterised by some as William's 'envy' serves to indicate the deep in-house division that devotion to Waltheof had come to symbolise.[29]

Although the cult had clearly taken on a momentum of its own, there were significant reasons to sympathise with William's attempts to stop the tide. The chapterhouse was one of the holiest places within the monastic precinct and, as such, general access to this area was limited to choir monks only.[30] The early secular dimension of the cult, seen in the cure of laymen in the second, third and fourth healing miracles, posed a threat to the cloistered life of the community – a danger apparently confirmed by the appearance of

---

23 'obnixius postulato'. *Ibid.*, 183.
24 'ad crebram denique & devotem ejusdem petitionem'. *Ibid.*, 183–4, 337–8.
25 *Ibid.*, 184, 338.
26 *Ibid.*, 185, 339.
27 *Ibid.*, 185–6, 339.
28 'obsecrando, plorando, implorando'. *Ibid.*, 186.
29 *Ibid.*, 186, 340.
30 There was also the more practical side of a healing cult to consider – as Henry Mayr-Harting remarked about the shrine of St Frideswide, the canons 'could have spent a great deal of time mopping up after miracles'. That such mess might occur in a monastic space used as frequently as the chapterhouse could have posed serious problems. Cassidy-Welch, *Monastic Spaces*, 105–6; Henry Mayr-Harting, 'Functions of a twelfth-century shrine: the miracles of St Frideswide', in *Studies in Medieval History Presented to R. H. C. Davis*, eds Henry Mayr-Harting and R. I. Moore (London, 1985), 193–206, at 195.

a clerk from distant lands. As the *Vita* itself states, William's actions represented the desire 'that the monasteries of the Cistercian order be free from endless crowds flowing in upon them from every side'.[31] Although in-house cults had developed around the memory of other early abbots, the Cistercian General Chapter had shown itself wary of the potential problems that a successful healing cult could bring.[32] Bernard's hostile feelings towards cults that had developed around the tombs of saints were well known and must have played a significant role in the decision made by the Cistercian leadership to stem the development of such a cult at Clairvaux following Bernard's death in 1153.[33] Consequently, the final version of the *Vita Prima*, which formed part of the material submitted for Bernard's canonisation in 1174, includes no posthumous *miracula*.[34] Even the later general miracle collection, the *Exordium Magnum Cisterciense* compiled between 1177 and 1221, records only four posthumous miracles relating to Bernard, three of which occurred before his burial. The third miracle, where a disabled man gained the power to stand on reaching Bernard's corpse, proved to be the final straw for the abbot of Cîteaux. Fearing that monastic discipline would be disrupted by subsequent hordes of pilgrims, he forbade the holy body itself from performing any more miracles.[35] While this may have provided a model for William's reaction, it did not make his decision any more palatable to the Melrose community. For the pro-Waltheof faction, it offered further evidence of William's overbearing arrogance. Not only was it a denial of one of the core Cistercian values of charity, in stifling the nascent cult, it formed a denial of God's works on earth, if not God himself. As the *Vita* stated, here was a man who had 'dared to block up the fount of mercy' and silence what the glory of heaven proclaimed to the world.[36]

---

[31] 'coenobitae Cisterc[i]ensis Ordinis turbarum undique confluentium carerent immoderata frequentia'. *Vita Waldevi*, 186, 340.

[32] For example, the *Vita* itself provides evidence of the cult that had grown up around William, the first abbot of Rievaulx. A cult had also developed around Robert, the first abbot of Newminster, while at Savigny, the community venerated five of the abbey's former monks, including their first abbot, Vitalis, and his successor, Geoffrey. *Vita Waldevi*, 145–7, 285–90; Peter Fergusson and Stuart Harrison, *Rievaulx Abbey: Community, Architecture, Memory, with Contributions from Glyn Coppack* (New Haven, 1999), 99; 'Vita S. Roberti Novi Monasterii in Anglia Abbatis', ed. Paul Grosjean, *Analecta Bollandiana* 57 (1939), 334–60; Lindy Grant, 'Savigny and its Saints', in *Perspectives for an Architecture of Solitude: Essays on Cistercians, Art and Architecture in Honour of Peter Fergusson*, ed. Terryl N. Kinder, Medieval Church Studies 11, Studia et Documenta 13 (Turnhout, 2004), 109–14, at 111; 'Vitae BB. Vitalis et Gaufridi Primi et Secundi Abbatum Saviniacensium in Normannia', ed. E. P. Sauvage, *Analecta Bollandiana* 1 (1882), 355–410.

[33] Bredero, *Bernard of Clairvaux*, 57–8, 70, 72–3.

[34] For Bredero's full argument about the lack of posthumous *miracula*, see *ibid.*, 65–73.

[35] The fourth posthumous miracle was an exorcism carried out using some of Bernard's beard hair, which explicitly references the abbot's prohibition of access to the dead body. *S. Bernardi Opera*, 447–9; Bredero, *Bernard of Clairvaux*, 68–70.

[36] 'misericordiae fontem audeat obstruere'. *Vita Waldevi*, 187, 340.

William's suppression of the cult seems to have alienated such a significant proportion of the community that he became unable to uphold the authority of his office.[37] Consequently, on 22 April 1170 William resigned his abbacy in favour of Prior Jocelin, who immediately took up his new post.[38] The swift replacement of William stands in marked contrast to the evidence for earlier and later abbatial successions at Melrose during this period and suggests that William's resignation was far from unexpected.[39] The *Vita*'s description of Prior Jocelin as one of William's principal adversaries and a man 'who loved St Waltheof and had been loved by him' suggests that he had become the figurehead for the opposition and the obvious choice as William's successor.[40] If we can recognise Waltheof's cult as being the key issue that divided the house against William, then Jocelin's immediate appointment as abbot represents the culmination of a long-recognised alternative. As Giles Constable states, the choice of abbot was one of the most important ways in which a monastic community could assert its wishes – by electing Jocelin, the monks reinstated Waltheof.[41]

That the replacement of Abbot William was directly related to the tensions surrounding the memory of Waltheof is confirmed by the subsequent action taken officially to authorise the cult. The *Vita* tells us that in 1171 Abbot Jocelin decided to replace the stone covering Waltheof's tomb with a new slab of marble that was more in keeping with the saint's sanctity and nobility.[42] It was to be no small ceremony. Bishop Ingram of Glasgow was invited to oversee the exchange of tombstones, while a number of abbots and priors

---

[37] Although the *Rule* stated that each monk owed absolute obedience to the abbot, Giles Constable argues that by the twelfth century the interpretation of this obedience had changed. He cites the mid-twelfth-century *Bridlington Dialogue*, which states that monks were by no means obliged to obey their abbot should he order them to commit wrongdoing. *Vita Waldevi*, 187, 341; *RB1980*, eds Fry et al., 180, 181, 184, 185, 188, 189; Giles Constable, 'The authority of superiors in religious communities', in his *Monks, Hermits and Crusaders in Medieval Europe*, Collected Studies Series 273 (London, 1988), ch. 3, 203–4.

[38] The events of April 1170 probably represent a forced resignation rather than a deposition. To suggest that a community had deposed its abbot was a serious charge and one that Jocelin had been careful to refute earlier in the text with regard to Waltheof's predecessor, Abbot Richard. *Chronicle of Melrose*, ed. Anderson et al., 38; 'The Chronicle of Melrose', trans. Stevenson, 132; *Vita Waldevi*, 119–20, 243–5.

[39] For example, William himself was elected to the abbacy just under four months after Waltheof's death in 1159. See also the appointments of new abbots in 1189, 1214, 1215 and 1216. Even when there is the suggestion that a change in leadership had been ordered by the abbot of Melrose's motherhouse, Rievaulx, as in 1194, the resignation of one abbot and the installation of another occurred on consecutive days. *Chronicle of Melrose*, eds Anderson et al., 35–6, 38, 47, 49, 58, 61, 63; 'Chronicle of Melrose', trans. Stevenson, 128, 132, 143, 146, 155, 160, 162–3.

[40] 'qui sancti Waltevi dilector & dilectus extitit'. *Vita Waldevi*, 187, 341.

[41] Constable, 'Authority of superiors', 197.

[42] Derek Baker incorrectly dates this event to 22 June 1170, just two months after Jocelin had been elected abbot. The *Chronicle of Melrose* is quite clear, however, that the discovery of Waltheof's incorruption was made on 22 May 1171. *Vita Waldevi*, 187–8, 341; Baker, 'Legend and reality', 70, n. 49; *Chronicle of Melrose*, eds Anderson et al., 39; 'Chronicle of Melrose', trans. Stevenson, 133.

were also present to witness the event.[43] The presence of the bishop suggests that the ceremony was intended formally to inaugurate Waltheof's sanctity. Although the papacy was extending its authority over the canonisation process during this time, the power of the bishop to authorise the veneration of minor saints still held strong before the end of the century.[44]

If there were doubts over the bishop's capacity to canonise the former abbot, then these were removed when the incorruption of the body proclaimed Waltheof's sanctity for him. The *Vita*'s account of this discovery draws immediate parallels with the rediscovery of St Cuthbert's incorrupt body in 1104.[45] That these parallels are present within the narrative structure rather than the phrasing of the text indicates that the *Vita*'s account reflects the story as the author had either heard or read it. Indeed, if we can accept this account as an accurate rendering of events, it seems that those present at the opening of Waltheof's tomb in 1171 reacted to the discovery in ways that consciously mimicked the account of St Cuthbert's examination in 1104. Taking the role played by the abbot of Seez in Durham, Bishop Ingram also tugged and pulled at the corpse in what Barbara Abou-El-Haj describes as 'a brutally tactile demonstration' of the saint's preservation.[46] Such actions were not for the fainthearted and both accounts record a similar level of horror

---

43 *Vita Waldevi*, 188, 341–2.

44 In 1102, the Council of Westminster decreed that episcopal approval was necessary for the veneration of saints. However, the impatience for official papal confirmation of Becket's sanctity following his martyrdom in 1170 shows that by this point, there was a strong perception in England that the right to canonise belonged to the *curia*. But it must be noted that Becket's martyrdom had attracted European-wide interest – it was clear that his cult was going to have a strong international following. The same cannot be said of Waltheof's cult. Eric Waldram Kemp, *Canonization and Authority in the Western Church* (Oxford, 1948), 53–4, 87–8; *Councils & Synods with Other Documents Relating to the English Church* vol. I , eds D. Whitelock, M. Brett and C. N. L. Brooke (Oxford, 1981), pt ii.678.

45 The anonymous account of the examination in 1104 was written at some point after 1123, possibly even after 1128. The testing of Waltheof's body may also have drawn on the accounts of Cuthbert's earlier examination in 698 found in the *vitae* written by an anonymous author (699×705) and by Bede (*ca* 721). Although Reginald of Durham's *Libellus de Admirandis Beati Cuthberti Virtutibus*, written between 1165 and 1172, gives an extremely detailed description of the corpse, its coverings and the coffin, he does not give an account of the examination of the body by the Abbot of Seez. *Symeonis Monachi Opera Omnia*, ed. Thomas Arnold, RS 75, 2 vols (London, 1882–5), I.248–61; 'The anonymous account of the translation of St. Cuthbert, 29 August 1104', trans. R. A. B. Mynors, in *The Relics of Saint Cuthbert*, ed. C. F. Battiscombe (Oxford, 1956), 99–107; *Two Lives of Saint Cuthbert: A Life by an Anonymous Monk of Lindisfarne and Bede's Prose Life*, ed. and trans. Bertram Colgrave (Cambridge, 1940), 13, 16, 130–3, 292, 293; *Reginaldi Monachi Dunelmensis, Libellus de admirandis beati Cuthberti virtutibus quae novellis patratae sunt temporibus*, ed. James Raine, Surtees Society 1 (1835), 84–90; 'Illustration [B]', in *The Church Historians of England*, trans. Stevenson, III pt ii.779–85; Bertram Colgrave, 'The post-Bedan miracles and translations of St Cuthbert', in *The Early Cultures of North-West Europe*, eds Cyril Fox and Bruce Dickins, H. M. Chadwick Memorial Studies (Cambridge, 1950), 329, 330.

46 Barbara Abou-El-Haj, 'Saint Cuthbert: the post-conquest appropriation of an Anglo-Saxon cult', in *Holy Men and Holy Women: Old English Prose Saints' Lives and Their Contexts*, ed. Paul E. Szarmach, SUNY Series in Medieval Studies (Albany, 1996), 177–206, at 192.

among the bystanders, with Melrose's Peter the cantor standing in for the anonymous disgruntled voices present at both Durham and Melrose. With his bathetic 'My lord bishop … you are handling the holy body more roughly than you ought', Peter's interjection forces the narrative on to the examiner's concluding statement.[47] Here, informing the convent that 'you have with you a companion for St Cuthbert, once a monk of Melrose', Ingram explicitly associates the two discoveries while hinting that this conforms to a preconceived expectation.[48] As both a former monk of Old Melrose and one of the major saints of the north, Cuthbert would have been a well known figure to the Melrose brethren and the ecclesiastics gathered there for the 1171 ceremony. On being presented with this unexpected blessing, those present at the ceremony recalled the examination of St Cuthbert in 1104 not only as a similar point of reference, but as a method of validating both their discovery and Waltheof's sanctity.[49]

Ingram's announcement that Waltheof had become 'a companion for St Cuthbert' seems to have been regarded as an official canonisation of the saint. This is supported by the account in the *Chronicle of Melrose* where the discovery of Waltheof's incorruption was accompanied by cries of 'truly this is a man of God' – an allusion to the words in Mark's Gospel which acknowledge Christ's true nature. The discovery of Waltheof's incorruption is presented as a similar revelation of status: Waltheof's sanctity was now made manifest.[50] That Ingram's declaration in the *Vita* is followed by

47 'Domine, inquit, episcope, salva reverentia vestra, durius quam decet sanctum corpus contrectas.' *Vita Waldevi*, 188–9.
48 *Vita Waldevi*, 189, 342–3; *Symeonis Monachi Opera*, ed. Arnold, I.259; 'Anonymous account', trans. Mynors, 105–6.
49 Their actions may also have been guided by other incorruption narratives, such as the account in Aelred's *Vita S. Edwardi*, that in Goscelin of Saint-Bertin's *Vita S. Wihtburge*, and the account of the examination of St Edmund's body given by William of Malmesbury in the *Gesta Pontificum* (although the manhandling of the corpse has negative repercussions in this narrative). However, given the local interest in Cuthbert, it is likely that the Durham accounts provided the main parallels for the Melrose discovery. *Beati Aelredi Abbatis Rievallensis Opera Omnia, PL*, CXCV.782–3; *Aelred of Rievaulx: The Historical Works*, trans. Jane Patricia Freeland and ed. Marsha L. Dutton, Cistercian Fathers Series 56 (Kalamazoo, 2005), 227–8; *Goscelin of Saint-Bertin, The Hagiography of the Female Saints of Ely*, ed. and trans. Rosalind C. Love, Oxford Medieval Texts (Oxford, 2004), 78–81; *William of Malmesbury, Gesta Pontificum Anglorum: The History of the English Bishops*, eds and trans. M. Winterbottom and R. M. Thomson, Oxford Medieval Texts, 2 vols (Oxford, 2007), I.246–9.
50 The account of this event in the *Chronicle* seems to be carefully worded to imply rather than proclaim Waltheof's sanctity. In addition to the allusion to the Gospel of St Mark, the text notes that the new tombstone was laid upon Waltheof's 'most holy body' ('sanctissime corporis'). Otherwise, the terms 'sanctus' and 'beatus' are notably absent from the *Chronicle*'s account of the discovery. This seems to reflect the fact that this stratum of the *Chronicle* was probably written in the first decade of the thirteenth century. This makes it directly contemporary with Jocelin's *Vita* and therefore unsurprising that the text conveys similar caution concerning the formal recognition of Waltheof's sanctity (see below). *Chronicle*: 'Vere hic homo dei est'; Mark 15:39: 'vere homo hic Filius Dei erat'. *Chronicle of Melrose*, eds Anderson et al., 39; Stevenson, 'Chronicle of Melrose', 133–4; *The Chronicle of Melrose: A Stratigraphic Edition vol. I, Introduction and*

a debate over where to place the shrine further confirms the official accept-ance of Waltheof's saintly status. As in 1159, the suggestion was again made, and again vetoed, that Waltheof's body should be transferred to the church. The *Vita* makes the reasoning behind this decision clear: the body should remain in the chapterhouse 'unless the authority of the pope or the consent and permission of the Cistercian Chapter should sanction otherwise'.[51] This statement makes a significant claim. Although it lends further support to the argument that papal authority over the translation of relics was widely recog-nised by this time, it also shows that this authority was far from absolute.[52] The *Vita* explicitly states that the Cistercian General Chapter was also able to authorise the translation of Waltheof's body – that in 1171, the power of the General Chapter to decide in this matter was seen as equivalent to that of the Pope.

The Vita *as a canonisation text*

However, by the time that the *Vita* was commissioned in the early thirteenth century, attitudes had changed. Over the course of Innocent III's reign (1198–1216) the papal hold over the process of canonisation had tightened and by 1206 the idea that the papacy alone could authorise a declaration of sanctity was being taught in the schools.[53] The investigation into the sanctity of Gilbert of Sempringham, initiated in 1200, had formalised this new canonisation procedure. At the request of the Gilbertine order, Archbishop Hubert Walter had commissioned an inquiry into the life and miracles of the saint. The report of this initial investigation, along with numerous letters of support for the case, was submitted for consideration at the *curia*. In response, the pope instituted a second inquiry whose report would include written statements of eyewitness testimony and be accompanied by a select group of eyewitnesses to testify in person. With the successful conclusion of these proceedings, Gilbert was canonised in 1202.[54] The same procedure was followed for the canonisation of Wulfstan of Worcester in the following year.[55] With the recent canonisation of two English saints and the significant involvement of the Cistercians in the application for the first, it seems unlikely that the Melrose

---

Facsimile Edition, eds Dauvit Broun and Julian Harrison, SHS Series 1 (Woodbridge, 2007), 129–30.

[51] 'donec auctoritate summi Pontificis, vel consensu & concessu capituli Cistercien[s]is aliud sanciretur.' *Vita Waldevi*, 189, 343.

[52] Kemp, *Canonization and Authority*, 80, 101–2.

[53] *Ibid.*, 102.

[54] *The Book of St Gilbert*, eds and trans. Raymonde Foreville and Gillian Keir, Oxford Medieval Texts (Oxford, 1987), xcvi–ix, 200–53.

[55] Kemp, *Canonization and Authority*, 105.

community would have been ignorant of the new developments in canonisation procedure.[56]

Indeed, it is clear that by the time the text was written, the Melrose community no longer viewed episcopal canonisation as sufficient authorisation of Waltheof's sanctity. As a result, the subsequent lack of any further attempts to promote the cult was viewed with no small disappointment. The perceived inaction of Abbot Jocelin, who was promoted to the bishopric of Glasgow in 1175, became a source of particular frustration. The *Vita* tells us that while he was 'a man in many ways to be praised, because he took no steps to canonize St Waltheof, who particularly loved, encouraged and advanced him, he is seen by many to be blameworthy'.[57] The simplest explanation for Jocelin's conduct is that he had felt no need to reconfirm what had already been authorised.[58] However, the *Vita*'s use of the present tense – 'is seen by many' – indicates that Jocelin was being judged by the standards of those who commissioned the text rather than the standards of those a few decades previously.

An earlier episode in the *Vita* shows further signs of the incorporation of contemporary concerns into the narrative. The first miracle to be recorded after the death of Waltheof is the vision of the king of Scotland's chancellor, Nicholas, while on business in Rome in 1159. Detained at the *curia* until late, Nicholas was offered hospitality at the papal palace rather than being forced to cross the dangerous streets of Rome at night. In his sleep, he saw a vision of Waltheof approaching the gates of heaven but being refused entry. The next morning, Nicholas recounted his vision to the pope who asked him to make a note of the date and to send him a letter on his return to Scotland so that the vision's full meaning could be understood. On Nicholas's

---

56 Cistercian abbots had been appointed to the panels of both the original inquiry and the one commissioned by the *curia* (although, in the case of the latter, the abbot of Wardon was unable to attend – he had already left for the General Chapter). It is possible that William, the abbot of Swineshead present at the initial inquiry, became abbot of Furness in the early thirteenth century and, if so, this may mean that the author of the *Vita*, Jocelin, was particularly well informed about contemporary canonisation procedures. However, the editors of *The Heads of Religious Houses* remain uncertain of the claims behind William's abbacy. *Book of St Gilbert*, eds and trans. Foreville and Keir, 200, 201 and n. 1, 234–7, 240, 241; D. Knowles, C. N. L. Brooke and Vera C. M. London, *The Heads of Religious Houses: England and Wales*, 2 vols, 2nd edn (Cambridge, 2001), I.134.

57 'vir in multis laudandus, sed in hoc, quod sanctum Waltevum, qui specialiter illum dilexit, erexit, provexit, canonizare non sategit, ut pluribus videtur, vituperandus.' *Vita Waldevi*, 190.

58 Although Duncan regards the 1171 ceremony as 'the first steps to canonisation', Bishop Jocelin's subsequent behaviour is most easily explained by the assumption that he felt it marked the end rather than beginning of this process. Baker's argument for an earlier, lapsed process of canonisation is largely based on the assumption that an earlier text written by Everard of Holmcultram was a *Vita* written primarily for canonisation purposes. However, there is no reason to assume that Everard's text formed an official hagiographical account of Waltheof's life. Duncan, 'Sources and uses', 150; Baker, 'Legend and reality', 66–72; Derek Baker, 'Waldef', in *ODNB*, LVI.765; Helen Birkett, 'The Hagiographical Works of Jocelin of Furness: Text and Context' (University of York, unpublished PhD thesis, 2008), 125–8.

return, he discovered that Waltheof had died on the day following his vision and Nicholas sent word to the *curia*. On the receipt of this news, the pope 'absolved [Waltheof's] soul and solemnly celebrated a mass for him and for all the faithful'.[59] That the account makes no mention of the papal changeover that occurred at this time – the pope to whom Nicholas sent his letter was not the same man as the pope to whom he had recounted his vision – underlines the main purpose of the narrative: to imply the papal approval of Waltheof's cult by the pope as an ongoing institution rather than an individual.[60] Although Jocelin is careful to state that the pope celebrated a mass for Waltheof *and* for the souls of the faithful, the text nevertheless insinuates that this mass was celebrated primarily in Waltheof's honour. The performance of a divine office to commemorate the saint had been an important feature of the canonisation procedure since the second century.[61] That it remained so is shown by the *Chronicle of Melrose*'s description of the canonisation of Thomas Becket in 1173, where it is noted that Pope Alexander sang the first mass in memory of the martyr.[62] By suggesting that the pope performed this same ritual for Waltheof, the *Vita* implies that the process of papal canonisation had already begun. The importance of this account is signalled in the extant manuscript copy of the text by the insertion of a rubric above the narrative which describes the episode as 'concerning the vision of a certain cleric that occurred in Rome'. Aside from those that introduce and conclude the *Vita*, this is the only such rubric to appear in the text.[63] The careful wording of this narrative – the implications of the account rather than its literal meaning – points to a divergence in the popular perception of the cult as papally endorsed versus an official recognition that it was not. Since concern for papal approval marks the later development of the cult rather than its earlier years, it seems that this narrative represents an early thirteenth-century interpretation of a much older story.

Other features of the text suggest that the *Vita* was written with a view to the papal canonisation of Waltheof. The presence of eyewitness accounts shows an appreciation of the new demands of the canonisation procedure. Of the twenty-two miracles included in the posthumous *miracula*, Jocelin cites direct first-hand sources – 'he told me', 'as he told me himself', 'as he himself told me more than once' – for six of the final seven miracles and

---

59 'Papa Deo gratis referens animam ejus absolvit, & pro eo & cunctis fidelibus Missam solemniter celebravit.' *Vita Waldevi*, 165–7, 315–18.

60 Waltheof's death occurred on 3 August and Pope Hadrian IV died just under a month later on 1 September. The *Chronicle of Melrose* records that Nicholas travelled on from Rome to Agnania to see Hadrian's successor, Pope Alexander, who had been elected on 7 September. *Chronicle of Melrose*, eds Anderson et al., 35–6; 'Chronicle of Melrose', trans. Stevenson, 128.

61 Kemp, *Canonization and Authority*, 2.

62 *Chronicle of Melrose*, ed. Anderson et al., 40; 'Chronicle of Melrose', trans. Stevenson, 134.

63 'de visione cuiusdam clerici roma existenti', Bibl. del Palacio Real, MS II 2097, fol. 59vb.

implies the existence of a living witness for another.[64] Although, as the case of Gilbert of Sempringham demonstrates, these accounts would not have been considered adequate testimony in themselves, as part of an initial application they would have provided evidence that such witnesses were available.

The vision of St Thomas of Canterbury recorded among the *miracula* also reveals much about the community's ambitions for the cult. Originally intending to visit Canterbury, a clerk of Westmorland redirected his journey after St Thomas appeared to him in his sleep. That Thomas should advise the clerk to visit Waltheof's tomb instead of his own shrine was praise enough. However, the *Vita* is careful to take full advantage of this celebrity endorsement and Thomas's final words to the clerk underscore the promotional nature of this story: 'Believe me, the day will come when [Waltheof's] name will be very famous and he will be honoured everywhere as one of the pre-eminent confessor saints of the Lord.'[65] The placing of this miracle immediately after the crucial eyewitness accounts and before the second discovery of Waltheof's incorruption emphasises the perceived importance of this narrative. Becket's martyrdom has been described by Robert Bartlett as 'the 1066 of English saintly cult' and St Thomas became the standard by which near-contemporary saints were measured.[66] We should not be surprised, therefore, that Becket's seal of approval was considered to be persuasive evidence for Waltheof's sanctity. The aligning of Waltheof with Becket also signalled the wider potential of the cult as a whole.

The *Vita*'s use of a specific biblical allusion in reference to Waltheof's sanctity also suggests that the text was written with papal canonisation in mind. Following Waltheof's earlier election as prior of the Augustinian house of Kirkham, Jocelin comments: 'No longer could the lamp that shed true light, be hidden under a bushel ... Therefore the lamp, raised upon the lampstand, offered the health-giving light to all in the house of the Lord over which he presided, and offered in himself the model of sanctity.'[67] This phrase

---

64 'mihi retulit', 'sicut ipse mihi retulit', and 'ut ipse mihi saepius referebat'. The two discoveries of Waltheof's incorruption are included in this count. The miracles for which Jocelin has eyewitness accounts are: a messenger, Henry, is saved from drowning; the miraculous cures of four Melrose brethren (Roger of Appleby, a second Roger, and the lay brothers Duramius and Henry); the discovery of Waltheof's tomb in 1206. Jocelin also tells us that the madman cured at Waltheof's tomb is still living, a statement that implies his potential availability as an eyewitness. The extant manuscript version of the text omits the statement 'sicut ipse mihi retulit' found in the *Acta Sanctorum* narrative concerning the cure of the second Brother Roger. *Vita Waldevi*, 191–5, 197–8, 345–50, 352–4; Bibl. del Palacio Real, MS. II 2097, fol. 66vb.

65 'Crede mihi, quia venient dies, in quibus nomen ejus celeberrimum habebitur, & ipse sicut unus de praecipuis sanctis Confessoribus Domini circumcirca honorabitur'. *Ibid.*, 195–6, 350–1.

66 Thomas makes similar appearances in a number of hagiographical narratives, see Robert Bartlett, 'The hagiography of Angevin England', in *Thirteenth Century England V, Proceedings of the Newcastle Upon Tyne Conference 1993*, eds P. R. Coss and S. D. Lloyd (Woodbridge, 1995), 37–52, at 40–1.

67 'Non potuit lucerna diutius, disponente vera luce, latere sub modio ... Lucerna ergo supra cande-

was one of several stock allusions that had come to mark canonisation bulls from the time of Pope Alexander III.[68] That this phrase was also cited in seven of the seventeen extant letters written in support of Gilbert's canonisation, the report of the initial inquiry and the bull of canonisation itself, indicates that by the early thirteenth century it had become a recognised part of canonisation discourse.[69] Jocelin's use of this allusion in specific reference to Waltheof's sanctity suggests that it should be understood in this context.[70] The carefully worded description of Waltheof's heavenly status also suggests that the text was destined for scrutiny by a higher authority. In a phrase that combines allusions to the Psalms and Ecclesiasticus, we are told that Waltheof had been 'led amid the splendour of the saints and made like them in glory'.[71] For those already convinced of Waltheof's sanctity, it read as an explicit confirmation of his status. For those yet to be convinced, it showed a careful deferral of judgement on this issue.

The dedication of the *Vita* to the Scottish royal house also has some bearing upon our understanding of the text as a potential canonisation document. At its most basic level, the *Vita* was written to raise the profile of Waltheof's cult. One of the most effective ways of doing this was to present the work to a prominent patron. As a result, rather than dedicating the text to the memory of the original commissioner of the work, the recently deceased Abbot Patrick, the *Vita* was dedicated to the most influential patrons in the land: the Scottish king, William the Lion; his heir, Alexander; and William's brother, Earl David. This shrewd piece of marketing not only drew on the ties of kinship between Waltheof and the Scottish royal house, but targeted

---

labrum levata lucem salutiferam omnibus in domo Domini, cui praeerat, praebebat, & semet sanctitatis exemplum expressum exhibebat.' The allusion to the light and bushel refers to Luke 11:33, Mark 4:21 and Matthew 5:15. Waltheof had been an Augustinian canon prior to his conversion to Cistercian monasticism. *Vita Waldevi*, 107–8.

68 Kemp, *Canonization and Authority*, 100.

69 This refers only to letters that are transmitted in full by the dossier (nos 5–22). *Book of St Gilbert*, eds and trans. Foreville and Keir, 202, 203, 210, 211, 214, 215, 216, 217, 224, 225, 228, 229, 230, 231, 232, 233, 244, 245.

70 This phrase also appears three times in Jocelin's earlier work, the *Vita S. Kentegerni*: once as part of a criticism of contemporary morals, once in relation to Kentigern's election to the bishopric of Glasgow and finally as background to the saint's meeting with Columba. Although the use of the phrase in reference to Kentigern's promotion is similar to its use in the *Vita Waldevi*, it is only in the latter that it seems to specifically refer to its associations with the canonisation process. It is interesting that this phrase is also used in reference to sanctity and the promotion to the head of the community in the *Vita S. Roberti Novi Monasterii* – this may indicate that the phrase formed part of a specific discourse within Cistercian hagiography. 'The life of S. Kentigern by Jocelinus, a Monk of Furness', in *Lives of S. Ninian and S. Kentigern, Compiled in the Twelfth Century*, ed. and trans. Alexander Penrose Forbes, Historians of Scotland 5 (Edinburgh, 1874), 27–119, 159–242, at 37, 54, 106, 165, 181, 229; 'Vita S. Roberti', ed. Grosjean, 345.

71 Psalms 109:3: 'in splendoribus sanctorum'; Ecclesiasticus 45:2: 'similem illum fecit in gloria sanctorum'. The text in the two versions of the *Vita* differs slightly. *Acta Sanctorum*: 'introductus in splendoribus Sanctorum, similis illis factus in gloria'. Madrid MS: 'introductus in splendoribus Sanctorum, similis in gloria'. *Vita Waldevi*, 200; Bibl. del Palacio Real, MS II 2097, fol. 68rb.

the family of Melrose's original founders.[72] It was also significant in terms of canonisation strategy. Royal support had proved influential in the requests to canonise Bernard of Clairvaux and Gilbert of Sempringham.[73] Such letters of support, accompanied by those from the wider ecclesiastical and religious community, provided the papacy with vital confirmation of the cult's potential for wide dissemination.[74] The financial implications of royal backing were also important. The cost of a journey to Rome, as well as the money needed to fund a prolonged stay in the city while the claim was pursued, meant that even the initial application for canonisation could be an expensive business. The *Vita S. Procopii*, written *ca* 1240, provides a useful account of such an attempt, suggesting not only the potential reluctance of the *curia* to canonise but the costs in time and money that such an application might entail. In 1203, Abbot Blasius of Sávaza experienced three visions in which St Procopius ordered him to seek his official canonisation. The abbot travelled to Rome to fulfil his holy commission but found Innocent III unmoved by the oral and written evidence presented before him. After remaining in the city for a year to pursue his case, lack of funds forced the abbot to withdraw. At this point Procopius took measures into his own hands and secured his sanctity by appearing in a vision to the pope himself.[75]

Although there is no proof that the *Vita* was ever submitted as part of an application for the papal canonisation of Waltheof, evidence within the text strongly suggests that this was its intended purpose. By the early thirteenth century, papal authority over the canonisation procedure had become widely accepted. Application to the papacy was recognised as the principal means of securing the official endorsement and universal recognition of a new cult. It was also a powerful indicator of the saint's perceived importance – and that of the community affiliated to him or her – in the wider religious landscape. Yet, the significance of papal canonisation should not be overstated. In terms of the Melrose community, it would have merely confirmed a sanctity that had been recognised by an increasing number of people since Waltheof's death in 1159 and, most probably, before.[76] Indeed, however desirable official endorsement might be, the long-term success of a cult remained dependent

---

72 Melrose was founded in 1136 by King David and his heir, Henry. *Chronicle of Melrose*, eds Anderson et al., 33; Stevenson, 'Chronicle of Melrose', 124; Broun and Harrison, *Chronicle of Melrose*, 1.

73 *S. Bernardi Opera*, 623; Bredero, *Bernard of Clairvaux*, 57; *Book of St Gilbert*, eds and trans. Foreville and Keir, 214, 215, 234, 235.

74 Bredero, *Bernard of Clairvaux*, 57.

75 *SV. Prokop, Jeho Klášter a Památka u Lidu*, ed. František Krasl (Prague, 1895), 499–500; Michael E. Goodich, 'Vision, dream and canonization policy under Pope Innocent III', in his *Lives and Miracles of the Saints: Studies in Medieval Latin Hagiography*, Collected Studies Series 798 (2004), ch. 12, 160–1.

76 As André Vauchez argues, papal canonisation officially authorised what was to many 'an evident reality'. André Vauchez, *Sainthood in the Later Middle Ages*, trans. Jean Birrell (Cambridge, 1997), 99.

on active support at a local level.[77] That Waltheof's cult had this in abundance, despite the apparent eventual failure to secure papal authorisation, is indicated by the reaction to the disappointing discovery in 1240 that the saint's body was no longer incorrupt. Far from sounding the metaphorical death-knell for the cult, the discovery was treated as an opportunity to expand Waltheof's profile through the distribution of relics – the immediate result being a sudden spate of healing miracles.[78] Indeed, the discovery itself seems to have been the result of a building scheme partly intended to provide easier access to Waltheof's tomb. It was also around this time that a shrine-like memorial was erected over the saint's resting place.[79] The continuing success of the cult shows that while papal authorisation was a desirable asset – so much so that the community appears to have commissioned a *Vita* in order to acquire it – it was more a way of keeping up with the ecclesiastical fashions of the day than the ultimate authenticator of Waltheof's status. The struggle to gain official recognition of Waltheof's sanctity during the late twelfth and early thirteenth centuries was, therefore, a battle that only needed to be waged rather than won.

---

[77] As the *Book of St Gilbert* states, papal canonisation did little to change the minds of those who had previously opposed the saint's veneration. *Book of St Gilbert*, eds and trans. Foreville and Keir, 6–9.

[78] *Chronicle of Melrose*, eds Anderson et al., 87; 'Chronicle of Melrose', trans. Stevenson, 182–3.

[79] Richard Fawcett and Richard Oram, *Melrose Abbey* (Stroud, 2004), 183–4, 186–8.

4

ROYAL AND ARISTOCRATIC ATTITUDES TO SAINTS AND THE VIRGIN MARY IN TWELFTH- AND THIRTEENTH-CENTURY SCOTLAND

Matthew H. Hammond

What follows is an attempt to contextualise the fragmentary and dispersed evidence on local and insular saints in the kingdom of the Scots in the central middle ages, and to understand better the ramifications of Europeanisation and other well known, sweeping changes on their cults. These changes, which included the restructuring of the church establishment under greater papal control, the massive growth of the Cistercians and other reformist monastic orders, and the expansion of power by the Norman and Angevin kings of England across Britain and Ireland, amounted to tectonic shifts in the religious life of a kingdom. How the *familiae* of saints like Columba, Cuthbert, Kentigern and lesser-known others maintained relationships with the kings, aristocracy and their newfound reformist brethren is the subject of this paper.[1]

Saints' cults in the kingdom of the Scots

It is well known that *familiae* devoted to various saints were commonplace throughout northern Britain in the early and central middle ages. Charters, *notitiae* of donations and foundation accounts make clear that gifts to communities at places like Durham, St Andrews, Abernethy, Loch Leven and Deer were often seen as donations made directly to the saint himself (or herself), rather than to institutions. Such gifts comprised an important element in the network of relationships which made these saints and their *familiae* central to medieval Scottish society. Chief among the duties of the members of these *familiae* (who could be monks, canons, *céli Dé* or simply clerics or brothers) were caring for their saint's relics and fostering what we may term the saint's public utility. In return for gifts of land, renders in kind or silver, wax for lighting the saint's altar, or other items, the saint was expected to intercede

---

[1] A version of this paper was given at the Scottish Catholic Archives at Columba House, Edinburgh, 24 March 2009. Thanks to Thomas Clancy, Simon Taylor and Gilbert Márkus for their invaluable comments.

in various ways, on behalf of the soul of the donor, his family and friends, to protect the souls of relatives already dead and those yet unborn, to ward off disease and heal the afflicted, to ensure the harvest, and to lead the army of the local province or kingdom in battle. Thus, a saint's *familia* was at the centre of a network of social expectations and responsibilities, and was part of the glue that held together society. The religious community protected the saint, and the saint protected the community.

Although the first charters of Scottish kings were written by Durham monks in the 1090s, there is still some evidence for the relationships of earlier rulers with saints' *familiae*. Thomas Owen Clancy has highlighted the importance of kings to the success of Columba's cult, noting the role of the saint's crozier, the *Cathbuaid*, for the protection of the tenth-century kingdom of Alba.[2] He has also drawn attention to the royal family's use of the name Mael Coluim ('servant of St Columba'). Although we have no pre-twelfth-century charters from the Scottish *familia* of Columba, there was clearly a tight relationship between the kings of Alba and the church which Cinaed mac Alpin seems to have built for Columba's relics at Dunkeld. King Mael Coluim III's grandfather, Crinán, was abbot of Dunkeld, a position later held by Mael Coluim's son, Ethelred.[3]

Devotion to St Columba did not prevent the kings of Scots from supporting other insular saints. Sources for this period are exceedingly rare, even for the most important religious centres. Narrative accounts of churches dedicated to St Brigit (at Abernethy) and St Andrew (at St Andrews) attribute their foundation to Pictish kings, but offer no evidence of their Scottish successors in the tenth and eleventh centuries.[4] Luckily, some evidence survives from two smaller church settlements. *Notitiae* recorded in the gospel-book of Deer in the mid-twelfth century reveal that Mael Coluim son of Cinaed, king of Alba (1005–34) as well as members of the rival Moravian royal dynasty supported a *familia* devoted to Drostan, a Pictish saint who lived around the

---

2 Thomas Owen Clancy, 'Scottish saints and national identities in the early middle ages', in *Local Saints and Local Churches in the Early Medieval West*, eds Alan Thacker and Richard Sharpe (Oxford, 2002), 397–421, at 408.

3 Thomas Owen Clancy, 'Columba, Adomnán and the cult of saints in Scotland', in *Spes Scotorum Hope of Scots. Saint Columba, Iona and Scotland*, eds Dauvit Broun and Thomas Owen Clancy (Edinburgh, 1999), 3–34, at 30.

4 Simon Taylor, 'The Abernethy Foundation Account and its place-names', *History Scotland* (July/August 2005), 14–16; Simon Taylor with Gilbert Márkus, *The Place-names of Fife, vol. III: St Andrews and the East Neuk* (Donnington, 2009), Appendix, 'The St Andrews Foundation Account B and the Augustinian's Account', 569–620. While Andrew was a major apostolic and universal saint, there is little to distinguish his cult in Scotland from that of a major insular saint such as Columba or Cuthbert. The author of the 'Augustinian's Account' (almost certainly Robert, first prior of St Andrews, 1140–60) reports that 'most Scots affirm that the blessed Apostle Andrew was here alive in the flesh'. Moreover, as with saints such as Columba, it is Andrew's ability to bring military victory to his earthly patrons that is emphasised in his foundation account.

year 700.[5] Similarly, *notitiae* relating to the *familia* of St Serf on an island in Loch Leven were copied into St Andrews Cathedral Priory's cartulary, recording gifts to the community of *céli Dé* there by individuals such as King Macbethad son of Findlaech ('Macbeth', 1040–57×58) and his wife Queen Gruoch, his successor, King Mael Coluim son of Donnchad ('Malcolm III', 1058–93) and his wife Queen Margaret, and Mael Coluim's brother King Domnall son of Donnchad ('Donald III Bane', 1094–7×99).[6]

From the 1090s, the evidence of Latin charters adds considerable depth and colour to our picture of saints' *familiae*. The sons of Mael Coluim and Margaret depended on the support of not only the English crown but also the church of Durham to face down their dynastic rivals in Scotland. In this, they were building on a relationship forged by their father, who had laid one of the foundation stones of the new cathedral, alongside the bishop and the prior.[7] The 'earliest Scottish charter', by King Donnchad son of Mael Coluim (Duncan II, 1094), is a donation of estates in East Lothian to St Cuthbert and his servants; the body of the text mentions Cuthbert twice much as if he were a living landholder and finishes with the saint's malediction on any who would oppose the gift.[8] The role of St Cuthbert in the re-establishment of a firm rule by the sons of Mael Coluim throws into relief the importance that kings of Scots placed on forging a successful 'relationship' with a saintly patron, not just for the kingdom, but for the kingship as exercised by that dynasty. In a sense, this is the experience of the social bond between a landholder and a saint, writ large. For a king, the expectations for saintly patronage and protection amounted to nothing less than the survival of a kingdom.

King Edgar (1097–1107) probably considered Cuthbert as fulfilling this role for him. On 29 August 1095, in the cemetery of the church of St Cuthbert at Norham, Edgar donated extensive lands in the shires of Berwick and Coldingham to the church of Durham in what looks like an anticipatory move presaging his successful acquisition of the kingship, which was not completed until 1097.[9] Later charters were produced, again donating many of the same lands to Durham and St Cuthbert, presumably after he was inaugurated as king. In one of these charters, Edgar refers to St Cuthbert as 'my lord'. Edgar was also present at the dedication of a new church of St Mary at

5   Thomas Owen Clancy, 'Deer and the early church in North-Eastern Scotland', in *Studies on the Book of Deer*, ed. Katherine Forsyth (Dublin, 2008), 363–97, at 382–5.

6   *St A. Lib.*, 113–18. My thanks to Simon Taylor for giving me access to his unpublished edition of this text.

7   Valerie Wall, 'Malcolm III and the foundation of Durham Cathedral', in *Anglo-Norman Durham, 1093–1193*, eds David Rollason, Margaret Harvey and Michael Prestwich (Woodbridge, 1998), 325–38; William M. Aird, *St Cuthbert and the Normans: The Church of Durham, 1071–1153* (Woodbridge, 1998), 238.

8   A. A. M. Duncan, 'The earliest Scottish charters', *SHR* 37 (1958), 103–35, at 119. Durham Cathedral Muniments, Miscellaneous Charters [DCM, Misc. Chs] no. 554.

9   A. A. M. Duncan, 'Yes, the earliest Scottish charters', *SHR* 78 (1999), 1–38, at 16 and 22–3. DCM, Misc. Chs, no. 559.

Coldingham, where he donated the estate of Swinton 'arranged by the will of the monks of St Cuthbert'.[10] Edgar's successors, Alexander I (1107–24) and David I (1124–53) were content merely to renew Edgar's gifts and made no new major benefactions.[11]

It would probably not be an exaggeration to suggest that the cult of St Cuthbert diminished considerably in the twelfth-century kingdom of the Scots. While it is not always clear to what extent the saint's *familia* at Durham had any dealings with the various parochial and local churches dedicated to Cuthbert across the kingdom, they still maintained some kind of claim to Old Melrose.[12] In setting up a Cistercian monastery nearby, King David gave Durham a church in Berwick dedicated to the Virgin Mary.[13] Moreover, most of Durham's possessions north of the border were packaged under the auspices of a new priory at Coldingham which continued that church's association with Mary.[14] Other churches and lands associated with Cuthbert were given to new reformed monastic establishments. For example, early in his reign, David made a donation to St Cuthbert's under the castle – which seems to have had quite a large *parochia*, but he later gave the church, its kirkton and other lands and its two chapels to his new Augustinian foundation dedicated to the Holy Cross.[15] To make matters worse, the size of St Cuthbert's *parochia* was slashed to make way for a new burghal church dedicated to St Giles.[16] Similarly, the new church of St Nicholas at Prestwick seems to have been carved out of the older parish of St Cuthbert's there, and given to Paisley Abbey.[17] Indeed, a cluster of Cuthbertine churches in the southwest were appropriated by various new monastic houses: Maybole, Girvan and Straiton, were given to North Berwick Priory, Crossraguel Abbey and Paisley Abbey, respectively.[18] At the same time, too much should not be read into these donations, as there is nothing to suggest that appropriation was accompanied by a diminution in reverence to a major insular saint like Cuthbert.

---

[10] *Early Scottish Charters Prior to A.D. 1153*, ed. Archibald C. Lawrie (Glasgow, 1905) [*ESC*], nos 18, 19, 20, 21, 22. DCM, Misc. Chs, nos 555, 556, 557, 558.

[11] *ESC*, nos 26, 27, 31; *The Chrs. David I: The Written Acts of David I King of Scots, 1124–53 and of his son Henry Earl of Northumberland, 1139–52*, ed. G. W. S. Barrow (Woodbridge, 1999), nos 9, 10, 11, 12, 31, 32; see also G. W. S. Barrow, 'The kings of Scotland and Durham', in *Anglo-Norman Durham*, eds Rollason et al., 311–23, at 317.

[12] *Ibid.*, 311–12; James Murray MacKinlay, *Ancient Church Dedications in Scotland, vol. II: Non-Scriptural Dedications* (Edinburgh, 1914), 243–57.

[13] *Chrs. David I*, no. 52.

[14] A. A. M. Duncan, 'The foundation of St Andrews Cathedral Priory, 1140', *SHR* 84 (2005), 1–37, at 34; *ESC*, no. 20.

[15] *Chrs. David I*, nos 71, 147.

[16] Ian B. Cowan, 'The emergence of the urban parish', in *The Scottish Medieval Town*, eds Michael Lynch et al. (Edinburgh, 1988), 82–98, at 90. David gave St Giles's to the order of St Lazarus of Jerusalem. *Chrs. David I*, no. 256.

[17] Ian B. Cowan, *The Parishes of Medieval Scotland* (Edinburgh, 1967), 167; Cowan, 'Urban parish', 94.

[18] MacKinlay, *Church Dedications: Non-Scriptural*, 256.

While it is clear that Edgar saw St Cuthbert as his chief patron, Professor Archie Duncan has suggested convincingly that his successor, Alexander I, directed his veneration towards the two main protectors of the kingdom's heartland, north of Forth: Andrew and Columba.[19] Even though Alexander was present at the translation of St Cuthbert's relics in 1104, as king, he merely confirmed his elder brother's gifts to that community.[20] Duncan argues persuasively that the period between Queen Sybilla's death and his own, 1122–4, saw the king seek to ensure the future of the churches of St Andrew and St Columba. The king's restoration of the Boar's Raik in East Fife to St Andrew was commemorated in a magnificent ceremony in which his Arabian warhorse and Turkish armaments were led down the aisle of the church to the altar of St Andrew, as described in the 'Augustinian's Account' and later chronicles. Duncan agrees with Walter Bower's assertion that this generous gift was meant to accompany the reform of the religious community there through the introduction of Augustinian canons, and that the election of Robert, prior of Scone, to the episcopate was part of this plan. In reality, this scheme did not come to fruition until 1140.[21]

Alexander seems to have wanted to impose a similar reform agenda on the community of St Columba. According to Donald Watt, 'it is likely that the abbacy [of Dunkeld] was at this stage allocated by King Alexander I on the death of his brother Abbot Ethelred as an endowment for a more permanent bishopric than had previously been based there'.[22] It is surely significant in this light that the first bishop associated with Dunkeld since the ninth century was Bishop Cormac, who witnessed two of Alexander's charters to Scone Priory.[23] As Professor Geoffrey Barrow has argued based on Myln's *Vitae Episcoporum Dunkeldensium*, David I probably granted various teinds of cains associated with the abbacy to Bishop Cormac.[24] Professor Duncan also accepts Walter Bower's statement (he was after all abbot of Inchcolm) that Alexander I founded the Augustinian priory at Inchcolm in the Firth of Forth in 1123.[25] Duncan suggests that the Augustinian house at Inchcolm may have been intended as a springboard for eventual establishment of canons regular at Dunkeld, much as the king seems to have intended Scone to lead to the

---

[19] Duncan, 'St Andrews'.

[20] Aird, *St Cuthbert*, 249.

[21] Duncan, 'St Andrews', 32–5.

[22] D. E. R. Watt, *Series episcoporum ecclesiae catholicae occidentalis: Ecclesia Scoticana* (Stuttgart, 1991), 41.

[23] *ESC*, nos 36, 49.

[24] *Chrs. David I*, no. 230; *RRS*, I.no. 65. Watt, *Series episcoporum*, 43.

[25] Duncan, 'St Andrews', 32; *Chron. Bower*, III.107, 111; Kenneth Veitch, '"Replanting paradise": Alexander I and the reform of the religious life in Scotland', *IR* 52 (2001), 136–66.

conversion of the St Andrews establishment.[26] All of this is indicative of a period of religious fervour and ambition which met resistance when arriving at the doors of the communities of saints. But there is independent evidence of Alexander's veneration of Columba. As Thomas Clancy has highlighted, a dedication poem in a copy of the *Vita S. Columbae* was written for that king.[27] Simeon, the poem's author, beseeched the saint: 'Increase King Alexander's virtue, bring him help and guard his salvation, for in your honour he commanded that your triumphs – see! – be written down.'[28] It is even possible that the poem's mention of an 'island of bishops' refers to Inchcolm.

Columba's position was still clearly very strong north of the Forth in the first half of the twelfth century. Thomas Clancy has highlighted the ways in which the church settlement at Deer, which seems to have first been dedicated to a Pictish saint named Drostan, added St Columba to their community's foundation legend and list of donations in an attempt to bolster support among a Gaelicised aristocracy and royalty. Strengthening this point is the appearance of Bishop Gregory, the head of the Columban community in Scotland, at the top of the witness list of King David's charter granting immunity from lay exaction to the clerics of Deer.[29] Furthermore, the establishment of a new twelfth-century church dedicated to Christ and St Peter, almost certainly at Peterugie (now Peterhead), 'reflects Europeanising'tendencies within twelfth-century Scotland'.[30] While it is not necessary to add much to Clancy's account, it is worthwhile to take a brief look at the Gaelic *notitiae*. In Text II, which records donations of the tenth and eleventh centuries, the recipients are expressed one time as Columba and Drostan, four times as Drostan alone, four times as God and Drostan, and six times with no recipient mentioned. Text V, evidently written after Text II but before Texts III, IV and VI, mentions two donations to Christ, Drostan and Columba. Text III, in the name of Gartnait son of Cainnech and Ete daughter of Gillemichel, dating to 1131×2, is to Columba and Drostan, for the consecration of a church to Christ and Peter the apostle, and Text IV, from the same individuals and dating to around the same time, is conceived as a gift to Christ, Columba and Drostan. It is interesting that we see here a twelfth-century re-emphasis on Christ's name, but it is difficult to know whether this should be seen as a strategy of survival in terms of a local community competing against outside Europeanising tendencies, or whether the relevant process is rather the spread of ideas of reform to the local clergy and their patrons. In any event, the relationship of Columba to Drostan serves as a salutary reminder that European reform

---

26 A. A. M. Duncan, *The Kingship of the Scots, 842–1292: Succession and Independence* (Edinburgh, 2002), 88.
27 Clancy, 'Scottish saints and national identities', 408.
28 *The Triumph Tree: Scotland's Earliest Poetry, AD 550–1350*, ed. Thomas Owen Clancy (Edinburgh, 1998), 185. Translation by Gilbert Márkus.
29 *Chrs. David I*, no. 136.
30 Clancy, 'Deer and the early church', 364.

and universal saints were not perhaps the only pressures that small religious communities venerating local saints had to cope with in order to survive.

The Royal Family: Driver of Trends

That donations to a small community of clerics, remote from the centres of royal power, would be interpreted around 1130 as gifts to Christ may be a remarkable indication of how widespread the spirit of reform was by that time. For in the late eleventh and early twelfth centuries, the challenge to insular saints and their *familiae* was coming not so much from 'universal' European saints as from a renewed emphasis on the worship of Christ, the three-fold divine expression as exhibited in the Trinity, and the Blessed Virgin Mary. In an eloquent monograph, Rachel Fulton has recently explored the nature of this renewed devotion to Christ and Mary across Europe. It should not surprise us that evidence of this turn, which seems to have affected many levels of society, should have come to Scotland by around 1100. Above all, Fulton highlights the example of St Anselm, the Italian abbot of Bec (1073–93) and archbishop of Canterbury (1093–1109), whose prayers reveal a renewed compassionate self-identification with the crucified Christ.[31] She adds,

> as Anselm's meditations and prayers circulated throughout the monasteries and pious households of Europe, as additional prayers were added and the whole collection rearranged, pious Christians would learn to think of their relationship to Christ in terms of an obligation to praise not simply the God-man but the man who had died in payment for their sins.[32]

As long ago as 1960, Professor Barrow noted the immediate impact which Anselm made on Scotland, sending monks from Benedictine Christ Church Cathedral at Canterbury to Dunfermline at the request of King Edgar, and corresponding with King Alexander.[33] Barrow also pointed out a miracle reported by Eadmer, the Canterbury monk elected to the see of St Andrews in 1120, in which a noblewoman named Eastrild 'had previously heard of the fame of Anselm's holiness', even before he healed her using Anselm's girdle.[34]

Even before Anselm's prayers, Queen Margaret has rightly been high-lighted as a devout figure whose influence must have made a profound

---

[31] Rachel Fulton, *From Judgment to Passion: Devotion to Christ and the Virgin Mary, 800–1200* (New York, 2002), 142; Saint Anselm, *Meditations and Prayers to the Holy Trinity and our Lord Jesus Christ* (Oxford, 1856); David Farmer, *The Oxford Dictionary of Saints*, 5th edn (Oxford, 2003), 25–7.

[32] Fulton, *From Judgment to Passion*, 190.

[33] G. W. S. Barrow, *The Kingdom of the Scots*, 2nd edn (Edinburgh, 2003), 174; *ESC*, no. 25.

[34] Barrow, *Kingdom of the Scots*, 175.

impact on her sons and daughters.[35] Turgot, her confidant, Benedictine prior of Durham (1087–1109) and bishop of St Andrews (1109–15), in the *Life of Queen Margaret* written between 1100 and 1107 for Margaret's daughter, Queen Matilda of England, noted that Margaret started the day with matins of the Holy Trinity, the Holy Cross and St Mary.[36] Furthermore, Turgot stressed that the queen 'filled on behalf of Christ the role of servant and most pious mother', that she 'delighted to venerate Christ through' people who 'enclosed themselves in little cells in diverse places', and that the king and queen would 'serve Christ' by feeding the poor.[37] Turgot added that she prayed with tears on behalf of her offspring, 'so that they might come to know their Creator in faith which works through love, and knowing, that they might worship, worshipping, that they might love him in everything'.[38]

Christ and the Holy Trinity

Canterbury must have had a profound influence on the foundation at Dunfermline, starting with Archbishop Lanfranc's letter to Queen Margaret (1070×89), describing the despatch of Goldwine and two brethren to the northern house.[39] Anselm sent more monks at Edgar's request, and kept in contact with Alexander I. Dunfermline's first abbot, Geoffrey, prior of Canterbury, was sent at the request of David I.[40] His links to Canterbury are illustrated by the fact that he was present at the dedication of the new cathedral church at Canterbury on 4 May 1130.[41] Furthermore, Dunfermline inherited its somewhat ambiguous dual dedication to both Christ and the Holy Trinity from Canterbury. This is not surprising, because devotion to Jesus led naturally to thoughts of the rest of the Trinity. Nevertheless, the association with the Trinity remained primary: all of David and Mael Coluim IV's charters to the abbey that mention a dedication refer to the Holy Trinity.[42] References to Dunfermline as Christ Church are more frequent in the late

---

35 *Ibid.*, 172–4.
36 Robert Bartlett, 'Turgot (*c.*1050–1115)', in *ODNB*, http://www.oxforddnb.com/view/article/27831 (accessed 22 March 2009); Turgot of Durham, 'Vita sanctae Margaritae Scotorum reginae', in *Symeonis Dunelmensis opera et collectanea*, ed. John Hodgson Hinde, Surtees Society (1868), 234–54.
37 Lois L. Huneycutt, *Matilda of Scotland: A Study in Medieval Queenship* (Woodbridge, 2003), 172–4.
38 *Ibid.*, 166. Note that Margaret's daughter, Edith/Matilda, founded a house of Augustinian canons dedicated to the Holy Trinity at Aldgate in 1107. Duncan, 'St Andrews', 8.
39 *ESC*, no. 9.
40 Barrow, *Kingdom of the Scots*, 174; *MRHS*, 58; *Chrs. David I*, no. 22.
41 'Houses of Benedictine monks: The cathedral priory of the Holy Trinity or Christ Church, Canterbury', in *A History of the County of Kent*, vol. II, ed. William Page (1926), 113–21; *Chrs. David I*, 39.
42 *Chrs. David I*, nos 44, 48, 50, 99, 131, 137, 138, 140, 141, 171, 172; *RRS*, I.nos 112, 118, 157, 164, 178, 213, 214, 229.

twelfth and early thirteenth centuries; these include two by King William as well as charters by Mael Coluim (I), earl of Fife, Saher de Quincy, Geoffrey de Maleville, Margaret of Ceres and Thomas of Restalrig, all of which refer to Christ Church.[43]

The Cantuarian influence on Dunfermline set the scene for further Trinitarian dedications throughout Scotland. This was perhaps most obvious in the northern region of Moray. Dunfermline's own cell or daughterhouse at Urquhart in Moray was also dedicated to the Holy Trinity: King David's charter of donation (1145×53) records a gift 'to God and the church of the Holy Trinity of Urquhart'.[44] The cathedral church of Moray was also dedicated to the Holy Trinity, by at least 1174.[45] Gregory, the earliest bishop of Moray on record, may have been active in the reign of Alexander I; there is little or no evidence for the dedication of the church in the twelfth century, but the church of the Holy Trinity at Spynie housed the bishopric in the early 1200s. It then moved to its permanent home at the church of the Holy Trinity at Elgin.[46] There is no indication of a pre-existing church or any hint of an earlier saintly dedication; this may be a genuine new establishment of the early twelfth century.[47]

So far, we have examined instances of new churches founded in the late eleventh and early twelfth centuries and dedicated to the Holy Trinity, but there has been little or no evidence of this being done explicitly to the detriment of existing saints' cults. Yet there can be no doubt that this also happened. The formation of a parochial structure under an episcopal hierarchy, coupled with the establishment of burghs, meant that new parish churches were being set up at this time. And it was in this way that the kings of Scots seemed to show a clear preference for christological devotion, even at the expense of the kingdom's two 'national saints', Columba and Andrew. A new parish church of the Holy Trinity was established at Dunkeld, the eastern centre of the Columban *familia*, at some point in the early twelfth century, and David I gave it to his 'court bishop', Bishop Andrew of Caithness. While King David's charter does not survive, the text of Bishop Andrew's gift of the church of the Holy Trinity of Dunkeld to the church of the Holy Trinity of Dunfermline

---

43 *RRS*, II.nos 321, 502; *Dunf. Reg.*, nos 144, 154, 158, 175, 188.
44 *Chrs. David I*, no. 185.
45 *RRS*, II.no. 139.
46 *MRHS*, 206; *Fasti Ecclesiae Scoticanae Medii Aevi Ad Annum 1638*, eds D. E. R. Watt and A. L. Murray, rev. edn, Scottish Record Society (Edinburgh, 2003), 278. Watt, *Series Episcoporum*, 64–5.
47 These comments should be seen in the context of Alex Woolf's suggestions about the interrelationship of St Andrews, Dunkeld, Mortlach and Rosemarkie in the early twelfth century. Alex Woolf, 'The cult of Moluag, the see of Mortlach and church organisation in northern Scotland in the eleventh and twelfth centuries', in *Fil súil nglais. A Grey Eye Looks Back: a Festschrift in honour of Colm Ó Baoill*, eds Sharon Arbuthnot and Kaarina Hollo (Callander, 2007), 299–310, at 308–9.

late in David's reign does survive in the Dunfermline abbey cartulary.[48] Strikingly, the first surviving charter text of a bishop of Dunkeld (in the 1160s) confirms this appropriation of a large parish in the heart of his own diocese to this Benedictine monastic house dedicated to the Trinity. Moreover, Bishop Gregory's confirmation refers to this as a gift of King Mael Coluim and Bishop Andrew, indicating a strong royal hand in the proceedings.[49] The other pre-eminent centre of a saint's cult north of the Forth experienced similar treatment. Bishop Robert of St Andrews's 1140 foundation charter of the Augustinian cathedral priory mentions for the first time a 'parish of Holy Trinity', but it is uncertain when the church was first founded.[50] Ian Cowan suggested that the church of the Holy Trinity pre-dated the episcopal burgh, noting that the church's bounds included the whole shire of Kilrymont, with rights both within and outwith the burgh.[51] As bishop-elect, Richard gave the parish church of Holy Trinity to the cathedral priory: this gift was confirmed by both King Mael Coluim in 1163 or 1164 and Richard himself after his consecration.[52]

One ulterior motive for making a dedication directly to God, in the form of Christ or the Holy Trinity, was precisely that one was not making a donation to an established local saint. This raised the thorny issue of who spoke for a saint like Andrew. The complex array of constituent parties at St Andrews with a claim to land and revenues in the early twelfth century included the bishop, a community of *céli Dé*, a pilgrims' hospital and several hereditary *personae*. If similar complications were evident at Dunkeld, then this may help add a pragmatic explanation, in addition to (rather than instead of or opposed to) purely devotional reasons, for why new parishes were dedicated to the Holy Trinity. The church of the Holy Trinity at St Andrews was, after all, in the possession of the Augustinian priory of St Andrews, and Dunfermline's acquisition of Dunkeld's parish church, while still perhaps surprising, can be attributed to Bishop Andrew's background as a 'native Scot' who had also been a monk at Dunfermline.[53] In other instances, cathedrals with local saints' cults of less prominent renown were overshadowed by new dedications. Brechin, which was served by a chapter of *céli Dé* in the second half of the twelfth century, seems to have been dedicated to a Saint Tarranan; Ralph of Strachan made a gift to 'God and St Terranan and the bishop of Brechin'.[54]

---

[48] *Dunf. Reg.*, no. 123; *Chrs. David I*, no. 255. The lands mentioned in Andrew's charter suggest a parish extending northwards to Dalmarnock, with detached portions at Bendochy and Couttie.

[49] *RRS*, I.no. 229; *Dunf. Reg.*, nos 36, 124.

[50] *St A. Lib.*, 122–3.

[51] Cowan, 'Urban parish', 87–8.

[52] *RRS*, I.no. 239; *St A. Lib.*, 132–3. Cowan, *Parishes*, 176. Matthew the archdeacon was apparently the *persona*.

[53] Marjorie O. Anderson, *Kings and Kingship in Early Scotland*, 2nd edn (Edinburgh, 1980), 242.

[54] *Registrum episcopatus Brechinensis*, ed. Cosmo Innes, Bannatyne Club, 2 vols (Aberdeen 1856) [*Brechin Reg.*], II.Appendix no. 1.

It seems very likely that this is the Saint Torannán or Ternan whom Thomas Clancy has discussed as having dedications in Kincardineshire.[55] Charters to the church of Brechin are rare, and the remaining thirteenth-century examples refer only to the bishop and canons, with no mention of a saint. By the early fourteenth century, however, Ternan was gone and it was the church of the Holy Trinity.[56] Similarly, the episcopal church of the bishops of Aberdeen, St Machar's Cathedral, was actually dedicated to the Virgin Mary and Machar by the early thirteenth century.[57]

The only new monastic foundation dedicated to the Holy Trinity that is likely to have been founded on the site of an existing church is Scone Abbey. Alexander I brought Augustinian canons to the royal manor of Scone from St Oswald's Priory, Nostell, probably between Christmas 1114 and 24 March 1115.[58] The foundation charter of Alexander and his wife, Queen Sybilla, begins with the phrase, 'in the name of the Holy and Indivisible Trinity, in which one God is adored and worshipped and believed', indicating a clear sense of devotion to the Trinity.[59] The charter expresses the foundation as a handing over of 'the church dedicated in honour of the Holy Trinity which is in Scone' to God, St Mary, St Michael, St John, St Laurence and St Augustine. These last three saints do not recur in the abbey's charters, but St Michael appears frequently. As with Dunfermline, royal charters refer to the church of the Holy Trinity at Scone.[60] Local landholders like Swain son of Thor, Thomas the king's doorward, and various burgesses of Perth from the late twelfth and early thirteenth centuries do make mention of St Michael.[61] Furthermore, while Walter Comyn son of William Comyn gave a stone of wax to the 'church of the Holy Trinity', the wax was to be collected on the feast day of St Michael.[62] It is likely that if there was a pre-existing church at Scone, it was probably dedicated to St Michael. It is known that Michael was venerated in Scotland prior to the twelfth century: one of the seven churches supposedly built at Kilrymont by St Rule was dedicated in honour of St Michael the Archangel and, as Simon Taylor has pointed out, there is independent evidence for the existence of a church of St Michael around the year 970.[63] While it can probably never be proven, Scone could provide an example of continuity in local recognition of an existing saint's cult despite a royal foundation focused primarily on the Trinity.

55 Clancy, 'Deer and the early church', 387.
56 *Brechin Reg.*, I.no. 8; *RRS*, V.no. 191.
57 *Abdn. Reg.*, I.16.
58 Duncan, *The Kingship of the Scots*, 82–6. Cf. *MRHS*, 97.
59 *Liber ecclesie de Scon*, ed. Cosmo Innes, Bannatyne Club (Edinburgh, 1843), no. 1. Translation by John Reuben Davies.
60 *Ibid.*, nos 2, 3, 4, 6–17.
61 *Ibid.*, nos 21, 22, 86, 87, 88, 89, 91, 125.
62 *Ibid.*, no. 98.
63 Taylor, *Place-names of Fife*, III.588.

Table 1. Monastic foundations in the Kingdom of the Scots, 1093–1250[64]

Foundations by kings and royal family				
Monastery	Founder(s)	Date founded	Order	Dedicatee(s)
Dunfermline	Queen Margaret	1070×93	Ben.	Trinity/Christ
Selkirk/ Kelso	David I	1113/1128	Tir.	(John)/Mary
Scone	Alexander I	1114×15	Aug.	Trinity/Michael
Inchcolm	Alexander I	1123	Aug.	Columba
Holyrood	David I	1128	Aug.	Holy Cross/Mary
Urquhart	David I	1130×50	Ben.	Trinity
Melrose	David I	1136	Cist.	Mary
Coldingham	David I	× 1139	Ben.	Mary/Cuthbert
Cambuskenneth	David I	1140×7	Aug.	Mary
Jedburgh	David I	1147×51	Aug.	Mary
Newbattle	David I	1140	Cist.	Mary
St Andrews	David I	1140	Aug.	Andrew
Lesmahagow	David I/John, bp Glasgow	1144	Tir.	Mary/Machutus
Loch Leven	David I	1152×3	Aug.	Serf
Isle of May	David I	× 1153	Ben.	All Saints
Kinloss	David I	1150	Cist.	Mary
Berwick	David I	× 1153	C.N.	Mary/Leonard
Restenneth	Mael Coluim IV	1161×2	Aug.	Peter
Manuel	Mael Coluim IV	× 1164	C.N.	(Mary)
Coupar Angus	Mael Coluim IV	1164	Cist.	Mary
Haddington	Countess Ada	× 1159	C.N.	(Mary)
Arbroath	William I	1178	Tir.	Thomas
Lindores	David, earl of Huntingdon	1190×1	Tir.	Mary/Andrew
Balmerino	Q. Ermengarde/ Alexander II	1227×9	Cist.	Edward/Mary
Pluscarden	Alexander II	1230×31	Vall.	Mary/Andrew

The Virgin Mary

Changes in devotional practices around the turn of the twelfth century were not restricted to Christ and the Trinity, however. Rachel Fulton also explores the ways in which figures like Archbishop Anselm and Eadmer, his biographer, and bishop-elect of St Andrews, were instrumental in spreading devotion to the Virgin Mary. Eadmer wrote a tract called *De conceptione beatae Mariae virginis*, defending the feast of her sinless conception.[65] Fulton argues convincingly that Mary's devotional prominence continued to grow,

---

[64] Exclusive of Galloway, Argyll and the Isles.
[65] Fulton, *Judgment to Passion*, 196, 530–1 n. 10.

because her story represented the 'appropriately human response to Christ's sacrifice, the fullest expression of love of which a human being was capable in thinking on and gazing upon the face of the God-man'.[66] This explains why Anselm wrote prayers to Mary that were as significant as his prayers to Christ: 'they spoke immediately to the contemporary anxiety over the coming of Christ in Judgment through an impassioned appeal to the image of Mary as Intercessor'.[67] Above all, the monastic foundations of King David I reveal a move towards the Virgin, rather than the Trinity or St Andrew, as his principal intercessor. Professor Duncan has noted that while David's 1113 foundation of Selkirk Abbey was made 'in honour of St Mary and St John the Evangelist', the figure of St John was dropped after the 1128 move to Kelso.[68] As Duncan has pointed out, with the exception of May Priory, whose initial endowment is unrecorded, all houses founded by David after Holyrood in 1128 were dedicated to the Virgin: this included houses of canons regular at Jedburgh and Cambuskenneth as well as four Cistercian houses, and even Holyrood's foundation mentioned 'Christ, the holy cross, the Virgin Mary and all the saints'.[69]

This turn towards Mary was not merely a result of the popularity of the Cistercian order, with its policy of mandatory Marian dedications. In addition to Cistercian foundations at Melrose (1136), Newbattle (1140) and Kinloss (1150), David also endowed Augustinian houses dedicated to Mary at Jedburgh and Cambuskenneth. David's descendants followed in this trend, with his daughter-in-law, Countess Ada, founding a house of nuns at Haddington, and his grandson, Mael Coluim IV, founding another Cistercian house at Coupar Angus and another nunnery at Manuel. Indeed, Countess Ada expressed her gift of a toft in Haddington to Dunfermline Abbey as a donation to Mary rather than to Christ Church or the Holy Trinity.[70] Mary, like the name of God or Jesus, could be evoked in charters regardless of the official dedication of the recipient church, and this fact places Mary in a separate class even from apostolic and national saints like Andrew. Remarkably, at least fifteen monasteries founded between 1124 and 1250 (excluding Galloway and Argyll) seem to have been dedicated exclusively to the Virgin Mary. A further twelve religious houses were dedicated to Mary along with one or more other saints (see tables). While the charter evidence is not always conclusive, it is clear that at least 80% of religious houses founded in Scotland at this time were associated with Mary in their dedications.

The belief in Mary as the most effective intercessory was not only evident in new foundations across Scotland, but also came to be exemplified in rela-

---

[66] *Ibid.*, 199–200.
[67] *Ibid.*, 204.
[68] *Chrs. David I*, nos 14, 70, 91; Duncan, 'St Andrews', 35 and n. 151.
[69] *Ibid.*, 35. *Chrs. David I*, no. 147.
[70] *Dunf. Reg.*, nos 151, 152.

tion to other saints. Mary's power and prestige were virtually ubiquitous; it became common to pair the Virgin up with other saints, whether universal or local, in monastic dedications. As we have seen, Coldingham Priory's dedication was to Mary and Cuthbert. Similarly, the church of St Machutus (or Malo) at Lesmahagow was made into a dependent cell of Kelso dedicated to Mary and Machutus.[71] King David also founded a house of nuns at Berwick which in the later thirteenth century was called 'the house of the Blessed Mary and St Leonard of South Berwick'.[72] Cases like that of the cathedral church of St Mary and St Machar at Old Aberdeen might lead one to believe that only small local saints were vulnerable to this treatment, but even Scotland's national, apostolic saint, Andrew, was paired up in second position to the Virgin Mary at both David, earl of Huntingdon's Tironensian foundation at Lindores (1190×1) and King Alexander II's Valliscaulian house at Pluscarden (1230×1).[73] Indeed, Mary was included in dual dedications of saints ranging from Uinniau (Finnian), Machutus, Machar and Serf to Andrew, James and John the Baptist. Indeed, this trend was so widespread that the absence of a Marian dedication stands out as the exception to the rule. This occurred at the most prominent cathedrals (Glasgow, Dunkeld, St Andrews) as well as at monasteries dedicated to Columba (Inchcolm), St Thomas Becket (Arbroath), All Saints (May) and possibly Peter (Restenneth). Nearly every other house was associated with either the Holy Trinity or the Virgin Mary.[74]

A change of direction: royal foundations, 1165–1249

By the time William the Lion came to the throne in 1165, the extraordinary phase of royal monastic patronage, which had seen the founding of no fewer than twenty religious houses of four orders, seemed to fizzle out. William made only one new foundation, the Tironensian house of Arbroath, endowed it with vast estates, and was buried there. His wife, Ermengarde, established a small Cistercian house at Balmerino in northern Fife where she was buried, with a relatively meagre endowment. Alexander II was interred at Melrose, a

---

[71] *Chrs. David I*, no. 130; *RRS*, II.no. 480; *Liber S. Marie de Calchou*, ed. Cosmo Innes, Bannatyne Club, 2 vols (Edinburgh, 1846)) [*Kelso Liber*], I.no. 182; *RRS*, V.nos 85, 401.

[72] *Chrs. David I*, no. 253; *MRHS*, 145; *Liber S. Marie de Dryburgh*, ed. William Fraser, Bannatyne Club (Edinburgh, 1847) [*Dryburgh Liber*], xv n.

[73] *Chartulary of the Abbey of Lindores: 1195–1479*, ed. John Dowden. SHS (Edinburgh, 1903) [*Lind. Cart.*], no. 5; S. R. Macphail, *History of the Religious House of Pluscardyn* (Edinburgh, 1881), 204–6.

[74] References to the Augustinian house at Loch Leven are few but refer primarily to St Serf. However, there was also a hospital of St Mary at Loch Leven. *St A. Lib.*, 175–6.

house which he favoured in his lifetime.[75] Nevertheless, it is hard to escape the conclusion that if the years between 1100 and 1165 were a period of rapid growth in monasticism, the following half century could be characterised as a phase of consolidation, during which most new foundations were smaller houses endowed by earls and other magnates. Alexander II is credited with ushering in a new phase of religious reform around 1230 with the establishment of friaries of various habit and the introduction of the austere new Valliscaulian order at Pluscarden in Moray. This stage in the religious history of Scotland has a slightly different flavour, and this was reflected in the attitudes of the kings and queens to the national and local saints of Scotland, particularly Andrew and Columba.

St Andrew and St Columba were both depicted in early medieval sources as winning battles for Pictish and Scottish kings, and the ability of these two 'national saints' to protect the kingdom was crucial to the royal support of their cults and *familiae*. There is much more evidence in the central middle ages for Columba as a 'battlefield saint' than Andrew. Nevertheless, the rifts which formed as a result of the controversy that followed King William's appointment of his chaplain Hugh as bishop of St Andrews in 1178, despite the canons' election of John Scot, must have affected the king's attitude towards the national patron; it clearly marked his feelings to Andrew's *familia*. It is possible to see the foundation of William's brother, Earl David, of a monastery at Lindores in Fife dedicated to Mary and Andrew, shortly after the resolution of the St Andrews controversy, as a cautious renewal of devotion to the saint, and it may be noteworthy that the earl's foundation charter – witnessed by the king and four bishops – was not written until after Bishop Roger of St Andrews' ten-year delay in consecration.[76] King Alexander's 1230 foundation at Pluscarden to Mary and Andrew renewed and continued the royal association with this apostolic national saint.

A much more serious crisis than the St Andrews debacle arose from the capture of King William at Alnwick on 13 July 1174. His imprisonment at Falaise and the subsequent debilitating arrangements by which he performed homage for Scotland and his nobles swore fealty to Henry II, hostages were given and castles were garrisoned by English troops, amounted to a personal and national humiliation. The capture of William at Alnwick held a special significance for Henry II, that of his own redemption after the slaying of Archbishop Thomas Becket. Contemporary chroniclers relate the story that William was captured on the same day that Henry II did penance for the murder in Canterbury Cathedral.[77] Alnwick, Falaise and their aftermath must

[75] *Liber Sancte Marie de Melros*, ed. Cosmo Innes, Bannatyne Club, 2 vols (Edinburgh, 1837), I.no. 173.
[76] *Lind. Cart.*, no. 2 (11 February 1198×17 March 1199).
[77] *Jordan Fantosme's Chronicle*, ed. Ronald C. Johnston (Oxford, 1981), 149; *Chronica Magistri Rogeri de Houedene*, ed. William Stubbs, RS 51, 4 vols (London 1868–71), II.61–3.

have seemed like a major failure for the intercessory powers of St Columba, and surely demonstrated the powers of the new saint, Thomas Becket. William's establishment of a generously endowed new monastery at Arbroath dedicated to St Thomas the Martyr within five years of his capture at Alnwick is remarkable and sends an unmistakable signal, of placating the figure who had been responsible for a personal and national disgrace. Given the afore-mentioned near-ubiquitous presence of the Virgin Mary, the sole dedication of Arbroath to St Thomas is particularly striking.[78] Highly symbolic of this eclipsing of St Columba by the new St Thomas is King William's grant of the custody of Columba's reliquary, the *Breccbennoch* ('speckled, peaked one'), to Arbroath Abbey on 28 June at some point between 1208 and 1211.[79] It is surely significant that this grant was made at a time of heightened tension between William and the English king, John which came to a head in the summer of 1209.[80] The charter suggests that the land of Forglen, Aberdeen-shire, had at some previous time been given to God, St Columba and the *Breccbennoch*, but that custody of the lands and the reliquary was now to be granted to the monks of Arbroath. The charter ends with an explicit instruc-tion that the monks (of Arbroath) were to perform military service in the king's army with the *Breccbennoch*. As the war-clouds gathered in 1209, it is likely that the army at William's back at Norham included monks of St Thomas who had been explicitly instructed to carry St Columba's reliquary. If Columba had failed the kings of Scots in 1174 because of St Thomas's intervention, this time was going to be different.

In the event, war was averted until after William the Lion's death, but his widow, Queen Ermengarde, displayed the same wariness towards tradi-tional Scottish saints. Like her husband, she turned to an English saint for her devotion. Whereas William's actions were aimed at the preservation of king and kingdom on the battlefield, Ermengarde's devotion to St Edward the Confessor seems at least in part to be explained by a desire to ensure the preservation of the kingdom in the marriage chamber.[81] Her son, Alexander II, married John's daughter, Joan, in 1221, but the couple remained childless. Ermengarde's establishment, with the help of her son, of a Cistercian house

---

78 *RRS*, II.no. 197.

79 *RRS*, II.no. 499. I disagree with Barrow's assertion that this charter dates probably to 1211. Even if it did not date to 1209, it is likely that the charter was written and/or dated the next time the king was in Aberdeen (perhaps 1210?), as the relevant lands of Forglen are situated in that county; the reliquary could have been physically given over to the monks prior to this. For a new, contro-versial, take on this topic, see David H. Caldwell, 'The Monymusk reliquary: the Breccbennach of St Columba?', *PSAS* 131 (2001), 267–82.

80 A. A. M. Duncan, 'John King of England and the Kings of Scots', in *King John: New Interpreta-tions*, ed. S. D. Church (Woodbridge, 1999), 247–71, esp. 256–65.

81 Ermengarde also supported a hospital of St Edward in Berwick around the same time. *Calendar of Writs preserved at Yester House 1166–1503*, eds Charles C. Harvey and John Macleod, Scottish Record Society (Edinburgh, 1930), no. 11; NAS, GD 28/11.

at Balmerino, Fife, coincided with the coming of age of the young queen.[82] The choice of an English royal saint was redolent in associations with the saintly Queen Margaret, a fruitful and holy exemplar of perfect queenship. Indeed, a Dunfermline continuation of Margaret's *vita* included a chapter on the visions of St Edward.[83] Moreover, the *Life of St Edward* contained the famous prophecy of the green tree, whereby the seed of two kingdoms flowed together peacefully. Ermengarde's actions seem aimed at promoting peace between the two kingdoms as well as ensuring the vital production of an heir. Ermengarde was buried at Balmerino after her death in 1233, and the figure of St Edward was phased out of the abbey's charters. In keeping with Cistercian tradition, Mary was introduced to the abbey's charters, and after the death of Queen Joan in 1238, Edward disappeared altogether from the charter dedications.[84] While Joan never produced an heir, the examples of Arbroath and Balmerino show clearly that, in terms of the royal family's need for successful 'relationships' with saints to ensure the preservation of their kingdom, there was a move away from both the traditional insular saints and the Christ/Trinity and Marian devotions of the early twelfth century, towards southern English saints with no previous tradition of devotion in Scotland. Still, the dedications to Thomas Becket and Edward the Confessor were products of their times, devoid of staying power. Ultimately, the need for a royal saintly patron remained unfilled.

The canonisation of Queen Margaret in 1249 or 1250 provided a resolution to this problem. Margaret can be seen as a focal point for many of the trends in royal devotion in the preceding 150 years: she was known for her devotion to Christ and the Trinity, she drew attention to the prestigious Anglo-Saxon royal blood, and, crucially, she acted as a national protector of both the royal dynasty and its realm. She had been venerated by local gentry for at least a century: as early as 1165×82, one local lord made a gift to Dunfermline Abbey 'for the love of God and St Margaret' which specifically requested the intercession of the 'holy queen'.[85] In the first half of the thirteenth century, aristocratic donations were referring to 'the church of St Margaret' and the 'Blessed Queen Margaret'.[86] The kings of Scots avoided such language until after canonisation, and Alexander III made a gift to 'the monastery of Blessed Queen Margaret of Dunfermline' in 1278.[87] Nevertheless, it is likely that Margaret was venerated as a saint by the royal

---

[82] *Liber S. Marie de Balmorinach*, ed. W. B. D. D. Turnbull, Abbotsford Club (Edinburgh, 1841), nos 1, 5, 6.

[83] Madrid, Biblioteca del Palacio Real MS II 2097, fol. 20b-v. I am grateful to Alice Taylor for giving me access to her transcription of this text.

[84] Matthew H. Hammond, 'Queen Ermengarde and the Abbey of St Edward, Balmerino', *Cîteaux: Commentarii cistercienses*, t. 59, fasc. 1–2 (2008), 11–36.

[85] *Dunf. Reg.*, no. 165.

[86] *Ibid.*, nos 166, 178, 202.

[87] *Ibid.*, no. 87.

family prior to 1250, even if they were wary of declaring this officially in charters. In 1199, Roger of Howden relates the tale that King William was dissuaded from invading England by a 'divine oracle' while spending the night at Margaret's tomb.[88] Margaret fulfilled in a much more successful way the role previously imagined for St Thomas and St Edward. At once English and Scottish, reformist and devout, Margaret was believed to have the power to protect the kingdom with wisdom, and, when necessary, force. In her *Miracula*, Margaret is depicted as having led the Scots to victory over the Norwegians at Largs in 1263. A local knight, John of Wemyss, had a vision of Margaret leading her husband and her three kingly sons to battle. 'For I have accepted this kingdom from God', she declares, 'and it is entrusted to me and my heirs for ever.'[89]

Aristocratic veneration and support for local saints

To a great degree, aristocrats in the Scottish kingdom followed the lead of the royal family, and engaged fully with the reform *zeitgeist*. For example, Earl Gillebrigte of Strathearn and his wife, Countess Matilda d'Aubigny, established an Augustinian monastery at Inchaffray on the site of an existing church dedicated to St John the Evangelist. Their foundation charter of 1200, which survives as an original single sheet, began with the phrase, 'in the name of the Lord Jesus Christ who is coequal and coeternal with God the father and the Holy Spirit', and specified that the donation was being made 'to our Lord Jesus Christ and blessed MARIE his mother (*genetrix*) and to St John the apostle'.[90] We should not find this surprising: the Gaelic names used by many Scottish earls in the twelfth and thirteenth centuries, such as Mael Isu, Gillecrist and Maeldomnaich, demonstate the importance of Jesus, Christ and the Lord respectively in Scottish society. The importance of the Virgin Mary as an intercessor was clearly not lost on aristocratic families of both 'native' and 'immigrant' backgrounds. Hugh de Moreville founded a Premonstratensian abbey dedicated to the Virgin Mary at Dryburgh in 1150.[91] The earls of Fife and Dunbar established houses of Cistercian nuns dedicated to Mary at North Berwick and Coldstream by 1154 and 1166, respectively.[92] Furthermore, Mary appears in a large number of dual or multiple dedications of monastic houses founded by aristocrats, matched with both apostolic and universal saints like James (Paisley), John the Evangelist (Inchaffray), John

---

[88] *Chronica Magistri Rogeri de Houedene*, ed. Stubbs, IV.100.

[89] *The Miracles of Saint Æbbe of Coldingham and Saint Margaret of Scotland*, ed. Robert Bartlett (Oxford, 2003), 86–9.

[90] *Inchaff. Chrs*, no. 9.

[91] *Dryburgh Liber*, no. 14; *Chrs. David I*, nos 191, 192, 193, 202, 204.

[92] *Carte monialium de Northberwic*, ed. Cosmo Innes, Bannatyne Club (Edinburgh, 1847), nos 3, 6; *Chartulary of the Cistercian Priory of Coldstream*, ed. Charles Rogers, Grampian Club (London, 1879), nos 8, 11.

the Baptist (Beauly) and Andrew (Lindores), as well as insular saints like Serf (Culross), Uinniau (Kilwinning) and Mirin (Paisley).

Aristocratic landholders of immigrant background sometimes expressed devotion for universal saints who had not previously been well known in Scotland, and sometimes they even brought local saints from their previous homes. The Cluniac establishment founded initially at Renfrew in 1162 or 1163 by Walter son of Alan I the steward, was moved within a few years to nearby Paisley. Walter's 'foundation charter' mentions only that the priory is 'to the honour of God', but a much fuller charter granting various endowments after the move to Paisley was made 'to God and St Mary and the church of St James and St Mirin and St Milburga of Paisley'.[93] Walter and the monks of Wenlock seem to have brought the dedication to St Milburga, an eighth-century Mercian princess and abbess, with them from Shropshire. The devotion to St James, rare in Scotland, seems to have been peculiar to the Stewart family, who certainly maintained the use of the personal name in their own family from the thirteenth century onwards.[94] Paisley may have been already associated with Mirin, a saint of purportedly Irish origin. So here we see the combination of an existing local saint, an imported local saint, an imported apostolic saint and the overarching figure of the Virgin. Perhaps unsurprisingly, the figure of Milburga dropped quickly from the abbey's charters, and grantors were able to choose freely between various options: 'the church of St James',[95] 'the church of St Mirin',[96] 'St James and St Mirin of Paisley',[97] and even 'the church of St Mary and Sts James and Mirin of Paisley'.[98]

Table 2. Monastic foundations in the Kingdom of the Scots, 1150–1250[99]

Foundations by aristocratic landholders				
Dryburgh	Hugh de Moreville	1150	Prem.	Mary
North Berwick	Duncan (I), earl of Fife	*ca* 1150	C.N.	Mary
Renfrew/Paisley	Walter son of Alan (I) the steward	*ca* 1163	Clun.	Mary/James/Mirin
Coldstream	Cospatric, earl of Dunbar	× 1166	C.N.	Mary
Kilwinning	Richard de Moreville?	1162×89	Tir.	Mary/Uinniau[100]

---

93 *Pais. Reg.*, 1–2, 5–6.
94 Geoffrey Barrow and Ann Royan, 'James, fifth Stewart of Scotland, 1260(?)–1309', in *Essays on the Nobility of Medieval Scotland*, ed. Keith Stringer (Edinburgh, 1985), 166–94, at 166 and n. 9.
95 *Pais. Reg.*, 11–15.
96 *RRS*, II.no. 220.
97 *Pais. Reg.*, 17–18, 20–1, 24; *RRS*, II.no. 518.
98 *RRS*, II.no. 378.
99 Exclusive of Galloway, Argyll and the Isles.
100 Evidence dates to 1320 (*RRS*, V.no. 165).

Inchaffray	Gillebrigte, earl of Strathearn	1200	Aug.	Mary/John Evangelist
Culross	Mael Coluim (I), earl of Fife	1217	Cist.	Mary/Serf
Deer	William Comyn, earl of Buchan	1219	Cist.	Mary
Fearn	Fearchar, e. Ross	1220s	Prem.	uncertain
Inchmahome	Walter Comyn, earl of Menteith	1238×58	Aug.	Mo-Cholmoc or Colmán[101]
Beauly	John Bisset	*ca* 1230	Vall.	Mary/John Bapt.
Blantyre	Patrick (II), e. Dunbar	1238×49	Aug.	uncertain
Monymusk	Earls of Mar	× 1245	Aug.	Mary
Crossraguel	Earls of Carrick?	1244×65	Clun.	Mary[102]

While the local dedication to St Mirin continues at Paisley to this day, there were other aristocratic foundations which seemingly failed to preserve previous associations with local saints. Despite the strategies employed by the community of St Drostan at Deer, such as the association with St Columba and the building of a church dedicated to Christ and Peter, the community drops 'off the radar' for over a half century. In 1219, we see William Comyn, earl of Buchan, establishing Cistercian monks at Deer. The few surviving charter texts suggest that Drostan was not given the treatment that Serf enjoyed at Culross, where, for example, the abbot tended to be called the 'abbot of St Serf'. Earl William's most extensive surviving charter text refers to 'God Omnipotent, the most Blessed Virgin Mary and all the Saints of God and the religious men of the abbot and monks of Deer', while two other thirteenth-century charters use the much more standard formula 'to God and St Mary of Deer and the monks'.[103] While Drostan certainly may have continued to be venerated by individuals in the Deer area or even by the monks themselves, it seems likely that his status was reduced to the level of not meriting his own religious house.

At Monymusk, also in Aberdeenshire, was a community of *céli Dé*, some charters to whom were written down in the thirteenth-century cartulary of St Andrews priory. Thomas Clancy has suggested that a monastery of Nér, dedicated to St Nechtan and perhaps also St Uinniau/Finnian, was located somewhere within the triangle formed by Monymusk, Fetternear and Abersnithock, and that Monymusk was an 'important ecclesiastical site in the early medieval period'.[104] Clancy claims that 'we may conjecture a seventh-century

---

[101] Potentially a hypocoristic form of Columba. For Colmán, see Máire Herbert, 'Saint Colmán of Dromore and Inchmahome', *Caindel Alban: Fèill-sgrìobhainn do Dhòmhnall E Meek*, eds Colm Ó Baoill and Nancy R. McGuire, *Scottish Gaelic Studies* 24 (2008), 253–65, esp. 260–1.

[102] Evidence dates to 1323 (*RRS*, V.no. 231).

[103] *Illustrations of the Topography and Antiquities of the Shires of Aberdeen and Banff*, vol. II, ed. Joseph Robertson, Spalding Club (Aberdeen, 1847), 426–8.

[104] Clancy, 'Deer and the early church', 371–4.

foundation at the roots of the ultimately Augustinian priory, with a *céli Dé* community present from some time in the period between 800 and 1200'.[105] The nearby church at Migvie was dedicated to St Fínán (or Uineus of Nér) in the mid-twelfth century.[106] Charters by earls of Mar and other local lords to Monymusk in the early thirteenth century explicitly identify the church of the *céli Dé* with the Virgin Mary.[107] The *céli Dé* converted to the Augustinian rule at some point between 1210 and 1245, but it is clear that the Marian dedication was in place before this conversion.[108] It is possible to interpret this in various ways, for example, that the dedication was thrust on the community by outside forces, such as bishop and earl, that the community adopted the Virgin as a survival strategy, or that the *céli Dé* were simply affected by the same reform impulses that touched many others in the kingdom.

Despite the aristocrats' underwriting of new monasteries dedicated to the Virgin Mary and universal saints and the Marian eclipsing of local saints at Deer and Monymusk, aristocratic patrons and donors, both native and immigrant, were much more likely to support the cults and *familiae* of insular saints in Scotland than were the royal family. Eschewing St Andrews, Dunfermline and Lindores, Earl Mael Coluim chose to endow the *fraternitas* of the premier comital family on the local St Serf, building a Cistercian monastery at Culross, probably as a burial place for the earls of Fife.[109] More striking is the decision of Walter Comyn, earl of Menteith, in 1238 to endow an Augustinian house at Inchmahome, the island of Mo-Cholmoc, probably a hypocoristic form of Columba.[110]

Earls may have felt tension between supporting the royal foundations dedicated to universal saints and the need to maintain longstanding cults of insular saints. The earls of Lennox provide a fascinating case in point. The earls supported insular saints such as Patrick: Earl Alwin gave lands 'to the honour of St Patrick' to the church of Old Kilpatrick in the late twelfth century.[111] It is the case of the church of Campsie, though, which is particularly instructive: in 1174, when David, earl of Huntingdon, held the earldom of Lennox, presumably in wardship, he gave the church of Campsie to Kelso Abbey.[112] Over thirty years later, Earl Alwin, 'for the sake of God and holy charity and love of Blessed Kentigern and for the souls of King David and Earl Henry and King Mael Coluim and for the health of the soul of his lord

---

105 *Ibid.*, 374.

106 *St A. Lib.*, 248–50.

107 *Ibid.*, 362–76.

108 *MRHS*, 93–4. Thomas Owen Clancy, 'Reformers to conservatives: Céli Dé communities in the North East', in *After Columba – After Calvin*, ed. James Porter (Aberdeen, 2000), 19–29, at 25–6.

109 *RRS*, V.no. 141.

110 William Fraser, *The Red Book of Menteith*, 2 vols (Edinburgh, 1880), II.326–9, no. 74.

111 *Pais. Reg.*, 157.

112 *Kelso Liber*, I.no. 226.

King William and Lady E[rmengarde] the queen, and his lord Alexander their son', gave the same church to St Kentigern and Glasgow Cathedral. A confirmation by Alwin's son, Maeldomnaich, was evidently produced at the same time.[113] The sycophantic *pro anima* clause and the accompanying confirmation charter suggest that Alwin was aware that shifting his patronage vis-à-vis the church of Campsie was risky. Indeed, shortly after Maeldomnaich became earl, he gave the church again to Kelso (using the 'gift' verb, *dare*), in a charter which recalled the original gift of Earl David and the confirmations by King William and Bishop Jocelin.[114] Nevertheless, the church of Campsie stayed with St Kentigern and Glasgow. Pope Honorius confirmed the church to Glasgow in 1216, and in a 1221 agreement, the abbot of Kelso resigned his claim.[115] Maeldomnaich evidently maintained a good relationship with Glasgow, confirming a tenant's gift 'to Blessed Kentigern'.[116] Unlike his father, however, he chose to cultivate *fraternitas* with the monks of St Thomas at Arbroath. His charters to Arbroath Abbey specify his *fraternitas*, and make explicit that his name and that of his brother, Amlaib, were to be written down in the abbey's *Martyrologium* or Book of Life. Maeldomnaich and Amlaib were also to be absolved annually by the monks in their chapterhouse.[117] As Professor Duncan has shown, Bishop Jocelin had a deliberate policy of associating Kentigern with St Thomas.[118] More practically, however, Maeldomnaich arranged to be buried at Paisley Abbey.[119]

If the prestige of St Columba diminished somewhat in the eyes of the Scottish king, this was certainly not the case among both native and immigrant aristocrats. Unfortunately, very little is known about the church of Dunkeld in the twelfth and early thirteenth centuries. It is clear that the bishop of Dunkeld was seen as the head of the Columban church in the kingdom; this was demonstrated by his close relationship with Inchcolm, the Island of St Columba in the Firth of Forth. Bishop Gregory held the island in custody until the Augustinian house could be built, and three bishops from this period were buried there.[120] Much of the endowment for the house came from the bishops

---

[113] *Glas. Reg.*, I.nos 101, 102.

[114] *Kelso Liber*, I.no. 222.

[115] *Glas. Reg.*, I.no. 116; *Kelso Liber*, I.no. 230; Cowan, *Parishes*, 26.

[116] *Glas. Reg.*, I.no. 178.

[117] *Liber S. Thome de Aberbrothoc*, eds Cosmo Innes and Patrick Chalmers, Bannatyne Club, 2 vols (Edinburgh, 1848–56), I.no. 133; BL, Add. MS 33245, fol. 141v.

[118] A. A. M. Duncan, 'St Kentigern at Glasgow Cathedral in the twelfth century', in *Medieval Art and Architecture in the Diocese of Glasgow*, ed. Richard Fawcett, The British Archaeological Association Transactions 23 (London, 1998), 9–24, at 11–12.

[119] *Pais. Reg.*, 158–9.

[120] *Charters of the Abbey of Inchcolm*, eds D. E. Easson and Angus MacDonald, SHS (Edinburgh, 1938), no. 1. Bishops Richard de Prebenda, John de Leicester, and Gilbert were buried on Inchcolm. *Chron. Bower*, V.81, 159. Their bones were moved in 1266. *Ibid.*, V.359.

of Dunkeld rather than the king.[121] Modern scholars have suggested that relics associated with the saint were kept on the island.[122] Brice (perhaps for Maelbrigte), prior of Inchcolm, and other canons and priests from the island witnessed the few surviving charter texts from the twelfth century.[123] The Columban cult in the east attracted the support of local lords of English and French descent. For example, David Uviet granted the church of Megginch, Perthshire, 'to God and St Columba and Bishop John'.[124] Inchcolm's donors included Robert de Quincy, Waltheof son of Cospatric, Richard son of Hugh de Camera, Thomas of Restalrig and John Avenel; moreover, Walter and Christina of Lundin, Fife, arranged for *fraternitas*.[125]

Little is known about the Columban community at Dunkeld itself before the constitution of a secular cathedral chapter and building of a new cathedral around 1230.[126] No episcopal cartulary survives, but an agreement made with the Cistercian abbey of Coupar Angus between 1203 and 1210 is instructive. In recognition for the assent of the 'canons of St Columba of the church of Dunkeld' to a donation made by the late Bishop John, the Cistercian monks agreed to pay one pound of incense at the church of Dunkeld on St Columba's Day.[127] The symbolism of these reformist monastic incomers making offerings to Columba on his feast day is hard to escape, and is a salutary reminder of the continuing high prestige of that saint. With the construction of the new cathedral, control of the parish of the Holy Trinity, formerly held by Dunfermline Abbey, reverted to the bishopric.[128] The thirteenth-century chapter seal shows the crozier and shrine of St Columba.[129] The original island of St Columba, Iona, meanwhile, lost control of its churches in Galloway in the 1170s, and a Benedictine abbey and Augustinian nunnery were established there, apparently by Rognvaldr (or Ranald) son of Somerled, ruler of *Innse Gall*.[130] The Irish *familia* of Columba responded by burning down the nascent monastery, and a contemporaneous poem has the saint lamenting the arrival of foreigners and cursing the line of Somerled.[131] A donation by Rognvaldr and his wife, Fonia, to Paisley Abbey, was accompanied by an oath on

121   *Inchcolm Chrs.*, no. 2.
122   Duncan, 'St Andrews', 33.
123   Shead, Scottish Episcopal Acta, I, nos 39–42. *Dunf. Reg.*, nos 124, 598; *Inchcolm Chrs.*, no. 1; *Registrum Monasterii S. Marie de Cambuskenneth*, ed. William Fraser, Grampian Club (Edinburgh, 1872), no. 12.
124   The church was later given to Holyrood Abbey. *Liber cartarum Sancte Crucis*, ed. Cosmo Innes, Bannatyne Club (Edinburgh, 1840), no. 66.
125   *Inchcolm Chrs.*, nos 2, 3, 4, 7, 11, 12, 13, 17.
126   Watt, *Series Episcoporum*, 41.
127   *Charters of the Abbey of Coupar Angus*, ed. D. E. Easson, SHS, 2 vols (Edinburgh, 1947), I.no. 15.
128   Cowan, 'Urban parish', 85; Cowan, *Parishes*, 53.
129   Peter Yeoman, *Pilgrimage in Medieval Scotland* (London, 1999), 86.
130   *RRS*, II.no. 141.
131   *MRHS*, 49; Clancy, 'The cult of saints', 32.

St Columba, suggesting that Rognvaldr might have characterised his attitude to the saint differently from the poet's depiction.[132]

A similar continuity in devotion is exemplified in the continuing popularity of the cult of St Cuthbert. The names of the kings of Scots, despite their interests in other institutions, continued to be entered into the *Liber Vitae* at Durham. The names of other Scots in this book suggest that the saint's prestige endured among the Scottish nobility both south and north of the Forth: visitors to the saint's shrine included earls of Dunbar, Fife and Atholl, the Abernethy family (former lay-abbots of St Brigit's church) and Dubgall, ruler of the Isles.[133] The comital family of Dunbar in particular, it seems, continued to venerate St Cuthbert. One good example of this comes from a 1231×2 charter of Patrick, future earl of Dunbar, in which he admits that his family has held the land of Swinewood without any right, and that, after seeing King Edgar's charter of donation, he had decided to resign his claim 'out of love and reverence for the glorious confessor Cuthbert whom his ancestors loved with a special love'.[134] Furthermore, the discovery of the body of St Æbbe and the building of a new oratory dedicated to her in 1188 offers an example of the renewal of a local saint's cult under the auspices of the Benedictine monks of Coldingham, a revival demonstrated by the inclusion of Æbbe's name alongside Mary and Cuthbert in a few charters of the earls of Dunbar.[135]

Despite the reformist turn towards veneration of Christ, the Trinity and Mary, the royal family's introduction of St Thomas and St Edward, and the emergence of the cult of St Margaret, devotion to local and insular saints remained fairly strong within the kingdom of the Scots, and these saints even attracted the patronage of Anglo-French incomers and their descendants. One is left with an impression of an underlying reservoir of tradition and custom relating to these figures, of which only glimpses can be attained from the surviving written texts. This conclusion fits well with the work of Julia Smith on local saints in Brittany, and it should not surprise us that local saints could disappear 'under the radar' of written record for decades, even centuries.[136] The figure of St Ethernan, venerated locally in Fife, demonstrates this tendency well. A charter by Cospatric, earl of Dunbar, records a gift to 'St Ethernan of May and the brethren serving God there', but this

---

132 *Pais. Reg.*, 125.
133 Geoffrey Barrow, 'Scots in the Durham *Liber Vitae*', in *The Durham Liber Vitae in Its Context*, eds David Rollason et al. (Woodbridge, 2004), 109–16.
134 DCM, Misc. Chs, no.736; J. Raine, *The History and Antiquities of North Durham* (London, 1852), Appendix, no. 127; For translation, see Elsa Hamilton, 'The Acts of the Earls of Dunbar Relating to Scotland c.1124–c.1289: A Study of Lordship in Scotland in the Twelfth and Thirteenth Centuries' (University of Glasgow, unpublished PhD thesis, 2003), 408.
135 Raine, *North Durham*, Appendix, nos 118, 125, 126; DCM, Misc. Chs, nos 733, 734, 741, 742, 769; Bartlett, *Miracles of Saint Æbbe*, xvii–xviii.
136 Julia M. H. Smith, 'Oral and written: saints, miracles and relics in Brittany, c. 850–1250', *Speculum*, 65 (1990), 309–43.

came on the cusp of the settlement or conversion there, probably in the 1140s, to the Benedictine order under the auspices of Reading Abbey.[137] This new house was dedicated to All Saints, and this is reflected in a succession of royal charters, which make no mention of Ethernan.[138] The next reference to that local saint emerges over a century later when Alexander Comyn, earl of Buchan, made a gift of wax for the lighting of St Ethernan of the Isle of May and the monks serving God and St Ethernan there.[139] Indeed, there is conclusive evidence that local and insular saints were venerated at reform monasteries: Serf, Cuthbert and Ninian had feasts in the Holyrood Abbey calendar (the sections covering the feast days of St Columba and St Kentigern are missing).[140] Furthermore, thirteenth-century offices for Kentigern have survived from Jedburgh Abbey, while offices for Brigit and Cuthbert were incorporated into the famous St Andrews Music Book.[141] Thus, while the tectonic plates of ecclesiastical structures, political hierarchies and religious worship moved constantly in the central middle ages, the underlying reservoir of veneration and devotion to local, insular saints remained intact, surviving in many ways until the Reformation.

---

[137] A. A. M. Duncan, 'Documents relating to the Priory of the Isle of May, c.1140–1313', *PSAS* 90 (1956–7), 52–80. For charter, see 74–5, no. 53.

[138] *Chrs. David I*, no. 165; *RRS*, I.no. 168; *RRS*, II.no. 8. References to All Saints also appear in the context of reform houses at Deer and Monymusk; it is likely that the concept of All Saints provided an acceptable umbrella for particularly obscure or undocumented local saints.

[139] *St A. Lib.*, 383.

[140] Francis Wormald, 'A fragment of a thirteenth-century calendar from Holyrood Abbey', *PSAS* 69 (1935), 471–9; David McRoberts, 'Scottish medieval liturgical books', *IR* 3 (1952), no. 11.

[141] McRoberts, 'Liturgical books', nos 6, 15; Henry George Farmer, 'A lost Scottish liturgical fragment', *IR* 5 (1954), 141; Warwick Edwards, 'Chant in Anglo-French Scotland', in Isobel Woods Preece, *'Our awin Scottis use': Music in the Scottish Church up to 1603*, ed. Sally Harper (Glasgow and Aberdeen, 2000), 201–24.

5

A SAINTLY SINNER? THE 'MARTYRDOM' OF DAVID, DUKE OF ROTHESAY

Steve Boardman

On 25 or 26 March 1402 David, duke of Rothesay, the eldest son and heir of the Scottish king Robert III, died in Falkland castle in Fife while in the custody of his uncle Robert, duke of Albany.[1] David's imprisonment and death were part of an intermittent but long-running struggle for control of the kingdom between the senior line of the royal dynasty represented by Robert III and his sons David and James (the future James I), and the cadet branch of the royal house headed by the duke of Albany. The rivalry between the royal house and the Albany Stewarts in the early fifteenth century goes some way to explain the dramatically divergent accounts of Rothesay's life, arrest and death that appeared after 1402. Men keen to inconvenience and embarrass the duke of Albany depicted Rothesay as a 'martyr', a young prince brutally and unjustly killed, starved to death on his uncle's orders in the dungeons of Falkland. Rothesay's supposedly cruel and lingering demise evidently provoked interest beyond the narrow circle of those actively involved in the arena of high politics, for the duke's tomb at Lindores Abbey seems to have become the centre of a miracle-working cult and a (perhaps short-lived) focus for popular pilgrimage in the early decades of the fifteenth century. However, the celebration of Rothesay as a saintly figure was hardly straightforward or universal, for a powerful counter-narrative existed, preserved in a series of fifteenth- and sixteenth-century texts, that characterised Duke David as an immoral, womanising degenerate who had had to be removed from power by his uncle in order to save the kingdom from the baleful effects of his rule. These very different interpretations of Rothesay's character, life and death would intersect and clash in a number of historical and literary works in the century and a half after the duke's demise, providing insights into aspects of political culture and popular piety in fifteenth- and sixteenth-century Scotland.

---

[1] *Chron. Bower*, VIII.39–40. For context, see Stephen Boardman, *The Early Stewart Kings, Robert II and Robert III, 1371–1406* (East Linton, 1996), 235–47.

It is, perhaps, appropriate to begin with a summary of the rather thin direct evidence for, or near contemporary comment on, the existence of a fully fledged cult focused on Rothesay. The first explicit indication that David's burial church was the site of 'miracles' came some twenty-five years after Rothesay's death, in a papal supplication from the abbot of Lindores. The tone of the document suggests that the miracle-working reputation of the prince's corporeal remains was by that stage well established in a local context. In 1427 the abbot, James Rossy, proudly informed the pope that in his abbey 'rests the body of David of happy memory, brother of James King of Scotland (which body is held as holy in those parts on account of the miracles [*divina miracula*] performed there)'.² It is worth noting the relatively cautious language employed by the abbot and the fact, understandable given that he was writing to the official arbiter of saintly status in late medieval Europe, that he did not describe Rothesay as a saint. Others were

---

2   Vatican City, Vatican Archives, Registrum Supplicationum, 215, fols 72v–73r; *CSSR 1423–1428*, ed. Annie I. Dunlop, SHS (Edinburgh, 1956), 166–7. Rossy became abbot shortly after the return of Rothesay's brother James I to the Scottish realm in 1424. It is thus possible that the reporting of 'miracles' at Lindores began, or became more acceptable, after 1424, encouraged by the re-establishment of the royal line and the appearance of a new abbot (for whom, see *The Heads of Religious Houses in Scotland from Twelfth to Sixteenth Centuries*, eds D. E. R. Watt and N. F. Shead (Edinburgh, 2001), 138). It is interesting that a similar application for the right to grant indulgences to visitors to Lindores by the previous abbot, John Steele, in 1414 made no mention of Rothesay. Significantly, perhaps, that supplication was accompanied by another relating to the annexation of a church to the abbey that was said to have had the support of Robert, duke of Albany. NAS, RH6/2, 'Vatican transcripts', II. nos 62, 63; *Calendar of Papal Letters to Scotland of Benedict XIII of Avignon, 1394–1419*, ed. Francis McGurk, SHS (Edinburgh, 1976), 293. The development of martyr devotions elsewhere, however, would suggest that the miracle-working aspect of the Rothesay cult was probably established in the immediate aftermath of the duke's death. It may be that Abbot Steele (who was transferred to Lindores from Coldingham sometime in 1402, and whose hold on the abbatial office encountered opposition from within the abbey itself – *Heads of Religious Houses*, eds Watt and Shead, 138; *CSSR, 1418–1422*, eds E. R. Lindsay and A. I. Cameron, SHS (Edinburgh, 1934), 246–8) had sought to suppress the cult on Albany's behalf.
    Abbot Rossy's 1427 supplication mentioned that 'in the Feast of the Nativity of St. Mary [8 September] and the octaves of the same, a great concourse of the faithful has been, and is, accustomed to flow to the said monastery, to which the said king bears singular affection'. There is no suggestion here that the 'great concourse' was made up of people whose primary purpose was to visit Rothesay's tomb, but there was surely some correlation between this reported traffic and the 'divina miracula' associated with the duke's corpse. Lindores was dedicated to the Virgin Mary, and the claimed popularity of the abbey as a destination for pilgrims on or around the feast of her nativity may simply have reflected this status as a Marian church (the 1414 supplication had also highlighted the significance of the Marian feasts of the Nativity and the Ascension for visitors to the abbey). The 8 September had, as far as can be told, no particular relevance to Duke David's life. However, Rothesay's death occurred either on, or the morning after, another (although less prominent) Marian celebration, the feast of the Annunciation of the Virgin Mary (25 March), so that a linkage between commemoration of the duke and the annual cycle of Marian devotion may have developed. Curiously, the 1427 Lindores supplication was recorded in the Registrum Supplicationum on 9 September, the day after the feast of the Nativity. It is possible, though perhaps unlikely given that the date is specified twice (and emphasised in the 1414 supplication), that the papal scribe inadvertently substituted the feast of the Nativity for the feast of the Annunciation. I am grateful to Eila Williamson for her thoughts on this issue.

less careful. That Rothesay was widely and openly celebrated as a saint in fifteenth-century Scotland is suggested by a garbled report given to the English antiquary William of Worcester in February 1478 by an anonymous Scottish visitor. Worcester (or his informant) was somewhat confused over the exact identity of the individual commemorated, but his note on a 'Sanctus David' (given the erroneous surname Bruce), the brother of James I, who died a martyr through starvation and was buried in Lindores Abbey near Newburgh, is clearly a reference to Rothesay.[3] Finally, a sequence of three sixteenth-century chronicles made mention of miracles occurring at Lindores following Rothesay's death. The earliest of these works was Hector Boece's Latin *Scotorum Historia* (1527).[4] John Bellenden's vernacular prose *Chronicles of Scotland* (1532) was largely (and explicitly) based on Boece's Latin history, as was William Stewart's vernacular verse *Buik of the Croniclis of Scotland* (1535).[5] Boece's summary of the history of the Rothesay cult was grudging and sceptical. There had been miracles at Rothesay's tomb, but according to Boece these had ceased after the duke's brother, James I, had obtained revenge for David's death, presumably a reference to the mass execution of the Albany Stewarts in 1425.[6] In essence, according to Boece, the events around Rothesay's tomb were the work of an uneasy spirit, a vengeful wraith, whose powers of intercession were weak and temporary. Boece, in fact, was rather more interested in the supposed moral failings of the royal duke which had been highlighted in a number of fifteenth-century texts, including Walter Bower's *Scotichronicon* (1441×9), one of Boece's principal sources, as an explanation of his downfall. The unhappy fate of rulers who did not maintain exemplary standards of personal probity was a major theme of Boece's work, and the tale of Rothesay's loss of power and ignominious death as a direct result of his debauched behaviour was clearly too tempting to ignore, even if the chronicler was also well aware of the

---

3   *William Worcestre: Itineraries*, ed. John H. Harvey (Oxford, 1969), 6–9.
4   Hector Boece, *Scotorum Historiae a prima gentis origine libri xvii* (Paris, 1527), 350. See also Nicola Royan, '*Scotichronicon* rewritten? Hector Boece's debt to Bower in the *Scotorum Historia*', in *Church, Chronicle and Learning in Medieval and Early Renaissance Scotland*, ed. Barbara E. Crawford (Edinburgh, 1999), 57–71, at 60–1.
5   *The Chronicles of Scotland, compiled by Hector Boece, translated into Scots by John Bellenden, 1531*, eds Edith C. Batho and H. Winifred Husbands, STS, 2 vols (Edinburgh, 1938–41) [hereafter *Chron. Bellenden*], II.361–2; William Stewart, *The Buik of the Croniclis of Scotland: or, a Metrical Version of the History of Hector Boece*, ed. William Turnbull, 3 vols (London, 1858), III.473–8.
6   Royan, '*Scotichronicon* rewritten?', 60–1; *Chron. Bellenden*, II.362. The supplication of 1427 suggests that miracles were still being reported after the death of the Albany Stewarts. The community at Lindores may, of course, have had a continuing financial interest in promoting the cult even if its 'political' relevance had disappeared with the fall of the Albany Stewarts. Whether Worcester's brief note should be read to indicate that Lindores was still an active cult centre in the 1470s is wholly unclear. For all the sixteenth-century chroniclers the cult was clearly an historic rather than an active phenomenon.

separate tradition that regarded Rothesay as a saint.[7] While John Bellenden replicated Boece's hostile summary of David's life, William Stewart openly disagreed with his 'author' and mounted a spirited and idiosyncratic defence of Rothesay's virtue as a prince.[8]

Taken together these isolated references tell us very little about the origins, nature or popularity of any devotion that grew up around the duke's tomb in Lindores Abbey. The general silence of the sources may lend some weight to the sixteenth-century chroniclers' view that the cult was not particularly long-lived or significant, for there is no trace of the devotional parapher-nalia that a widely popular and long-lasting pilgrimage cult might have been expected to produce.[9] However, the few direct statements on the cult can be supplemented through analysis of other administrative, chronicle and literary sources that shed a tangential light on the contentious debate over Rothesay's fate and posthumous status in the first half of the fifteenth century.

It was evident that rumours and accusations about the manner of the duke's death were in circulation almost as soon as the young prince had expired. A general council held in May 1402 determined that Rothesay had died by 'divine providence, and not otherwise' and Robert III, perhaps reluctantly, publicly forgave the duke of Albany and his accomplice in the arrest and detention of Rothesay, Archibald, fourth earl of Douglas, and granted both men and their supporters legal immunity from any charges, including lese majesty, that might have arisen from their actions.[10] The king's proclamation also urged that his subjects should 'not slander the said Robert and Archibald and their participants, accomplices or adherents in this deed, as aforesaid, by word or action, nor murmur against them in any way whereby their good reputation is hurt'.[11] The 'murmuring' against Albany and Douglas no doubt centred on the straightforward accusation that the young duke had, in fact, been deliberately starved to death in Falkland castle. That tales emphasising the pitiful circumstances of Rothesay's demise were circulating within and outwith Scotland in the early decades of the fifteenth century is suggested by accounts of the episode included in two very different works. Walter Bower, the abbot of Inchcolm, compiled and revised his massive Latin history, the *Scotichronicon*, in the period 1441×9.[12] *The Dethe of the Kynge of Scotis*,

---

7   *Chron. Bower*, VIII.38–41. See Royan, '*Scotichronicon* rewritten?', for general comment on the relationship between the work of Bower and Boece.

8   Stewart, *The Buik of the Croniclis*, ed. Turnbull, III.473–8, esp. 475. See below, 100–1.

9   There are, for example, no lives of the saint, no specific records of acts of devotion at Lindores or elsewhere, no surviving pilgrimage badges or other pictorial representations of the 'passion' of the martyr saint, no commemoration of the date of David's death in any of the extant calendars or litanies produced or used in late medieval Scotland, and no surviving liturgical material relating to 'Sanctus David'.

10 Records of the Parliaments of Scotland to 1707 [1402/5/1], http://www.rps.ac.uk/ (accessed 6 February 2009).

11 *Ibid.*

12 *Chron. Bower*, IX.204–8 (for a biography of Bower).

meanwhile, was penned by the well known English scribe and copyist John Shirley, who claimed to have translated the work into English from a Latin 'original'.[13] The *Dethe* included a short commentary on the duke's fate as a preamble to its discussion of the life and assassination of David's younger brother, James I. The provenance and date of Shirley's source remains unclear, but it seems likely that his translation was undertaken fairly shortly after James I's murder.[14] Although varying in tone, purpose and level of detail the two texts seem to have similarities in their discussion of Rothesay's downfall. It seems improbable that either of the authors had direct access to the work of the other, and it is likely that the shared elements in the narratives they laid out were derived from an earlier (and now lost) account of Rothesay's demise.[15] In the *Dethe*, David is presented as a dissolute and irresponsible prince brought down by his own folly, whose death was nonetheless so horrifying that it demanded sympathy and pity. Taking advantage of his father's infirmity, the duke was said to have unlawfully seized control of royal government after which 'he wex fulle viceous in his liveing, as in depucelling and defouling of yong maydenys' and 'breking the ordre of wedloke be his foule ambycious lust of aduoutrie'.[16] Alarmed by the prospect of such a malign figure ruling as king after his father's death because of the 'many inconveniencez, infortunez, and vengeancez' that might fall on the land as a result 'of his lyff soo opnly knowen vicious [that is, vice-filled]', the *Dethe* narrates that the Scottish nobility, led by Albany and the earl of Douglas, imprisoned Rothesay in Falkland. There, 'by dures of ffamyn [famine] hee eate his owne handez and died in grete distress and myserie ... ageinst Goddez lawe and mannez lawe'.[17]

At first glance Bower's ostensibly more sober, cautious and detailed narrative seems to reflect a pro-Albany and Douglas account that effectively exonerated the two men from the charge that they had deliberately set out to kill the young heir to the throne.[18] The prince is said to have been detained by Albany on Robert III's orders, after the young man had spurned a 'council of

13 There are two modern editions of the *Dethe*. *Death and Dissent: Two Fifteenth-century Chronicles*, ed. Lister M. Matheson (Woodbridge, 1999), 23–56; Margaret Connolly, 'The *dethe of the kynge of Scotis*: a new edition', *SHR* 71 (1992), 46–69. See also the discussion of the text in M. H. Brown, 'Crown-magnate relations in the personal rule of James I of Scotland' (University of St Andrews, unpublished PhD thesis, 1991), 500–13.

14 *The Dethe*, ed. Matheson, 10–13, 20–1.

15 Brown points out that at least some elements of Shirley's account of Rothesay could theoretically have been derived from a reading of Bower's *Scotichronicon* (the claimed Latin original?), but that Bower does not seem to have been the source for the bulk of the material relating to James I and that, in any case, the date of composition/translation of the *Dethe* must have been fairly close to, or pre-dated, the final compilation of the *Scotichronicon*. There would thus seem to have been little opportunity for any direct borrowing, in either direction.

16 *The Dethe*, ed. Matheson, 23–4.

17 *Ibid.*

18 It is conceivable that Bower had access to the otherwise lost general council debate of May 1402 which cleared Albany and Douglas of any responsibility for David's demise.

honourable men' that the king had assigned to advise him. The hope, claimed Bower, was that the prince's wayward behaviour could be curbed by a spell of corrective custody. This plan had gone horribly awry as a result of the duke's accidental death from dysentery while under temporary arrest in Falkland.[19]

There were, however, elements of Bower's treatment of the episode that clearly chimed with the more sensational interpretation offered by the *Dethe*. First, although it was not treated in Bower's account as the principal reason for the action taken against Rothesay, Abbot Walter did highlight problems caused by the duke's various romantic liaisons. The fall of princes through their departure from wise council and descent into carnal vice and wickedness was, of course, a standard theme for late medieval writers in a variety of genres.[20] In Rothesay's case, however, accusations that he had disregarded marriage vows and treated sexual partners inappropriately were demonstrably in circulation prior to his arrest. In a famous letter to the English king Henry IV in 1400, George Dunbar, earl of March, explicitly accused the prince of 'defowling' his daughter Elizabeth through breaking the marriage he had contracted (and consummated) with her and going on to wed Mary Douglas, sister of Archibald, fourth earl of Douglas.[21] The annulment of the Dunbar marriage was only one part of a wider political rift between the earl of March and Rothesay, but the failure to honour his obligation to Elizabeth could clearly be highlighted by the duke's opponents as a character flaw that had had serious consequences for the realm. George Dunbar, disenchanted with the Rothesay led regime, opened negotiations with King Henry and, when these were exposed, the earl and his family had been forced into exile. Dunbar's expulsion directly contributed to a full-scale invasion of the south of Scotland mounted by the English king in 1400.[22] Aside from discussing Rothesay's abortive betrothal to Elizabeth Dunbar, Bower also suggested that

---

19   *Chron. Bower*, VIII.36–41.

20   See, for example, Sally Mapstone, 'Bower on kingship', in *Chron. Bower*, IX.321–38; Joanna Martin, *Kingship and Love in Scottish Poetry, 1424–1540* (Aldershot, 2008), 2–8 for useful summaries of the way in which the medieval 'advice to princes' tradition manifested itself in fifteenth-century Scottish chronicles and poetry.

21   BL, Cotton Vespasian F. VII. fol. 22; *Facsimiles of the National Manuscripts of Scotland*, ed. Cosmo Innes, 3 parts (Southampton, 1867–71), pt ii. no. liii. In the *Dethe*, Rothesay was also accused of 'defouling ... yong maydenys'. 'Defoul' had various meanings, including 'to disgrace, bring discredit or shame on' or to 'defile by immorality'. See the *Dictionary of the Scots Language*, http://www.dsl.ac.uk/dsl/. It is intriguing to note that Elizabeth Dunbar was effectively withdrawn from the marriage market after her encounter with Rothesay, perhaps because her social disgrace made her unattractive to potential partners of appropriate rank. She seems to have entered Holy Orders and ended her days as prioress of the house of Augustinian canonesses at St Leonard's in Perth. NAS, Records of King James VI Hospital, Perth, GD 79/2/6 and 79/4/79; Robert Scott Fittis, *Ecclesiastical Annals of Perth, to the Period of the Reformation* (Edinburgh, 1885), 278–9; *Heads of Religious Houses*, eds Watt and Shead, 177. Some garbled awareness of Elizabeth's later clerical career may partly explain the Boece/Bellenden claims that Rothesay's excesses included the defilement of nuns.

22   Boardman, *Early Stewart Kings*, 226–9; Alastair J. Macdonald, *Border Bloodshed* (East Linton, 2000), 137–40.

one of the men who arrested David, William Lindsay of Rossie, had developed a dislike of the prince because he had promised marriage to William's sister Euphemia, but 'had repudiated her in … subsequent attempted marriages to other ladies'.[23] Rothesay's dalliances with Euphemia Lindsay and Elizabeth Dunbar encouraged Bower to misapply a hostile mid-fourteenth-century passage from the so-called 'Bridlington Prophecies', actually relating to the alleged promiscuity of David II (1329–71), to the young duke.[24] It is, perhaps, not surprising that Rothesay's demise was interpreted by some as a consequence of, and punishment for, his apparently dissolute behaviour. It is impossible to say whether those who moved against him in 1401 actually argued at the time, as the account in the *Dethe* implies, that their action was justified because, in line with conventional theorising, the duke's immorality and 'frivolity' had demonstrably threatened, and continued to threaten, the safety of the realm.[25] It seems likely, however, that this rationalisation of events, with its emphasis on Rothesay's debased nature, would have become increasingly significant for the duke's one-time adversaries as attempts to portray David as a martyr gained ground.

Although Bower privileged the explanation that Rothesay had died as a result of dysentery, he also openly acknowledged that others claimed that the duke had been starved.[26] In short, the *Scotichronicon* narrative displayed

---

[23] *Chron. Bower*, VIII.30–3 (for the Dunbar marriage and its aftermath); 40–1 (for Euphemia Lindsay).

[24] *Ibid.*, VIII.40–1, 167.

[25] As Rothesay's new marriage partner in 1400 was the sister of Archibald, fourth earl of Douglas, it is difficult to see how the Douglas earl, at least, could have presented himself as outraged at the duke's abandonment of Elizabeth Dunbar.

[26] *Chron. Bower*, VIII.38–40. Intriguingly, one of the fifteenth-century manuscript copies of the *Scotichronicon* – BL, Harleian MS 4764 (MS FE) – abandoned Abbot Walter's neutral tone, omitted the possibility that dysentery had killed the duke, criticised Albany for his role in his nephew's death and described the men who had arrested Rothesay as traitors. The text preserved in the Harleian MS seems to have been written at Dunkeld for Bishop George Brown sometime between 1497 and 1515. See *Chron. Bower*, IX.197–8, for the description of Harleian MS 4764. *Chron. Bower*, v.460 n. 50 (for the provenance of the MS); *Ibid.*, VIII.intro. xvi, 138, 166–7 (under 53–4), 211 (under 4). George Brown was a Dundonian who maintained strong links to that burgh's parish church throughout his life (for this, see Steve Boardman, 'The cult of St George in Scotland', in *Saints' Cults in the Celtic World*, eds Steve Boardman, John Reuben Davies and Eila Williamson (Woodbridge, 2009), 146–59, at 156). The right of presentation to the vicarage of Dundee parish church was, in the fifteenth century, held by the abbot and community of Lindores. Moreover, in February 1405, Robert III had granted a 100 shilling annuity to the chaplain of St Saviour's altar in Dundee to support masses for the soul of his deceased son David. *CSSR 1447–71*, eds James Kirk, Roland J. Tanner and Annie I. Dunlop (Glasgow, 1997), no. 572 (for the abbot of Lindores as patron of the vicariate of Dundee); *Charters, Writs and Public Documents of the Royal Burgh of Dundee*, ed. W. Hay (Dundee, 1880), 26 (and unnumbered inserts); *ER*, III.626, 631 (for the 1405 annuity). If the Harleian MS's discussion of Rothesay and Albany reflected Brown's views in any way, then these might have been shaped by the bishop's early connections to Dundee and (indirectly) Lindores. It is unknown whether Brown received his initial education at the burgh's grammar school, another institution that had historical links to the abbey of Lindores, but the chronicler Hector Boece certainly did. It seems possible, then, that Lindores' association

an awareness of accounts that must have been very similar in import to that underlying the *Dethe*, centred on Rothesay's sexual incontinence as an explanation of the animosity displayed towards the duke, and certain that he had been starved to death.

At no point in either the *Dethe* or the *Scotichronicon* was it suggested that Rothesay deserved or enjoyed a posthumous reputation as a saint and there was certainly no aspect of his short life as depicted in these texts that could be viewed as conventionally 'virtuous'. In late medieval Europe the official ecclesiastical criteria for recognition of sainthood normally required the display of virtue and piety in life and miracles after death, so that a saint acted as both example and intercessor.[27] However, as scholars such as André Vauchez have emphasised, 'popular' sanctity could be imagined for, and bestowed on, anyone who was thought to have been killed as a martyr, that is through a process of prolonged and unjust physical torment. The nature of the death, rather than the nature of the life, could encourage and secure identification as a 'saint'.[28] Moreover, the narrative framework of christian martyr tales carried with it certain ideas and expectations that might naturally be mapped onto political struggles. The martyr's story typically 'developed through the confrontation of the saint with worldly authorities in the form of an evil tyrant'.[29] Despite their suffering and physical death, martyr saints were ultimately triumphant through the posthumous miracles they performed and their attainment of a state of perfect bliss. Martyr tales thus held out the almost prophetic prospect of eventual victory over the tyrannical and unjust secular leaders responsible for the torture and execution of the saint, and thereby acted to sustain support for the martyr's cause beyond their death.

The establishment of miracle-working cults around the tombs and relics of 'political' martyrs was a not infrequent occurrence in the late medieval English realm.[30] The most prominent and enduring of these English cults,

---

with Dundee meant that men such as Brown and Boece were well aware of the historic martyr cult centred on the abbey and the partisan account of the duke's death that had sustained it.

The abbreviated re-working of the *Scotichronicon* found in the so-called Book of Pluscarden (dating to the 1460s) also explicitly embraced the idea that Rothesay had been starved to death at Albany's behest. *Liber Pluscardensis*, ed. F. J. H. Skene, Historians of Scotland 7 and 10, 2 vols (Edinburgh, 1877–80) [hereafter *Chron. Pluscarden*], I.342; II.258. Even within the fifteenth-century chronicle tradition based on Bower's work, then, there was obvious accommodation with a narrative that portrayed Rothesay as a prince maliciously and unjustly slain by his uncle.

27 Aviad M. Kleinberg, 'Proving sanctity: selection and authentication of saints in the later middle ages', *Viator* 20 (1980), 183–205, at 188–90; E. W. Kemp, *Canonisation and Authority in the Western Church* (Oxford, 1948), 79, 104.

28 André Vauchez, *Sainthood in the Later Middle Ages*, trans. Jean Birrell (Cambridge, 1997), 148–56; Kleinberg, 'Proving sanctity'.

29 *St Katherine of Alexandria: The Late Middle English Prose Legend in Southwell Minster MS 7*, eds Saara Nevanlinna and Irma Taavitsainen (Cambridge, 1993), 18.

30 For general surveys of this phenomenon, see Danna Piroyansky, *Martyrs in the Making. Political Martyrdom in Late Medieval England* (Basingstoke, 2008); Simon Walker, 'Political saints in later medieval England', in *Political Culture in Later Medieval England; Essays by Simon Walker*, ed. Michael J. Braddick (Manchester, 2006), 198–222 (first published in *The McFarlane Legacy:*

such as those focused on Simon de Montfort (killed in battle in 1265), Thomas of Lancaster (executed 1322), Archbishop Richard Scrope (executed 1405) and Henry VI (murdered 1471), all had their origins in the violent deaths or ignominious executions of men actively engaged in the affairs of the world.[31] They were also often distinguished by the notion that the individual commemorated and venerated had died because of their commitment to a distinct set of political principles and concerns.[32] The presentation of prominent political figures killed on the battlefield or scaffold as martyrs was a compelling way to keep the cause or set of interests for which they had supposedly fought and died alive in the imagination of the devotees attracted to their shrines. Late medieval English rulers were well aware of the very real and immediate threat presented by cults centred on the tombs of their former adversaries. Henry III's settlement with supporters of the deceased Simon de Montfort in October 1266 (the so-called *Dictum de Kenilworth*) insisted that Earl Simon had performed no posthumous miracles and threatened those who claimed otherwise with corporal punishment.[33] Similarly, Edward II's advisors were said to have ordered that steps should be taken to prevent pilgrimage to Thomas of Lancaster's tomb and execution site in Pontefract for otherwise they and the king 'shulde be in grete sclaundre [th] rou[gh]-out al Cristendome for the de[th] of Thomas of Lancaster'.[34] The duke of Albany's obvious sensitivity in the general council of 1402 about the 'murmuring' against him and the earl of Douglas might indicate a compa-

Studies in Late Medieval Politics and Society, eds Richard H. Britnell and Anthony J. Pollard (Stroud, 1995), 77–106; John M. Theilmann, 'Political canonization and political symbolism in medieval England', *The Journal of British Studies* 29 (1990), 241–66.

31 For studies of individual cults, see, inter alia, Claire Valente, 'Simon de Montfort, Earl of Leicester, and the utility of sanctity in thirteenth-century England', *JMH* 21 (1995), 27–49; John McQuilton, 'Who was St Thomas of Lancaster? New manuscript evidence', in *Fourteenth Century England IV*, ed. Jeffrey S. Hamilton (Woodbridge, 2006), 1–25; J. W. McKenna, 'Popular canonisation as political propaganda: the cult of Archbishop Scrope', *Speculum* 45 (1970), 608–23; Douglas Biggs, 'Archbishop Scrope's Manifesto of 1405: "naïve nonsense" or reflections of political reality?', *JMH* 33 (2007), 358–71.

32 Montfort, Lancaster and, to a lesser extent, Scrope, were all regarded as having died because of their leadership of, or involvement in, opposition to unjust or arbitrary kingship. However, as Walker's skilfully nuanced study points out, the most successful and long-lived of these cults escaped their particular and partisan origins to act as a means of reconciliation for the wider political community, and all (with the exception of the relatively short-lived devotion to Simon de Montfort) came to enjoy significant royal patronage and support. Walker, 'Political saints', 205–14. For Walker, then, the political martyr cults of late medieval England did not arise (or rather endure) because of a general trend towards the 'canonisation of opposition to the Crown', but because they served to reconcile king and subjects and to restore the harmony of a political community in which the acceptance of royal sacrality was a key (and increasingly stressed) element.

33 *Documents of the Baronial Movement of Reform and Rebellion, 1258–1267*, eds and trans. R. F. Treharne and I. Sanders (Oxford, 1973), 322–3.

34 *The Brut or the Chronicles of England*, ed. Friedrich W. D. Brie, EETS, 2 vols (London, 1906–8), I.228–31. For similar attempts to forcibly suppress commemoration at the tomb of Archbishop Scrope, see Ronald C. Finucane, *Miracles and Pilgrims* (Basingstoke, 1977), 33.

rable anxiety arising from the presentation of Rothesay as a man unjustly done to death at Duke Robert's instigation.

While the determination of Albany's opponents to make sure Duke David's death and Albany's iniquity were not forgotten might have provided a powerful impetus for the commemoration of Rothesay as a saint, political support by itself was not sufficient to create veneration, for a cult required devotees who firmly believed in the effectiveness of their patron as an intercessor. Even if a large number of people could be persuaded that Rothesay had indeed been brutally murdered, what aspects of his life or death might have encouraged the conviction that his tomb at Lindores was a place where posthumous miracles were likely to occur?

There were a number of circumstances, real or imagined, surrounding Rothesay's death that could have promoted popular belief both in the duke's status as a martyr cruelly done to death and his potential effectiveness as an intercessor. Most significant, of course, was the appalling way in which the duke was said to have met his end. The notion that extreme hunger had forced Rothesay to eat his own hands is first attested in the *Dethe*. Although it is possible that this horrific detail was invented by John Shirley, the fact that the same story was later found in Boece's chronicle might suggest that it was an early and integral part of the tale as established in fifteenth-century Scotland.[35] In 1402, moreover, the political community in Scotland was likely to be especially sensitive to the possibility of starvation as a form of political assassination given the claimed fate of the deposed English king, Richard II, in February 1400.

Another factor was Rothesay's status as heir to the throne. In medieval Europe men and women of royal blood were rather more likely to have their claims to sanctity recognised, officially and unofficially, than members of other social groups. This was only partly explained by the fact that they invariably left behind them powerful kinsmen to promote their posthumous reputation. There seems, rather, to have been a general expectation that those who wielded secular authority in this life were more liable to carry this power

---

[35] There is no evidence that manuscript versions of the *Dethe* were known, or circulated, in fifteenth- and sixteenth-century Scotland. For discussion of the extant manuscripts, see *The Dethe*, ed. Matheson, 3–10, 12–20. Although imprisonment and starvation featured as an ordeal experienced by a number of saints, few were said to have been martyred by this method, and it is highly unlikely that this episode derived from a hagiographical source. Often, as in the tale of St Katherine, attempted starvation was overcome by a miraculous divine intervention (in Katherine's case being fed while in prison by a dove sent by Christ) or stoically endured. Rothesay's reported self-consumption hardly fitted into the hagiographical framework of delivery through divine grace or a willingly sought death. A possible literary parallel for the episode may have been Chaucer's 'The Monk's Tale' which described the fate of the Pisan nobleman, Count Ugolino, imprisoned and starved to death with his young children on the orders of his political rivals. In Chaucer's work Ugolino is described as biting his own arms, but this would appear to be through grief at the death of his infant son rather than hunger per se. *The Riverside Chaucer*, ed. Larry D. Benson, 3rd edn (Oxford, 1988), 247–8. My thanks to Thomas Clancy for bringing Ugolino's tale to my attention.

beyond the grave and, therefore, more likely to be successful intercessors. It might be significant in this regard that William of Worcester's informant seems to have conflated Rothesay with David II (1329–71), making the saint commemorated at Lindores a straightforwardly 'kingly' figure.[36]

An association of Rothesay with otherworldly powers would also have been encouraged by the date of his death and the astronomical portents surrounding it. Bower reported that the prince died either on the evening of 25 March or the morning of 26 March. March 25 was the feast of the Annunciation of the Virgin Mary, while in 1402 Easter Day fell on Sunday 26 March, so that David expired either on, or the evening before, the holiest day in the christian calendar.[37] Sudden deaths on or around important religious festivals could encourage the notion that the deceased had the capacity to act as a powerful intercessor, and those called to paradise on a particularly auspicious occasion could very rapidly become the subject of popular devotion.[38] Even more strikingly, the early months of 1402 saw the appearance of a spectacular comet, visible during daylight hours, in the skies above Europe and Asia. Comets were traditionally regarded as foreshadowing the death of princes or ruinous war, and the comet of 1402 was indeed specifically linked to Rothesay's demise by Walter Bower.[39] The contemporary observations of Jacobus Angelus of Ulm in Swabia and a number of Asian astronomers confirm that the comet of 1402 disappeared from view in the skies of northern Europe around the feast of Easter, coinciding almost exactly with Rothesay's death.[40] In terms of exciting interest in Rothesay as a figure around whom strange and mysterious forces were at work, it is difficult to think of a more potent mix, for here was a royal prince, 'martyred' on Easter Day, his fate foretold and echoed in the heavens. Given the additional fact that many powerful figures in Scotland wanted Rothesay's memory sustained as a political challenge and rebuke to the Albany Stewarts, it seems unsurprising that some form of commemoration of the duke flourished in the early decades of the fifteenth century.

---

[36] Vauchez, *Sainthood*, 157–63; see also McQuilton, 'Who was St Thomas of Lancaster?', 22, for the importance of Lancaster's royal blood and aristocratic status in the establishment of his cult.

[37] *Chron. Bower*, VIII.39–40. The close proximity of the feasts linked to Christ's conception and resurrection is striking.

[38] See, for example, Guibert of Nogent's (*ob.* 1124) outraged description of the popular veneration accorded a young boy who had died by accident on Good Friday. Guibert of Nogent, *De sanctis et eorum pigneribus in Opera varia*, ed. R. B. C. Huygens, Corpus Christianorum, Continuatio Mediaeualis 127 (Turnholt, 1993), 97. Again, I should like to thank Thomas Clancy for alerting me to this account.

[39] *Chron. Bower*, VIII.40–1.

[40] Jane L. Jervis, *Cometary Theory in Fifteenth-Century Europe*, Studia Copernicana 26 (1985), 37–42; Ho Peng Yoke, 'Ancient and mediaeval observations of comets and novae in Chinese sources', *Vistas in Astronomy* 5 (1962), 127–225, at 200; Gary W. Kronk, *Cometography, A Catalog of Comets*, vol. 1 (Cambridge, 1999), 260–4.

Attempts to portray Rothesay as a saint, however, clearly held little attraction for Walter Bower, a career cleric, the leader of a monastic community, and a man well aware of the ecclesiastical criteria for formal canonisation. As we have seen, he was hardly an apologist for David, refuting the charge that he had been deliberately starved to death on his uncle's orders and accepting that it was largely the young duke's own failings that had brought about his fall from power. Despite this, some of the detail provided by Bower in relation to the duke's arrest and its immediate aftermath may have been derived from a narrative designed to present David in a rather more sympathetic light. From the account preserved in the *Scotichronicon* we learn that Rothesay was arrested by William Lindsay of Rossie and Sir John Ramornie on the approach to the castle of St Andrews, between Nydie and Strathtyrum, as he rode with a small escort 'with no evil in mind'.[41] Taken by force to St Andrews, Rothesay was kept in the episcopal castle while Albany and his council met further south in Fife at Culross to decide what should be done with the young prince. Albany and Archibald, fourth earl of Douglas, then 'forcibly moved him to the tower of Falkland mounted on a mule [*jumentum*] and dressed in a russet tunic'.[42] Bower offers no explanation as to why Rothesay was treated in this manner, although the humiliating ride is clearly difficult to reconcile with the chronicler's wider assertion of the essentially benign aims of those involved in the arrest and imprisonment. The 'Book of Pluscarden' suggested that the prince was disguised as a 'varlet, so that he might not be noticed on the way'.[43] The notion of a surreptitious smuggling of Rothesay to a location where he was beyond hope of rescue or escape was consistent with the Pluscardine chronicler's view that Albany and Douglas aimed from the outset to kill Duke David.[44] An alternative interpretation is that the move to Falkland involved a calculated and public degradation of a defeated political opponent. The use of a low status beast of burden and the wearing of a russet tunic

---

[41] *Chron. Bower*, VIII.38–9. The 'Book of Pluscarden', suggested that the arrest took place at the 'great cross' beside Strathtyrum. *Chron. Pluscarden*, I.342. In a 1405 perambulation this cross was named as *Sluthariscors*. *St A. Lib.*, 422. Simon Taylor has pointed out (personal communication) that this form could contain a twelfth-century personal name (Sluthagh) or, perhaps, a variant on 'slutheroun' or 'slut', a 'slovenly or sluttish, immoral' person (could the cross have been a traditional site for the public punishment of sexual crimes such as adultery?). The latter possible derivation is intriguing given Rothesay's reputation, although it is perhaps unlikely either that the cross would have been given a new name to commemorate the duke's supposed arrest there only three years before the perambulation or that his captors chose to make their move against the duke at a symbolically appropriate location.

[42] *Chron. Bower*, VIII.38–9. 'Jumentum' could indicate variously a mule (as in the modern translation of the *Scotichronicon*), a low status pack horse, or a similar beast of burden. Russet was a rough cloth not considered appropriate for noble dress. Its lowly associations led to russet being adopted by the Lollards as an outward expression and affirmation of their humility and piety.

[43] *Chron. Pluscarden*, II.258; I.342.

[44] A similar clandestine ride was a feature of some accounts of the last days of the deposed Richard II, taken to Leeds castle in Kent disguised as a woodcutter. *Chronique de la traison et mort de Richart II*, ed. B. Williams (London, 1846), 228.

struck at the heart of, and in a sense denied, the duke's identity as a knight and nobleman. The formal humbling of adversaries, the symbolic stripping away of social dignities, was very often part of the punishment imposed on vanquished opponents for their alleged 'crimes', especially that of treason.[45] If we assume for a moment that the ride did take place as described, then the charge that Rothesay had unlawfully usurped his father's 'royal' authority could have justified a measure of public disgrace.[46]

There is, however, a more fundamental issue relating to Bower's account of the events of 1401–2. The source available to Abbot Walter clearly preserved very specific details about Rothesay's final movements and the names of those who were responsible for the initial arrest (John Ramornie and William Lindsay of Rossie), the consideration of his fate at Culross (Albany and the earl of Douglas), and his fatal imprisonment in Falkland (John Selkirk and John Wright). The identification of these men and the commemoration of their role in the controversial demise of the prince were hardly likely to be features of a pro-Albany narrative. The story, in fact, has a number of similarities to accounts of the last days, effectively the 'passion' tales, of other figures regarded as martyrs. One interesting parallel was with the cult based around Thomas, earl of Lancaster, the cousin and rival of Edward II, executed after the defeat of his rebellion against that king at the battle of Boroughbridge in 1322.[47] After his capture the earl was imprisoned in Ponte- fract castle, tried by a court of dubious legality, 'unjustly' sentenced to death as a traitor and rebel, and led 'on a lene white palfray, ful unsemeliche, and ek al bare, wi[th] an olde bridel' to a hill outside Pontefract where he was beheaded.[48] Remembrance of these episodes and injustices became central to the commemoration of Lancaster as a martyr saint, with devotional plaques and pilgrimage badges effectively retelling the critical elements of this story in visual form.[49]

Accounts emanating from supporters of a supposed martyr might, then, emphasise (or invent) episodes of dishonourable or unjust treatment as an integral part of the martyrdom narrative, stressing the suffering endured before death. They might also map out a devotional landscape by indicating

---

[45] See Danielle Westerhof, 'Deconstructing identities on the scaffold: the execution of Hugh Despenser the Younger, 1326', *JMH* 33 (2007), 87–106, at 92, 97, 103, 106.

[46] The loss of any record of the justification of David's arrest provided by Albany and Douglas in the general council of May 1402 is obviously unfortunate. In defending themselves before the king's council the two men claimed that their actions had been 'for the public good', but any detailed explanation was not recorded in the indemnity granted to them by the king. See http://www.rps. ac.uk/ [1402/5/1].

[47] J. R. Maddicott, *Thomas of Lancaster, 1307–1322* (Oxford, 1970), 311–12.

[48] *The Brut*, ed. Brie, II.223. This was a notably pro-Lancastrian account.

[49] Hugh Tait, 'Pilgrim-signs and Thomas, Earl of Lancaster', *The British Museum Quarterly* 20 (1955–6), 39–47; John Edwards, 'The cult of "St." Thomas of Lancaster and its iconography', *Yorkshire Archaeological Journal* 64 (1992), 103–22; Brian Spencer, *Pilgrim Souvenirs and Secular Badges* (London, 1998), 199–201.

those sites associated with the subject's arrest, judgement, humiliation, death and burial. It thus seems possible that the source of Bower's detailed information about the events of 1401–2 was a pro-Rothesay narrative that described the duke's death in a way typical of the passion stories that underpinned the cults of other political saints by highlighting the treacherous nature of his arrest, naming the men who decided on his death (an unjust judgement?), and tracing his degradation by his opponents.

Even if the *Scotichronicon* does provide a passing glimpse of material that reflected and encouraged popular veneration of Rothesay as a martyr, it is clear that his cult did not achieve within Scotland a formal status or wide following comparable to that enjoyed by the more successful and long-lasting of the devotions centred on 'political' or 'episcopal' martyr saints in late medieval England. The cult of Thomas of Lancaster, for example, remained significant (although fulfilling rather different devotional functions as it evolved) for almost two centuries after 1322. In terms of its lifespan the Lindores cult seems more akin to the devotion that grew up around Simon de Montfort after 1265, and which had effectively petered out by the end of the thirteenth century.

There were a number of factors that may have acted to restrict the appeal of the Rothesay cult, particularly within the Scottish political elite. There was, most obviously, understandable unease about the nature of David's life before his death. The duke's 'martyrdom' may have ushered him from the world in a way appropriate to a saint, but his life as reported in nearly all fifteenth- and sixteenth-century texts could hardly be held up as a model of christian morality to be emulated by other secular princes, nor did he appear as a figure of public virtue, in the manner of Lancaster and Montfort, worthy of remembrance as an exemplar of political probity.[50]

The tension between Rothesay's status as a worker of posthumous miracles and his apparently dissolute and degenerate life was particularly vexing for William Stewart, the author of the vernacular verse *Buik of the Croniclis*.[51] Stewart mused on what he clearly regarded as an impossible contradiction; Rothesay's miracle-working power and reputation after death indicated

---

[50] D. W. Burton, 'Politics, Propaganda and Public Opinion in the Reigns of Henry III and Edward I' (University of Oxford, unpublished D.Phil. thesis, 1985), 126–7, makes the point that Simon de Montfort was represented, even before his death, as a deeply pious man who fought in the political sphere to 'preserve the people of England from oppression'; for general discussion, see Piroyansky, *Martyrs*.

[51] For comment on the career of the William Stewart usually thought to be the author of the chronicle, see Stewart, *The Buik of the Croniclis*, ed. Turnbull, intro., and A. A. MacDonald, 'William Stewart and the court poetry of the reign of James V', in *Stewart Style 1513–1542. Essays on the Court of James V*, ed. Janet Hadley Williams (East Linton, 1996), 179–200. However, M. P. McDiarmid, 'The metrical chronicles and non-alliterative romances', in *History of Scottish Literature, vol. I: Origins to 1660*, ed. R. D. S. Jack (Aberdeen, 1988), 27–38, at 36, argues that the chronicle was in fact the work of the William Stewart (*ca* 1490–1545) who ended his days as bishop of Aberdeen.

that he was a saint, but a saint, by Stewart's understanding, should have led a pious and exemplary christian life. From Stewart's theologically orthodox perspective a sinner could not become a saint through an unfortunate and grisly death.

> I can nocht wit how thir tua ma accord
> Be ony ressoune weill to be defendit;
> Ane vicius man with vices apprehendit,
> Syne for his vice in presoun maid to die,
> Efter his deid ane sanct syne for to be.[52]

The chronicler decided that the depiction of Rothesay as a reprobate simply had to be mistaken and found a number of justifications for his position. First, he claimed to have met, while a young man, a 'woman of grit eild and age' who had known Rothesay and vouched for his 'gentres, vertu, and . . . hie prudence/ Into his tyme aboue all uther prence'.[53] Second, he pointed out that Albany had every incentive to spread untruths about his nephew in order to justify his arrest and death. Last, Stewart returned to what he clearly regarded as the most important and irrefutable proof of Rothesay's sanctity.

> Efter his deid tha held him for ane sanct
> For sindrie singis [that is, signs, miracles] of him that wes sene,
> Dum men gat speech and blynd men gat their ene,
> And mony seik men to their helth restord.[54]

Stewart's account reflected the wider uncertainty or unease about the nature of sanctity in medieval Europe when the models of appropriate conduct endorsed and encouraged by ecclesiastical authorities did not align with the powerful evidence provided by effective intercession and miraculous cures. The contrast was likely to be especially acute in cults centred on men who had lived and died as great secular lords. Ranulf Higden's mid-fourteenth-century *Polychronicon*, for example, highlighted the fact that there was 'ofte greet stryf among comoun peple' in regard to Thomas of Lancaster and 'whe[th] er he schulde be accounted for seyntes o[th]er none'.[55] On the one hand, the chronicler noted that Lancaster had been generous with alms, respectful of religious men, that he 'mayntened a trewe querel [cause]' to the end of his life and that the enemies (a reference to the Despensers) who brought about his downfall died a shameful death shortly thereafter. However, Lancaster was

---

52 Stewart, *The Buik of the Croniclis*, ed. Turnbull, III.473–5.
53 *Ibid.*, III.474. It seems highly likely, given that William Stewart the poet is thought to have been born *ca* 1481, that this encounter was imagined. *Ibid.*, x, xxiv. MacDiarmid's putative author William Stewart, the bishop, was born *ca* 1490, making such a meeting even more unlikely in his case.
54 *Ibid.*, III.474–5.
55 *Polychronicon Ranulphi Higden, monachi Cestrensis*, eds Churchill Babington and Joseph Rawson Lumby, RS, 9 vols (London, 1865–86), VIII.312–15. The quotations are from John Trevisa's fourteenth-century English translation of Higden's Latin text.

also reputed to have been unfaithful to his wife and to have 'defouled a greet multitude of [gentil] women and of gentil wenches', to have killed men who had offended him, and to have protected evil doers he favoured from legal sanctions.[56] In effect, the debate over Lancaster's claim to saintly status as reported by Higden was couched in terms of his public and private morality, his adherence to, or disregard for, accepted or expected models of aristocratic political and social behaviour. In the end, however, the chronicler finished his summary of the objections to Lancaster's claim to sanctity by observing that 'offrynges and liknes of myracles' were occurring where Thomas had been executed and that 'what issue [th]ey schuld take, it schal be knowe after [th] is tyme'.[57] That is, the ultimate proof of Thomas's sainthood lay, as William Stewart would later argue for Rothesay, in the prolonged display of effective intercession through the performance of miracles and the continued recognition and support of devotees.[58]

While Rothesay's unsavoury reputation clearly presented a potential obstacle to widespread acceptance of his standing as a saint, then, it was not necessarily an insurmountable one. As recent studies of political martyrdom in England have stressed, there was no one template that determined or guaranteed the creation and success of particular devotions. Individual martyr cults might arise from a variety of political and social contexts and circumstances, and fulfil diverse and changing roles according to the evolving needs and expectations of the devout.[59] Equally, not every victim of political violence, however 'innocent' or worthy, was certain to attract posthumous reverence. Intriguingly, Rothesay was the only secular figure in fourteenth- or fifteenth-century Scotland around whom anything like a miracle-working cult can be shown to have developed, although the young duke was certainly not alone in dying in distressing or controversial circumstances. The mass execution of the Albany Stewarts in 1425, the brutal assassination of James I in 1437, the bloody slaughter of William, eighth earl of Douglas by James II and his courtiers in 1452, the slaying of John, earl of Mar in 1479, and the killing of James III in battle in 1488, were all events that seem to have provoked contemporary outrage and disquiet. There were, admittedly, accounts that used the language and vocabulary of martyrdom to describe the fate of some of these casualties of political bloodshed, but there was absolutely no indica-

---

[56] *Ibid.*, VIII.315. The charge of defouling 'gentil wenches' provides a direct point of comparison with criticism of Rothesay. In addition, Higden suggested that Lancaster's flight from Edward II's forces rather than fighting to the death in a good cause (that is, embracing death willingly as a martyr) was another argument used to deny his status as a saint.

[57] *Ibid.*

[58] Although Stewart followed Boece in suggesting that the miracles at Lindores ceased after James I had revenged his brother's death.

[59] Piroyansky, *Martyrs*, 119–32. This study also suggests that across the fourteenth and fifteenth centuries there was a gradual shift in the bestowal of devotion and sympathy that came to place greater value on the demonstrated 'sanctity' of the individual venerated rather than their transformation through 'martyrdom'.

tion of temporary, let alone sustained, popular devotion growing up around their tombs or the sites where they were judged or killed.[60]

The apparently limited reach and relatively swift waning of the Rothesay cult was, perhaps, not entirely surprising in a polity where the veneration of secular martyrs seems to have had no special or enduring place or function in public political discourse, as has been claimed for the martyr cults of late medieval England. A long-established view of the structural role of these cults in the southern kingdom from the twelfth to the end of the fourteenth century was that they provided a means of articulating and justifying opposition to oppressive or tyrannical kings whose authority was based on the claimed sanctity of their office as well as their practical financial, judicial and military powers.[61] More recently, Simon Walker's re-assessment of the phenomenon has suggested that the most important of these devotions, such as the Lancaster cult, acted to re-unify the English polity after periods of rupture and discord; that is, they eventually became symbols of political unity, forgiveness and reconciliation that ultimately acted to restore and bolster the spiritual authority of English monarchs. The apparent contrast between the English and Scottish engagement with martyr cults raises general questions, outwith the scope of the present study, about the structures and expectations that governed political life in late medieval Scotland. It seems that the development of cults centred on figures killed in the course of political disputes was far less common, indeed almost unknown, in late medieval Scotland. In particular, there were no examples of 'martyrs' who were held to have died because of their opposition to unjust or arbitrary royal government (unless

---

[60] The most obvious example is provided by the highly coloured account of James I's death in the 'Book of Pluscarden'. Here, James was portrayed meeting his fate 'like an innocent lamb', calling for God's mercy and with his arms outstretched to heaven. 'This persecution [a very significant term in martyr narratives] he suffered for righteousness' sake.' The same chronicle suggested that the papal nuncio resident in Scotland at the time of James I's assassination [Anthony, bishop of Urbino] had, on seeing James' body, 'kissed his piteous wounds: and … said … that he would stake his soul on his [James] having died in a state of grace, like a martyr, for his defence of the common weal and his administration of justice'. *Chron. Pluscarden*, I.390; II.290. Other chronicles suggested that James's blood-stained shirt had been sent to the Pope. *The Dethe*, ed. Matheson, 58.

The sixteenth-century chronicler George Buchanan claimed that another blood-stained shirt, that of James III who was killed at Sauchieburn in 1488, was used as a banner by the leaders of a rebellion in 1489 against the regime established through that act of regicide.

There is no suggestion of any prolonged commemoration of non-royal figures such as William, eighth earl of Douglas or the Albany Stewarts, although the sixteenth-century *Extracta E Variis Cronicis Scocie* preserves a short narrative that presented the dying Earl William in a sympathetic light. 'The earl, having been laid out in a coffin, could not give up his spirit until a certain serving girl, following Douglas's instructions, took a cross from his neck, whereupon his spirit immediately departed.' *Extracta e Variis Cronicis Scocie*, ed. W. B. D. D. Turnbull, Abbotsford Club (Edinburgh, 1842), 242.

[61] The earliest exploration of the topic was provided by Josiah Cox Russell, 'The canonization of opposition to the king in Angevin England', in his *Twelfth Century Studies* (New York, 1978), 248–60. First published in *Anniversary Essays in Mediaeval History by Students of Charles Homer Haskins*, ed. C. H. Taylor (Boston, 1929), 279–90; Theilmann, 'Political canonization'.

fourteenth-century figures such as William Wallace and Simon Fraser, who were executed because of their opposition to the English dynasty's claims in Scotland, can be viewed as such). In many ways the situation in Scotland was quite typical of the experience of other European polities, where political martyr cults were similarly rare; in that sense, the anomaly here may be the political and devotional culture of late medieval England.

Moreover, as we have seen, the young duke's life was hardly likely to excite the interests of later clerical commentators as a 'mirror for princes', except as a warning of the price of youthful folly and immorality and an illustration of the fate of rulers who failed to live according to christian precepts. Boece and his sixteenth-century translators may well have been right to link James I's destruction of the Albany Stewarts with the fading of devotion to Rothesay. The cult had probably served to keep alive the memory and interests of the dynastic line removed from power by Albany's 1402 coup throughout the eighteen-year exile of James I in England. By 1425, however, the political/dynastic cause linked to veneration of Rothesay had effectively triumphed within Scotland and victory, sometimes more than defeat, could threaten the relevance and status of a martyr. In the end, the Rothesay cult simply failed to grow beyond its particular political origin and purpose to secure a more permanent and meaningful place in the affections and spiritual lives of fifteenth-century Scots.

6

WO/MEN ONLY? MARIAN DEVOTION IN MEDIEVAL PERTH

Mark A. Hall

A recent study of Marian iconography in relation to *The Lord of the Rings* pithily notes that Mary, 'in many respects is the central figure of the Middle Ages'.[1] There is a vast body of surviving texts, statues, pictures, rosaries, misericords, icons, etc., relating to Mary, and even in their vastness they are but a small portion of what existed during the middle ages. This fact underpins this exploration of Marian devotion, which aims to see what sense can be made of the varied but fragmentary evidence for that practice in medieval Perth. It assesses how that evidence fits the broad pattern of such devotion in medieval Europe and whether we can see any kind of gender dimension to that devotional practice. Mary is a figure both human and quasi-divine, both a virgin and a mother, the Church's feminine ideal. As Marina Warner observed, women are equal in God's eyes but not in men's, and 'Whether we regard the Virgin Mary as the most sublime and beautiful image in man's struggle towards the good and the pure or the most pitiable production of ignorance and superstition, she represents a central theme in the history of western attitudes to women.'[2]

The nature of Mary has evolved and changed in Church teaching. Of the four key Marian dogmas of the Catholic Church, only two – her divine motherhood and her virginity – stem from early Church teachings and Council declarations. The other two – her Immaculate Conception (that is, with no trace of original sin) and her Assumption, body and soul, into heaven – were only officially sanctioned by the papacy in 1854 and 1950 respectively. The popular belief in Mary however has never been confined by Church dogma – the Immaculate Conception and the Assumption were flourishing medieval cults. This is not the place to rehearse in full the various incarnations of

---

[1] Michael W. Maher, '"A land without stain": medieval images of Mary and their use in the characterization of Galadriel', in *Tolkien the Medievalist*, ed. Jane Chance (London, 2003), 225–36, at 226.
[2] Marina Warner, *Alone of All Her Sex, The Myth and Cult of the Virgin Mary* (London, 1976; rev. 2000), xxvi–xxvii.

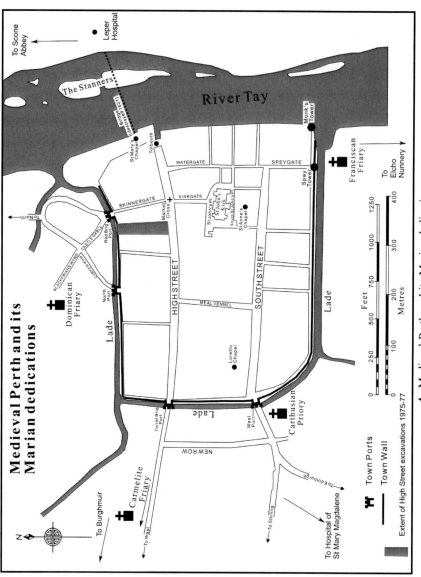

4. Medieval Perth and its Marian dedications

Mary.[3] Suffice to say here that the perception of her and her role changed as Church teaching changed and as society changed in a complex intertwining. There is a clear linkage between her motherly love for humankind and the expectation that this view should serve as a role model for women as gentle, humble, domestic creatures. Mary acts positively through Christ, the main man in her life, and in a largely patriarchal medieval society women were expected to emulate her.[4] While there is a clear element of self-evident truth to this we nevertheless need to be wary of over-generalising from it, and on its own it does not come to grips with the full complexity of the fact that there seems to be no universal gender-specific generalisation to be made between the Virgin and her believers. Four brief, diverse examples help to emphasise this gender complexity: Aldhelm of Malmesbury's seventh-century treatise, *On Virginity*, accepted that a woman could gain the state of chastity, after marriage, if she retired to a nunnery. He further redefined virginity as a state of mind: 'Pure virginity is preserved only in the fortress of the mind rather than the strict confines of the flesh.'[5] Medieval society had no great difficulty in celebrating Mary's natural biological function of breast-feeding in her image as Maria Lactans. Indeed, in the twelfth century Bernard of Clairvaux refined Anselm of Canterbury's notion of Mary's wisdom-giving milk to the extent that he suggested it was possible to pray to God as the great mother.[6] The early thirteenth-century *Exempla* of Jacques de Vitry often invoked the Virgin in an intercessionary role in the salvation of robbers. All christians were entitled to salvation, no matter how greatly they had sinned, if they died in great repentance.[7] Fundamental to the popularity of Marian devotion was the late medieval view that veneration did not rely so much upon 'the need to do good and to be good', as upon 'the brightly painted and beautiful images' demonstrating 'the overflowing abundance of God's grace, even to

---

3   *Ibid*. and Eamon Duffy, *The Stripping of the Altars: Traditional Religion in England 1450–1580* (London, 1992). For a cogent summary, see James Hall, *Dictionary of Subjects and Symbols in Art* (London, 1996), 323–35. By the fifteenth century women were seen as the first teachers of children, male or female, as symbolised in the images of Mary with the Christ Child and a Book of Hours and of St Anne teaching Mary (her daughter) to read; see M. T. Clanchy, *From Memory to Written Record: England 1066–1307*, 2nd edn (Oxford, 1993), 13; and Michael Camille, *Mirror in Parchment: The Luttrell Psalter and the Making of Medieval England* (London, 1998), 161–2. For an example of the range and depth of Marian imagery in the fifteenth century, see the analysis of Jan van Eyck's 'The Madonna and Chancellor Rolin', in Richard Foster and Pamela Tudor-Craig, *The Secret Life of Paintings* (Woodbridge, 1986), esp. 4–8.

4   Warner, *Virgin Mary*, 286 ff.

5   Henrietta Leyser, *Medieval Women: A Social History of Women in England 450–1500*, rev. edn (London, 2001), 34, quoting from *Aldhelm: The Prose Works*, trans. Michael Lapidge and Michael Herren (Cambridge, 1979), 62. Aldhelm's treatise was written specifically for the nunnery at Barking.

6   Warner, *Alone of All Her Sex*, 196–8.

7   This exempla-established role of the Virgin was carried over into popular tales such as those of Robin Hood. Robin's devotion to the Virgin marks him out as a redeemable outlaw and is further testimony to the socially pervasive nature of Marian devotion. For a full discussion, see Trevor Dean, *Crime in Medieval Europe* (London, 2002), 151–3.

the undeserving, from whom they required only love'.[8] By the late fifteenth century the Church could seemingly tolerate Jean Fouquet's *Melun Diptych* (*ca* 1450). Commissioned by Etienne Chevalier, Charles VI's treasurer, it is a portrait of Agnès Sorel, Charles's mistress (with whom Etienne was infatuated), as the enthroned Virgin, offering a breast to the Christ child on her knee.[9]

Marian Scotland

In what we now call Scotland, the earliest known surviving examples of Marian devotion are from Iona: a hymn to the Virgin written in the early eighth century, *Cantemus in Omni Dei*, followed within fifty years by the carving of St Martin's Cross, with its Virgin and Child panel. Both hymn and sculpture echo *Physiologus* in presenting the notion of God concealed in Mary, of the Saviour concealing his Godhead through incarnation in the Virgin's womb.[10] The conjunction of hymn and sculpture in the first half of the eighth century are widely accepted as evidence for a Virgin cult on Iona,[11] and Henderson suggests that the evidence is strong enough to imply that the monks of Iona sang the hymn in procession around the St Martin's Cross.[12] The importance of Mary to Iona is further illustrated by two other crosses sculpted with her image, St Oran's and St John's, and by the Virgin and Child folio of the *Book of Kells*, possibly painted in the Iona scriptorium.[13] The influence of Iona and its mission may possibly be seen in other Virgin and Child sculptures. Through the seventh to tenth centuries we can see Virgin and Child imagery on crosses in Kildalton, Islay; on Canna; and in Brechin,

---

[8] Duffy, *Stripping of the Altars*, 187, 256–65.

[9] For the Fouquet painting and anecdote, see Warner, *Alone of All Her Sex*, pl. 28. In a similar vein, François Rabelais wrote a letter in 1536 to Bishop Geoffrey d'Estissac, noting that the then Pope, Paul III, was the bastard son of Pope Alexander VI and his sister and that in the pope's palace built by Alexander there hung a portrait of Alexander's sister, Paul's mother as a portrait of Our Lady; see *The Complete Works of François Rabelais*, ed. and trans. Donald M. Frame (London, 1991), 774.

[10] Isabel Henderson, *Pictish Monsters: Symbol, Text and Image* (Cambridge, 1997), 7–8.

[11] For the hymn, see Thomas Owen Clancy and Gilbert Márkus, *Iona: The Earliest Poetry of a Celtic Monastery* (Edinburgh, 1994), 177–85. For the Virgin cult, see RCAHMS, *Argyll IV: Iona* (Edinburgh, 1982), 47 and 267, summarised in Ian Fisher, *Early Medieval Sculpture in the West Highlands and Islands* (Edinburgh, 2001), 18.

[12] Henderson, *Pictish Monsters*, 8.

[13] For the attribution to Iona, see George Henderson, *From Durrow to Kells: The Insular Gospel Books 650–800* (London, 1987), ch. 6, and see 153–5 for a discussion of the Virgin illumination. See also Jane Hawkes, 'Columban Virgins: iconic images of the Virgin and Child in insular sculpture', in *Studies in the Cult of Saint Columba*, ed. Cormac Bourke (Dublin, 1997), 107–35. The most accessible reproduction of the Kells Virgin and Child (fol. 7v) is Bernard Meehan, *The Book of Kells* (Dublin, 1994), pl. 7.

Angus, their shared Marian iconography read as a Columban link by several writers.[14]

So although depictions of the Virgin are comparatively rare in Insular art they survive in sufficient numbers to suggest, as might be expected, that Marian teaching and devotion was a key element of both the protracted conversion discourse and of monastic life.[15] The association of Mother and Child in early medieval times clearly implies Mary's motherhood but this was less important than emphasising her queenly, hieratic status. Across Europe Mary gradually became a less hieratic figure, as devotion to her increased. Across Scotland a huge number of dedications ensued which do not require discussion here save to note that Perth can be seen as a typical example.[16]

---

[14] RCAHMS, *Argyll 5: Islay, Jura, Colonsay and Oronsay* (Edinburgh, 1984), 208 (Kildalton); RCAHMS, *Canna, the Archaeology of a Hebridean Landscape*, Broadsheet 5 (Edinburgh, 1999); Isabel Henderson, 'Towards defining the function of sculpture in Alba: the evidence of St Andrews, Brechin and Rosemarkie', in *Kings, Clerics and Chronicles in Scotland 500–1297: Essays in Honour of Marjorie Ogilvie Anderson on the Occasion of her Ninetieth Birthday*, ed. Simon Taylor (Dublin, 2000), 35–46, at 41–2 (Brechin). See also Hawkes, 'Columban Virgins'. All three along with the Iona crosses are comparatively drawn together in Fisher, *Early Medieval Sculpture*. The strength of Marian devotion at Lindisfarne, Northumberland, is evidenced by the Virgin and Child carved on St Cuthbert's (*ob.* AD 698) wooden coffin – in part this may be a further reflection of Columban sponsorship of the Virgin cult, Lindisfarne having been founded from Iona around AD 635.

[15] A selective reading list for Insular Marian iconography would additionally include Jane Hawkes, *The Sandbach Crosses: Sign and Significance in Anglo-Saxon Sculpture* (Dublin, 2002), 30–8, 81–5, 110–13; Dorothy Kelly, 'The Virgin and Child in Irish sculpture', in *From the Isles of the North: Early Medieval Art in Ireland and Britain*, ed. Cormac Bourke (Belfast, 1995), 197–204; Jane Hawkes, 'Mary and the Cycle of Resurrection: the iconography of the Hovingham Panel', in *The Age of Migrating Ideas: Early Medieval Art in Northern Britain and Ireland*, eds R. Michael Spearman and John Higgitt (Edinburgh, 1993), 254–60; Michael O' Carroll, 'Our Lady in early medieval Ireland', in *Seanchas: Studies in Early and Medieval Irish Archaeology, History and Literature in Honour of Francis J. Byrne*, ed. Alfred P. Smyth (Dublin, 2000), 178–81; Mary Clayton, *The Cult of the Virgin Mary in Anglo-Saxon England* (Cambridge, 1990) and Ross Trench-Jellicoe, 'A missing figure on the slab fragment no. 2 from Monifieth, Angus, the a'Chill Cross, Canna and some implications of the development of a variant form of the Virgin's hairstyle and dress in early medieval Scotland', *PSAS* 129 (1999), 597–647.

[16] James Murray Mackinlay, *Ancient Church Dedications in Scotland vol. I: Scriptural Dedications* (Edinburgh, 1910), 70–179. In addition to the formal church dedications there is a range of place-name evidence that reveals the extent of Marian devotion generally. Many holy wells carry Marian dedications including Ladywell in Muthill parish, Perthshire (with the nearby Knock Mary, or 'Mary's Hill') and Ladywell in Rait Parish, Perthshire. The place-name Gilmerton can be found throughout eastern Scotland, in Lothian, Perthshire and Fife. It derives from the Gaelic *Gille Moire*, 'servant of (the Virgin) Mary', and it also survives as a personal name in the form Gilmour, Gilmer and Gilmore. Gillemure the deacon from Strathearn and Gillemure the seneschal from Atholl are known from charter evidence in the twelfth century. See Angus Watson, 'Place-names, Land and Lordship in the Medieval earldom of Strathearn' (University of St Andrews, unpublished Ph.D. thesis, 2002), 407; W. J. Watson, *The History of the Celtic Place-names of Scotland* (Edinburgh, 1926), 134–5; George F. Black, *The Surnames of Scotland: Their Origin, Meaning and History* (Edinburgh, 1946), 308; and Simon Taylor, 'Settlement-names in Fife' (University of Edinburgh, unpublished PhD thesis, 1995), 210.

Worshipping women

Before considering in detail the evidence for Marian devotion in medieval Perth it is appropriate to outline something of what is known of the wider picture of the lives of medieval women in Perth, and Scottish burghs generally. Judy Stevenson's analysis of working women in medieval London showed that their options were limited.[17] There were no female guilds (unlike in Paris, for example, which had a female silk-weavers' guild). A married woman working in her husband's trade had no legal or independent rights. Women could become apprentices but not full guild members in their own right. However, some women were able to work as sole traders in their own right, hiring and training staff and being financially accountable. Such women, with a skill or business, were highly marriageable and this gave some women an outlet, through their husbands, to voice political and fraternal grievances. Independent survival for a single woman was also feasible.

This general pattern seems to be borne out by the more fragmentary evidence for active women in Perth. For example, looking at the entries in the Perth Guildry Book for 1452–1601 we can note that of 1136 entries, 182 mention women: for the years 1452–1500 there are sixteen named, and for the years 1500–50 there are thirty-eight named (leaving 128 for the end of the sixteenth century). Only nine women are named independently of men; the rest are named (though some are not even named) and then defined in relation to a man, either as daughter of ..., wife of ... or daughter and wife of....[18] The pithy substance of the entries reveal these women paying for their burial rights, pursuing fishing rights on the Tay, maintaining a spouse's business or craft and as Guild members through their male connections. This is a picture corroborated by the surviving details from property rentals. Rentals and annuals (several detailed in the following discussion) relating to a variety of institutions in and around late medieval Perth, including Scone Abbey, Our Lady of Consolation altar, the Holy Blood altar, St Bride's altar, St Stephen's altar, St Adamnan's altar, the Confraternity altar and Blackfriars monastery, all name women (usually as wives, but not always) as benefactors and property owners.[19] Elizabeth Ewan's wider study of Scottish towns in the fourteenth century confirms this as a general picture at that time, with women legally entitled to own property, generally through a male connection. They clearly played an important part in the economic life of the burgh and were often, for example, a town's brewers. They could also achieve pivotal roles in

---

[17] Judy Stevenson, 'Working women in medieval London', in *Women in Industry and Technology From Prehistory to the Present Day: Current Research and the Museum Experience, Proceedings from the 1994 WHAM Conference*, eds Amanda Devonshire and Barbara Wood (London, 1996), 95–100.

[18] The entries analysed are all in *The Perth Guildry Book 1452–1601*, ed. Marion L. Stavert, Scottish Record Society (Edinburgh, 1993), which includes useful indexes, including of personal names.

[19] For the rentals, see *Rental Books of King James VI Hospital, Perth*, ed. R. Milne (Perth, 1891).

a burgh's customs system, as happened in Dundee when Marjorie Schireham became the burgh custumar, an office bestowed by royal government and whose returns were entered in the Exchequer Rolls.[20]

Marian Perth

The history of Perth as a royal burgh from the twelfth century (when it was granted its royal charter) is well known.[21] Archaeological evidence is increasingly extending our understanding of Perth before the twelfth century, so much so that it can be argued that there was a church in existence by the end of the tenth century.[22] This church may have preceded or followed the economic and political development that made Perth a desirable and flourishing settlement. It is likely to have always carried its dedication to St John the Baptist and given his importance as one of Christ's immediate family on Earth it is even more likely that the church had some element of Marian devotion from an early date.

The evidence for later medieval Perth and the social functioning of St John's Kirk, the parish church, is somewhat clearer and more plentiful. During the twelfth to fifteenth centuries it was joined by several other ecclesiastical institutions – chapels, monasteries, and hospitals. Indeed by the fifteenth century we can visualise Perth as marked out by a network of Marian dedications through and around the town. Within the immediate confines of the walled burgh, St John's Kirk lay at the centre, with several altars and chantries dedicated to various aspects of the Virgin. Immediately south of St John's lay the chapel and hospital of St Anne, who was, of course, the mother of Mary and a key element in the later medieval aspect of Mary's cult that emphasised her humanity.[23] At the eastern end of the High Street (or North

---

20 Elizabeth Ewan, *Townlife in Fourteenth-Century Scotland* (Edinburgh, 1990), 93, 105–6 (legal position), 32, 67, 81 (economic contribution) and 128 (Marjorie Schireham).

21 A. A. M. Duncan, 'Perth: the first century of the burgh', *Transactions of the Perthshire Society of Natural Science, Special Issue* (1973), 30–50 and *idem, Scotland the Making of the Kingdom* (Edinburgh, 1975), 467–9.

22 The evidence has been summarised in a short paper, Mark A. Hall, 'Cultural interaction on the medieval burgh of Perth, Scotland 1200–1600', in *Medieval Europe Basel 2002, Pre-printed Papers Volume 1*, eds G. Helmig, B. Scholkman and M. Untermann (Hertingen, 2002), 290–301. The evidence has now been extended by the C-14 dating of pottery samples from Perth, producing a cluster of ten dates between AD 940 and 1020, see Mark Hall, Derek Hall and Gordon Cook, 'What's Cooking? New radiocarbon dates from the earliest phases of the Perth High Street excavations and the question of Perth's early medieval origin', *PSAS* 135 (2005), 273–85.

23 Warner, *Alone of All Her Sex*, 30–1, 242–3 and Duffy, *Stripping of the Altars*, 181–3. Excavations in St Anne's Lane, Perth in 1974, recovered 158 small glass beads – see Lisbeth M. Thoms, 'Trial excavation at St Ann's Lane Perth', *PSAS* 112 (1982), 437–54, at 449 – which I now suggest are likely to be prayer/rosary beads, possibly connected with the chapel of St Anne. A more detailed discussion of them will be found in Mark A. Hall, 'Liminality and loss: the material culture of St Serf's Priory, Loch Leven, Kinross-shire, Scotland', in *West Over Sea: Studies in Scandinavian Sea-Borne Expansion and Settlement Before 1300: A Festschrift in Honour of Dr. Barbara*

Street as it was then) stood Our Lady's Chapel (a regular meeting place of the royal exchequer during the later fourteenth century) at the western end of the timber bridge across the Tay.[24] To the southwest of St John's stood the Loreto Chapel, dedicated to the Virgin's holy house where she received the Annunciation. On the limits of the walled town were several monasteries:[25]

On the northern edge lay 'Blackfriars', the Dominican friary founded in 1231 and dedicated to the Virgin and St Dominic, and with an altar to the Blessed Virgin Mary.[26]

On the southern edge lay 'Greyfriars', the Observant Franciscan friary founded in 1460 and probably dedicated to the Virgin and St Francis.[27] Both the Franciscans and the Dominicans preached a strong Marian message but they were bitter opponents over the status of the cult of the Immaculate Conception. The Franciscans were strongly in favour, the Dominicans bitterly opposed.[28]

On the western edge lay the 'Charterhouse', or Carthusian Priory (the only one in Scotland), founded in 1429 and dedicated to the Virgin Mary and St John the Baptist.

In addition, at a slightly further remove were the following religious houses:

Approximately one mile to the northeast lay 'Whitefriars', the Carmelite Friary of the Order of Our Lady of Carmel (with all its churches so dedicated). It was founded in 1361, probably on the route from the town to the Burghmuir, used as a public space for fairs, performances and the administering of justice.

Approximately one mile to the southwest lay St Leonard's Nunnery and Hospital, possibly a twelfth-century foundation. Initially this may (doubtfully) have been a Cistercian house but by the mid–late thirteenth century was Augustinian. The Prioresses' seal of the late thirteenth century showed

---

E. Crawford, eds Beverley Ballin Smith, Simon Taylor and Gareth Williams (Leiden, 2007), 379–400.

24 *ER*, II.4. I am grateful to Archie Duncan for drawing this to my attention and for a number of other useful comments made on this chapter.

25 For the various Perth monastic houses, see *MRHS*, 86, 119, 132, 151, 187–8, 199; for Scone, *ibid.*, 97; for Elcho, *ibid.*, 146 and A. G. Reid and D. M. Lye, 'Elcho Nunnery', in *Pitmiddle Village and Elcho Nunnery: Research and Excavation on Tayside*, Perthshire Society of Natural Science (Perth, 1988).

26 *Ca* 1420, Thomas de Lyn endowed the Blackfriars for the celebration of three masses every week, 'only before the altar of the Blessed Mary in the church of the said Convent', from a Blackfriars charter translated in John Parker Lawson, *The Book of Perth* (Edinburgh, 1847), 13.

27 Records indicating the dedication of Greyfriars do not survive but one that included at least Mary and St Francis would be consistent with Franciscan policy in Scotland: the friaries in Aberdeen and Dumfries were so dedicated and that in Ayr had a miraculous statue of the Virgin; see Mackinlay, *Dedications*, 172–3.

28 For the Dominican-Franciscan dispute, see Warner, *Alone of Her Sex*, 236–54.

the Virgin and Child. The Nunnery passed to the Carthusian Priory in the fifteenth century.

Approximately two and a half miles to the southwest lay St Mary Magdalene's Hospital. This was in existence by 1390 and is included in this list because of Magdalene's close association with Christ's family. This hospital was also conferred on the Carthusian Priory in the fifteenth century.

Approximately three miles to the north-northeast and across the river Tay lay Scone Abbey, re-founded as an Augustinian house in the twelfth century and dedicated to the Blessed Virgin Mary, St John, St Laurence and St Augustine.

Approximately three miles to the southeast lay Elcho Nunnery, a Cistercian house (and so dedicated to the Virgin), founded in *ca* 1247.

Thus, within a three-mile radius of Perth and by the mid-fifteenth century we have a very notable grouping of Marian dedications, undoubtedly perceived as having a protective aura. It is further noteworthy that three of the houses were of preaching friars who no doubt reinforced Marian devotion in their preaching and teaching. The dedications of the monastic establishments were not unique to Perth, of course, being the general dedications of their monastic orders, making a further linkage from Perth into the Europe-wide pattern of such devotional dedications. For several of those establishments the Marian dedication was reinforced by the iconography of their seal matrices, an impression of which would have accompanied every document they issued (the wax impressions, like later casts, are important sources of information where matrices no longer exist and also for the extent of usage and so dispersal of imagery). Elcho, Whitefriars, Blackfriars and St Leonard's all had seal matrices depicting the Virgin and Child. The Elcho seal shows a standing Virgin and Child, the fifteenth-century Whitefriars seal shows the Virgin feeding the Child (illustration 3) and the late fifteenth-century Blackfriars seal shows the crowned Virgin holding the Child on her left arm (both the Whitefriars and Blackfriars matrices have kneeling friars below the main image) and the Carthusians matrix shows the Coronation of the Virgin as Queen of Heaven (above a kneeling figure of James I, the Friary's founder-patron).[29]

---

[29] The Blackfriars seal matrix is in the collections of the NMS, see David Caldwell, *Angels, Nobles and Unicorns: Art and Patronage in Medieval Scotland* (Edinburgh, 1982), 99 cat. E99 and Virginia Glenn, *Romanesque & Gothic Decorative Metalwork and Ivory Carvings in the Museum of Scotland* (Edinburgh, 2003), 135. The Whitefriars seal matrix is in the collections of Perth Museum; see *Three Scottish Carmelite Friaries: Excavations at Aberdeen, Linlithgow and Perth 1980–1986*, ed. J. A. Stones (Edinburgh, 1989), 154. The St Leonard's seal matrix is no longer extant but is known from the seal impression added by the Prioress ('Thephanie de Ederdman') of St Leonard's to the Ragman Roll in 1296, swearing fealty to Edward I; see Mackinlay, *Dedications*, 153 and Bruce A. McAndrew, 'The sigillography of the Ragman Roll', *PSAS* 129

3. The seal matrix of the prior of the Perth Carmelites, showing the Madonna and Child. © and courtesy of Perth Museum & Art Gallery, Perth & Kinross Council, Scotland

All this seal imagery is suggestive of altars/shrine arrangements within churches where the faithful could be encouraged to pray to the Virgin. The strength of institutional dedications is reinforced when we turn to look at the altars within those institutions. I will focus on St John's Kirk, where the pattern seems clearest.

In his study of religious practice in England in the century and a half before the Reformation, Duffy showed that around two-thirds of all English parish churches underwent rebuilding programmes and so observed that 'if we can take it as an axiom that where your money is your heart is, then the hearts of late medieval and early Tudor Englishmen and women were in their churches'.[30] The evidence from Perth would seem to fit this picture.

(1999), 663–752, at 690, no. 1280. The Elcho seal is also no longer extant but is known from an impression on a 1539 charter; see Henry Laing, *Supplemental Descriptive Catalogue of Ancient Scottish Seals* (Edinburgh, 1866), no. 1140. For the critical impact of the Cistercians on spreading the Virgin cult, see Warner, *Alone of Her Sex*, 131. The Carthusian matrix is no longer extant but its impression is known from Carthusian charters; see Lawson, *Book of Perth*, plate opp. 40, and Walter de Gray Birch, *History of Scottish Seals vol. II: Ecclesiastical and Monastic Seals of Scotland* (Stirling, 1907), 105.

[30] Duffy, *Stripping of the Altars*, 132.

The parish church underwent an extensive renovation programme in the later fifteenth century and this was accompanied by a series of altar and chantry dedications and re-dedications, part of a pattern of community investment that lasted down to the Reformation. As late as 1557 the Perth Glover Incorporation had painted a portrait of its patron, St Bartholomew, probably for its altar in St John's Kirk. The nature of guild patronage of St John's Kirk is dealt with elsewhere; here I will confine myself to the diversity of patronage visible in the Marian altar dedications.[31]

The earliest dated Marian dedication known is to the altar of Our Lady, founded in 1431/2 by Alan de Myrtoun. On 9 July 1491 Robert Chalmers founded an altar in honour of the Presentation of the Virgin, at the existing altar of St Andrew. Chalmers was a burgess, he married Catherine de Kinnaird and both agreed to found the altar. It seems likely that this was in fact a re-foundation of the altar of the Holy Presentation, founded in 1470–1 by Marjory Gray, wife of John Chalmers. Also in 1491, the altar of Our Lady of Consolation was founded by James Fentoun, chamberlain to Bishop George of Dunkeld, precentor at Dunkeld Cathedral and vicar of Tibbermuir church. He founded it for the welfare of his soul, the soul of his relative, the late Janet Fentoun (a Lady Portioner at Baky, Forfarshire) and the souls of his other relatives. As part of the altar foundation he paid for two chaplaincies and 'a ... reredos ... antemural ... sedilia and ceiling suitably designed for the chapel'.[32] Into the sixteenth century, we see the foundation, in 1513, by Patrick Wellis, Provost, of the altar of the Salvation of Our Lady and St Gabriel, clearly connected with the celebration of the feast of the Annunciation. The final altar we need to mention in St John's is that of the Visitation of Our Lady's Grace, endowed by the chaplain Sir Simon Young in 1514 and patronised by the burgh council. The council kept charge of the vestments, chalices and ornaments, as listed in a detailed inventory of 1544. This included mention of six chandeliers, of varying type, including one of brass.[33] All this material is now lost but a Flemish brass chandelier (illustration 4) of the fifteenth century still hangs in St John's Kirk. It may originally have been associated with the Lady Chapel at the east end of the choir or with one of the Marian altars but what is known of its history links it with the patronage of the skinner and shoemaker incorporations. Certainly its iconography does

---

[31] Mark A. Hall, 'Burgh mentalities: a town-in-the-country case study of Perth, Scotland', in *Town and Country in the Middle Ages: Contrasts, Contacts and Interconnections, 1100–1500*, eds Kate Giles and Christopher Dyer, Society of Medieval Archaeology Monograph 22 (Leeds, 2005), 211–28. For the rebuilding programme at St John's, see Richard Fawcett, *A History of St John's Kirk Perth* (Perth, 1987). The details of the altar dedications and patronage are taken from Robert Scott Fittis, *Ecclesiastical Annals of Perth, to the Period of the Reformation* (Edinburgh, 1885), 298 ff.; Lawson, *Book of Perth*, 56–74 and *James VI Hospital*, ed. Milne, 455–6, 464, 494–7.

[32] *Rentale Dunkeldense: Being Accounts of the Bishopric A.D. 1505–1517, with Myln's 'Lives of the Bishops' A.D. 1483–1517*, trans. and ed. Robert Kerr Hannay, SHS (Edinburgh, 1915), 322–3.

[33] Fittis, *Ecclesiastical Annals*, 299–300, gives the full details of the inventory, which clearly included some sumptuous vestments.

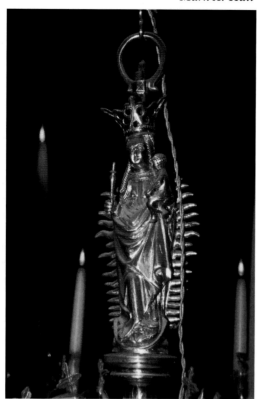

4. Detail of the Flemish chandelier in St John's Kirk, showing the central figure of the Virgin (with the Child) as Our Lady of the Sun. © and courtesy of Perth Museum & Art Gallery, Perth & Kinross Council, Scotland

not match the known Marian altar dedications suggesting that it may have been for a non-Marian altar as a way of demonstrating Marian devotion by its patron(s).[34] It is a chandelier of twelve branches (probably symbolising the Twelve Apostles) with a Virgin and Child set in a sunburst at its apex. It is thus a depiction of the 'Beata Maria in Sole' – Our Lady of the Sun. This appellation derives from the Book of Revelation, where chapter 12 verse 1 describes a figure interpreted as the Madonna as 'clothed with the sun and having the moon under her feet and stars about her head'. One final object associated with the Virgin cult at St John's deserves mention here: the Ave Maria Bell. This dates from *ca* 1340 and its surviving inscription runs *Ave*

---

[34] The chandelier is part of the collections of Perth Museum and is currently on loan to St John's Kirk. Of several such chandeliers known to have been imported into Scotland from the Low Countries this is the only one to survive. For its history, see Thomas Hunter, *St John's Kirk, Perth: A History* (Perth, 1932); Fawcett, *History of St John's Kirk*; and Caldwell, *Angels, Nobles and Unicorns*, 116 cat. F23. For a general discussion of such Marian chandeliers, see M. Q. Smith, 'Medieval chandeliers in Britain and their symbolism', *The Connoisseur* 190 (1975), 266–71, which does not note the Perth example.

Maria Gracie Plena Dominus Tecum ('Hail Mary Full of Grace the Lord is With You'), the opening words of the 'Hail Mary' prayer and one of the commonest amuletic and apotropaic phrases of the middle ages and in this case likely to represent the Virgin's power called to protect the kirk whenever the bell was rung.[35]

To return to the altars, there are two further examples in St John's of related interest. The first is that of St John the Evangelist, founded in 1448 (its upkeep deriving from rents from property in Northgate (High Street) owned by Violet Anderson and Richard Fernie). St John was particularly associated with the Virgin in her role as the Mater Dolorossa. The second is that of St Joseph, more fully the altar of St Joseph, Confessor and Husband of the Virgin Mary, founded in 1524 by Sir John Tyrie at the existing altar of St Michael the Archangel.

Leaving the kirk the two key, non-monastic dedications in the town about which details survive are Our Lady's Chapel on the bridge and the Loreto Chapel. The Chapel of Our Lady (with similarly styled altar inside) stood at the west end of the bridge that spanned the Tay from the foot of Northgate. An early version of the chapel was swept away by the great flood of 1209 and a new chapel built, which was endowed with a resident priest. Mary's protection of the bridge and its users was perhaps particularly looked for in a town subject to the tremendous flooding force of the river Tay. Beside the chapel, perhaps part of its external decoration, stood a statue of the Virgin, mentioned in a brief poem probably written *ca* 1453 (anonymously) in the Perth Guildry Book. It offers a rare insight into a creative, literate culture in Perth and to individual Marian devotion. The poem was the chosen medium by which its author expressed his thoughts to give an account of the washing away of the bridge during a later flooding episode. Within the poem the writer accepts that some may be sceptical of what is written but nevertheless maintains that a miracle took place in the flood leaving the statue of the Virgin unscathed:

> Nor do I pass over in silence when the Tay flooded in revenge and breached the timberwork of the bridge. ... The wall next to the chapel was broken down, but an image of the Virgin stood unmoved and still stands, as can be seen, fixed to its base by no nail and no hand. Anyone can make what he wishes of this, I am amazed and include it among miracles by the merits of the wondrous mother ...[36]

In a European context such an (admittedly minor) miracle story as this seems less distinctive. By the fifteenth century thousands of miracle stories were circulating through Europe. They serve as evidence of both piety and a

---

35 For details of the bell, see R. W. M. Clouston, 'The bells of Perthshire: St John's Kirk, Perth', *PSAS* 124 (1994), 525–41, at 531–2.

36 For the full text of the poem, see Stavert, *Guildry Book*, 493. Her note, at 528, suggests that the hand of a royal clerk wrote it and entry 1059 concerning the operation of the royal mint in Perth. For the bridge generally, see Fittis, *Ecclesiastical Annals*, 270–2.

5. One side of the pewter ampulla from the Shrine of Our Lady of Walsingham, showing her coronation as Queen of Heaven. © and courtesy of Perth Museum & Art Gallery, Perth & Kinross Council, Scotland

desire for salvation but were also frequently circulated to encourage further pilgrimage to particular shrines. The latter is not readily apparent in Perth, though we should remember that it was a nodal communication point, critical to pilgrimage routes to Scone and St Andrews, for example, and it did possess relics, including of the Holy Blood and of St Eloy.[37]

The first documentary reference to Perth's Loreto Chapel is 1528, when the founder was granted land for its building, by James V who was clearly inclined towards this cult, making a pilgrimage to Our Lady of Loreto's Chapel in Musselburgh in 1530. In Perth the precise location of the chapel is unknown but the evidence suggests it was off South Street, to the west of St John's Kirk.[38] Loreto Chapels take their name from the House of Loreto in Italy, the shrine of the Holy House where the Virgin Mary was Annunciated. Originally, this house was located in Nazareth but was miraculously moved

---

[37] A full selection of Marian miracle stories is given in *Medieval Popular Religion 1000–1500: A Reader*, ed. John Shinners (Peterborough, Ont., 1997), 113–48; and see Jacobus de Voragine, *The Golden Legend: Readings on the Saints*, trans. William Granger Ryan, 2 vols (Princeton, 1993), I.143, 196; II.77, 149.

[38] Fittis, *Ecclesiastical Annals*, 295; *RMS*, III.157 no. 722. The 1862 OS Map marks the chapel site as in this area; in 1947 two skeletons were found in Loreto Court – the chapel is said to have had a burying ground on its north side and a garden on its west.

by angels in 1291, finally settling at Loreto, near Ancona, Italy in 1295. This legend was first written down in Italian in 1472. Miracles followed and its popularity was such that in 1476 Pope Sixtus IV declared it an example of sacral transfer from Palestine to Italy and committed the Papacy to 'ownership and patronage of the cult of the Holy House of Nazareth at Loreto and to make the oratory of the Virgin there into a papal chapel'.[39] In 1507 Pope Julius II approved it as a place of pilgrimage and its popularity increased further.[40] It became the richest and most popular shrine in Italy and Holy Houses were erected in imitation across Europe, each supposed to obtain from Loreto a stone which was a portion of the one on which the Angel Gabriel had stood when breaking the news to Mary. Generally hand-in-hand with the Holy House went the Loreto Litany, listing the many personifications and qualities of the Virgin. Litanies were prayers in which a reader (lay or religious) invoked a set of petitions to which the congregation made specific responses. During the sixteenth century the Loreto Litany became hugely popular, and details over forty titles given to Mary.[41]

I have recorded in some detail the European Loreto phenomenon because in the absence of direct evidence for what transpired in the Perth Loreto it gives us a possible handle on how such devotion may have been practised in Perth. Excavation in the Loreto part of town may yet add significant evidence to our understanding of the Chapel. We do though know that pilgrims from Perth were demonstrably in tune with European practice. Excavations elsewhere in the town have recovered a number of pilgrim badges and other souvenirs, relating to a variety of shrines, including St Andrews, Canterbury and Santiago.[42] The most significant of the souvenirs in the context of this study is the thirteenth-century pewter ampulla (illustration 5) from a shrine of Our Lady, probably Walsingham, Norfolk.[43]

It takes the form of a church, with the neck being the tower and the body the rest of the church and with a pitched roof clearly visible. The gable-ends

39   Eamonn O' Carragain, '*Ut Poesis Pictura*: the transformation of the Roman landscape in Botticelli's *Punishment of Korah*', in *New Offerings, Ancient Treasures: Studies in Medieval Art for George Henderson*, eds Paul Binski and William Noel (Stroud, 2001), 492–518, n. 66. Sixtus IV was the patron of the Sistine Chapel, dedicated to the Blessed Virgin Mary.

40   Warner, *Alone of All Her Sex*, 295.

41   The details of the Litany come from Maher, 'A land without stain', 225–36. The Litany was printed in 1558 by the Jesuit, Peter Canisius, an example of prayer books circulating throughout Europe despite the Reformation.

42   The pilgrim badges and other souvenirs are largely from the as yet unpublished excavations on the Perth High Street; see N.Q. Bogdan et al., *Perth High Street Excavations 1975–78*, forthcoming. A summary of the evidence can be found in Hall, 'Cultural interaction' and *idem*, 'Burgh mentalities: a town-in-the-country case study of Perth, Scotland', in *Town and Country in the Middle Ages Contrasts, Contacts and Interconnections 1100–1500*, eds Dyer and Giles, 211–28.

43   The identification of the ampulla was made by the late Brian Spencer (and will appear in Bogdan, forthcoming). It is referred to in his discussion of Walsingham: Brian Spencer, *Pilgrim Souvenirs and Secular Badges*, Medieval Finds from Excavations in London 7 (London, 1998), 135–48, esp. 145–6; see also Leyser, *Medieval Women*, 222–3.

of the transepts are shown on either side, and beneath each gable is shown the Virgin and Child enthroned on one side and the Coronation of the Virgin on the other. Both scenes are supported by illiterate Latin inscriptions, fitted to the available space around each scene and alluding to the scene (only one is fully legible and translates as 'Behold, God Himself Crowns His Mother With His Right Hand').

Walsingham was the pre-eminent English shrine by the early sixteenth century. As well as the Virgin shrine and a number of relics it also boasted a Holy House, but one that predates the Loreto cult. In 1061 widowed gentlewoman Richelde de Fervaques had the copy of the House built after a vision of Mary, which told her to do so and gave her the dimensions of the original. Walsingham started then, as a place of private devotion but it became so popular it needed a religious foundation, an Augustinian Priory, to look after it.[44]

The only other Marian pilgrimage souvenirs so far known from Scotland comprise:

A fifteenth-century, north European clay plaque bearing Virgin and Child and the garbled inscription 'MON C(U)ER AVERDMON CUER AVE GARDE', with the intended meaning 'My Heart, Hail to the Queen My Heart, Hail Guard ...' This was found at the chapel of St Mary, Markle, East Lothian, where it may have been used to make papier-mâché devotional plaques, either for Markle or the nearby Marian shrine at Whitekirk, near Dunbar.[45]

From excavations at Fast Castle, Berwickshire, come two items, one certainly a pilgrimage souvenir and the other probably so. The first is a late fifteenth-century pewter badge showing the assumption of the Virgin Mary. This could relate to the shrine of the Blessed Mary of the Assumption at Eton College, Eton, Bedfordshire, but again it could also relate to the Whitekirk shrine. The second item is certainly connected to Marian devotion; it is a pipe clay figurine of the late fifteenth century depicting the Madonna and Child, possibly acquired as a pilgrimage souvenir.[46]

[44] Spencer, *Pilgrim Souvenirs*, 137.
[45] For the plaque, see Caldwell, *Angels, Nobles and Unicorns*, 97, cat. E94, illus. 98. For a more detailed analysis, see D. Fox and C. Bowman, 'A fifteenth century clay mould found in Scotland and the Master E.S.', *Pantheon* (June 1982), 225–9.
[46] *Fast Castle: Excavations, 1971–86*, eds Keith L. Mitchell, K. Robin Murdoch and John R. Ward (Edinburgh, 2001), 97 (badge), 88 (pipeclay figurine); Peter Yeoman, *Pilgrimage in Medieval Scotland* (London, 1999), 48, 50–1 (Whitekirk); Spencer, *Pilgrim Souvenirs*, 148–9 (Eton). The shrine at Whitekirk was also associated with a holy well dedicated to the Virgin. Late medieval dedications of such wells to Our Lady form much the biggest grouping, with at least 234 throughout Britain, another key indicator of popular devotion; in 1413 Whitekirk received 15,663 pilgrims, see James Rattue, *The Living Stream: Holy Wells in Historical Context* (Woodbridge, 1995), 71, 82–3. East Lothian has a longer history of Marian cult as indicated by the church of St Mary Wedale, possibly in existence by the tenth century and later boasting fragments of an image of the Virgin reputedly brought back from the Holy Land by King Arthur. See G. W. S.

In the parish church of Dunning (St Serf's), Perthshire, survives a bell cast in 1526 by Willem van den Ghein of the Low Countries' Mechline Foundry. It includes within its casting a badge of the Madonna and Child with a small crucifix to her left within a pointed oval or vessica and presumably from a Continental shrine (this badge is accompanied by one of St James of Compostella).[47]

Pilgrim badges, in expressing devotion also fulfilled another role, as protective amulets. Malcolm Jones has demonstrated that the late medieval mind was clear that badges from Marian shrines were seen to bring good luck. Jones also showed that christian faith could be interwoven with long-established folk practices, particularly in relation to amulets. Red coral beads and various fossil stones were widespread as amulets against the evil eye. Italian Virgin and Child paintings of the fourteenth and fifteenth centuries frequently show the Child wearing a red coral branch. In 1488 James III is known to have owned 'four serpents tongues' (that is, fossil sharks' teeth). The two forms of good luck, religious and secular, were deliberately amalgamated to reinforce each other. There is some evidence from Perth to show that secular amulets were in use and they probably can be seen as reinforcing the religious amulets, such as the Walsingham brooch, and vice versa. One of the commoner varieties of European late medieval annular brooches is the variety carrying the widely used apotropaic phrase 'Ave Maria Gracia Plena', usually in a garbled illiterate form. They do not necessarily indicate particular devotion to Mary but a desire to have her protection. An incomplete example, with very garbled legend, was recovered by excavation in Perth.[48] The Dunning badge referred to above was, as stated, cast into the fabric of the bell, a Low Countries tradition that exploited the apotropaic

---

Barrow, *The Kingdom of the Scots* (Edinburgh, 1973), 154 and 160. A recent metal-detector find from this area may be of pilgrimage significance and certainly extends the range of Marian devotional material. It is a fifteenth-century silver gilt figurine of the Madonna and Child, a probable composite piece applied to a portable shrine, casket or similar. It was found close to the church of St Mary, Aberlady, see J. Shiels, 'Aberlady – 15th century silver gilt figurine', in *Discovery and Excavation in Scotland* 7, eds E. McAdam and P. Milburn (2006), 58.

47 See R. W. M. Clouston, 'The bells of Perthshire', *PSAS* 122 (1992), 453–508, at 479–80 and E. van Loon-van de Moosdijk, 'Pelgrim Insignes op Nederlandse klokken', in *Heilig en Profaan 2: 1200 Laatmiddeleeuwse insignes uit openbare en particuliere collecties*, eds H. J. E. van Beuningen, A. M. Koldeweij and D. Kicken (Cothen, 2001), 112–27, illus. 10. As this chapter was finalised, excavations in Aberdeen (the St Nicholas project) in 2006 recovered a lead alloy pendant-like object bearing a depiction of the Mater Dolorossa, which may be a pilgrimage souvenir or possibly some form of medical-token/amulet. It was found in a possibly fifteenth-century grave, under the pelvic area of a female skeleton with evidence of osteomalacia (adult rickets). I am grateful to Alison Cameron for bringing it to my attention.

48 A study of the Perth annular brooch is forthcoming in Bogdan et al. For comparable material, see *Heilig en Profaan: 1000 Laatmiddeleeuwse insignes uit de collectie H. J. van Beuningen*, eds H. J. E. van Beuningen and A. M. Koldeweij (Cothen, 1993), cat. 879 and 881, and *Heilig en Profaan 2*, eds van Beuningen et al., cat. 2144, 2146, 2150, 2152, 2153 and in particular 2149 (almost identical to the Perth example).

power of pilgrim badges, enabling its dispersion over a community through the sound of the bell.[49]

There were also purpose-made secular badges which reveal that Marian devotion was open to parody and satire. A Low Countries (found in Brugge), pewter badge of *ca* 1400, in the form of a vulva wearing a crown with a tri-phallic diadem, borne upon a litter by three phalli walking on human legs, is interpreted by Malcolm Jones as an attack upon Marian relic processions.[50] While it could be a proto-Reformation reflex, it could equally have been a badge only worn at times of carnival or world-turned upside-down; an acceptable humorous parody and a mutually reinforcing fusion of apotropaic sexual imagery, and Marian and Trinitarian imagery. In any event such a superficially scurrilous image would no doubt have upset Church authorities but the average believer on the street may have been less offended – we have already seen how popular (and sometimes authorised) belief could seemingly absorb such contradictions. At the level of widespread social practice such irreverence could indeed be connected with christianity, certainly with the cult of relics. As a foundation stone of popular christianity it saw millions of pilgrims criss-crossing Europe in search of saintly body parts and it seems highly likely that this would have given rise to and fuelled irreverent humour and beliefs (many connected to body parts and functions).

One further object from Fast Castle can serve to lead us back to Perth. It is an incomplete set of twenty bone beads, possibly part of a rosary.[51] From Perth we have a jet crucifix pendant with tin inlay which could have been part of a rosary, along with a jet bead from Elcho Nunnery. This has recently been shown to be made from jet from northwest Spain, and probably represents a pilgrimage souvenir from Compostella.[52] Rosary beads are known from before the twelfth century but they did not achieve widespread popularity until the fifteenth century. In *ca* 1470 the Dominican priest Alanus de Rupe

---

49 Malcolm Jones, *The Secret Middle Ages* (Stroud, 2002), 13–19; for the Perth context, see Hall, 'Cultural interaction'. For the Low Countries tradition of bells incorporating badges, see van Loon-van de Moosdijk, 'Pelgrim Insignes'.

50 Jones, *Secret Middle Ages*, 255. There is now a second such badge, possibly from Paris. It is in the collections of the Musée National du Moyen Age, Paris (registration number Cl. 23653). Marian relics were circulating in the Insular world by at least the ninth century and included hair, clothing fragments and milk; see Raghnall O'Floinn, 'Insignia Columbae I', in *Studies in the Cult of Saint Columba*, ed. Bourke, 136–61, at 148. I am not suggesting in the above discussion that Marian imagery or devotion was never contested. In *ca* 1220 Gautier de Coincy, in his *Miracles de Notre Dame*, rebuked clergy for being as likely to have images/statues of the folk-tale fox Isengrim and his wife in their rooms as statues of the Virgin; see Jones, *Secret Middle Ages*, 194, n. 101, 102. In the 1440s Walter Bower, wrote his *Scotichronicon*. Chapter 42 of Book VIII details an episode at the siege of Châteauroux where a losing dice player angrily breaks a statue of the Virgin Mary. A miracle ensues but the underlying concern is focused on discouraging such blasphemous attentions; see *Chron. Bower*, IV.375 (lines 52–71).

51 *Fast Castle*, eds Mitchell et al., 149.

52 The XRF analysis was carried out courtesy of Fraser Hunter at NMS; see n. 7 in Hall, 'Cultural interaction', which also gives references to the original publications of the jet artefacts.

published his *De Utilitate Psalteri Mariae*, later officially approved by Pope Alexander VI in 1495. It was probably Rupe who invented the tradition that St Dominic, founder of the Order, had been given the rosary in a vision by the Virgin herself, telling him that christian men and women should invoke her aid on the beads.[53] The rosary was so popular that it reached beyond the personal possession of beads to the provision of communal beads in churches. A prayer survives from an East Anglian source imploring the reader to say a Psalter or series of 150 Hail Marys and to use the rosary beads provided if they do not have their own. There was a recognition that not everyone could afford rosary beads, and the prayer goes on to ask that if used the beads should be left where found for others to use – clearly as a powerful amulet the beads were attractive to steal. It shows too that although the act of prayer was a very personal one it could take place in a communal context.[54]

We know little about the individual lives of women in medieval Perth. What we do know largely reflects their legal identity as extensions to their men-folk. It is equally true that the endowments of Marian altars were neither exclusively male nor female: endowers could be male or female or both in partnership and they could be endowed by men for women. Though the surviving evidence indicates a male lead here on Earth (respecting gender-biased social structures), it seems clear enough that salvation was not contingent upon gender. It is also equally true that we do not know a great deal about many of the men in Perth either, certainly below a certain social level (allowing for some generic information provided by archaeology, which applies to both men and women).[55] One contributory factor is the relatively poor survival of sources but even with fuller sources of evidence the lives of many socially inferior individuals would remain opaque (and some Church teaching in emphasising rigid social order helped to keep people in their place and so opaque).

Medieval culture was held in common across Europe but was not uniform, though it was frequently broadly inclusive and able to escape the confines of social hierarchy. Religious practice in particular is often seen, looking back, as having theological uniformity on the one hand, or as being pregnant

---

[53] Warner, *Alone of Her Sex*, 305–8 for the development of the rosary.

[54] Shinners, *Medieval Popular Religion*, 369, no. 90.

[55] I know of no one comparable, for example, to the English knight Sir Geoffrey Luttrell. In his will Luttrell not only left money for masses to be said for his soul in his local church but in several other churches throughout England. He also left money to images, many of them of Mary, including in St Paul's Cathedral, London; Canterbury Cathedral; St Mary's Abbey, York and the Marian shrine at Walsingham. The Luttrell Psalter, commissioned by Sir Geoffrey, includes a number of Marian miracle stories and an image depicting the statue of the Virgin and Child under an elaborate canopy; see Camille, *Mirror in Parchment*, 136–9. This Psalter was not unique. European-made Books of Hours and other books, with Marian images included, are known (if in much less detail) from Scottish contexts (including the Perth Psalter), several with female owners; see, for example, Caldwell, *Angels, Nobles and Unicorns*, 75–88 and David McRoberts, *Catalogue of Scottish Medieval Liturgical Books and Fragments* (Glasgow, 1953).

with Protestant Reform on the other. In fact, uniformity was never the case, even for the ecclesiastical elite (witness the calculation of Easter dispute, the clear divide between those who saw purpose and those who saw no purpose in Church ornamentation and the Dominican-Franciscan dispute over the Immaculate Conception). More widely theological consistency of faith was always mitigated by social structures and connections, politics, environment, doubt, and disbelief. We have seen a number of examples where papal proclamation of the faith followed established popular practice rather than leading it. Believers did not necessarily oblige the Church Fathers by accepting models of behaviour their teaching put forward. Mary's subordination to her son, Christ, won her the sympathies of people subordinate to a rigid spiritual and social hierarchy. When the Spanish colonised Peru, they took with them the popular cult of the Virgin Mary. It fused readily with the Peruvian maternal cult of Pachama, '... as the Immaculate Protectoress she' (Mary) 'was the natural refuge from the manifold tragedies of disease, death and social exclusion that came with the invasion'.[56]

Mary was a valued and popular route to salvation whose adherents could subvert Church dogma and both delight in and satirise the blessed intercession of the Virgin. The nature of the evidence from Perth allows us to see the practice of Marian devotion in both its more formal ecclesiastical context: the dedications of churches and chapels (and their altars), the use of seals on documents from some of these institutions and the work of their preaching friars and in its more popular context: the patronage of altars (particularly in St John's Kirk), the attestation of at least one miracle, pilgrimage and the celebration of feast days and litanies. The two were woven together to form a locally distinctive pattern but one that was in tune with a common practice across Europe, one which Perth's inhabitants informed and were informed by. Marian devotion seems to have been as popular here as throughout Europe. Its local uniqueness comes in its particular physical and religious setting and encompassed both genders and probably all social classes.

---

[56] T. Laughton, 'Spirits of the mountains', in *Mythology: The Illustrated Anthology of World Myth and Storytelling*, ed. C. Scott Littleton (London, 2002), 617.

7

IS EAGAL LIOM LÁ NA HAGRA:
DEVOTION TO THE VIRGIN IN THE LATER
MEDIEVAL GÀIDHEALTACHD[1]

Sìm R. Innes

The later medieval Scottish poet Maol-Domhnaigh mac Mhághnais Mhuile-adhaigh (Maol-Domhnaigh son of Magnus of Mull), in his poem *Ná léig mo mhealladh, a Mhuire* (Do not allow me to be deceived, O Mary), addresses the Blessed Virgin Mary in the hope that she will intervene with God on Judgement Day to save his soul:

> Is eagal liom lá na hagra,
> a inghean Anna an fhoilt tais;
> i n-aghaidh Dé ní fhoil aighneas,
> goir mé óm aimhleas ar m'ais.

> (I fear the day of accusation, O daughter of Anne of the soft hair;
> recall me from harm since there is no pleading against God.)[2]

This chapter seeks to introduce some of the material which can be used to gain an understanding of devotion to the Virgin in the later medieval *Gàid-healtachd*.[3] The Virgin is crucial to any study of christian piety and devotion in the later middle ages.[4] How then was she conceptualised by the Gaels of Scotland during that period? We will begin with an introductory survey of some of the available material, before concentrating on Gaelic poetry which

---

[1]   This chapter is based on some of the work completed for my, as yet unfinished, doctoral thesis with the Department of Celtic and Gaelic at the University of Glasgow, funded by the AHRC. I would like to thank Susan Cameron, the Celtic Collection Librarian at St Francis Xavier University, Nova Scotia for helping me to access materials while I re-drafted this chapter.

[2]   David Greene, 'Ná Léig mo mhealladh, a Mhuire', *Scottish Gaelic Studies* 9 (1962), 105–15.

[3]   While we will not be considering place-name and personal name evidence in this chapter it is acknowledged that further work on both would add to our understanding of the importance of the Virgin in the later medieval *Gàidhealtachd*.

[4]   For the earlier origins, see Mary Clayton, *The Cult of the Virgin Mary in Anglo-Saxon England* (Cambridge, 1990). Regional studies include Peter O' Dwyer, *Mary: A History of Devotion in Ireland* (Dublin, 1988); Bridget Heal, *The Cult of the Virgin Mary in Early Modern Germany: Protestant and Catholic Piety, 1500–1648* (Cambridge, 2007); Linda B. Hall, *Mary, Mother and Warrior: The Virgin in Spain and the Americas* (Austin, TX, 2004); *La dévotion mariale de l'an mil à nos jours*, eds Bruno Béthouart and Alain Lottin (Arras, 2005).

focuses on the Virgin and miracles performed by her for her devotees. Miracle tales including the Virgin are often seen as 'excessive' and scholarly reaction to medieval Marian miracles is very mixed. It will also be shown how this debate is relevant to the Gaelic material. It is well recognised that Gaelic Scotland suffers from a lack of sources which would traditionally be used to study devotion and popular religion in the later medieval period. However, although we lack testaments and the like, occasional sources survive which suggest that devotion to the Virgin appears to have run along similar lines to the rest of later medieval Europe. An obvious starting point is the liturgical year.

Marian Feasts

The major Marian feasts are all contained in one fifteenth-century calendar thought to be from Argyll. This is the calendar from the Glenorchy Psalter.[5] It contains a fascinating mix of traditional and more recent European saints such as St Bernardino of Siena, canonised in 1450, and Gaelic saints of local importance such as Fillan, Monan and Maol Rubha. It also contains all of the major Marian festivals: Purification on 2 February, the Annunciation on 25 March (here labelled Annunciation of the Lord), Assumption to Heaven on 15 August, Nativity of the Virgin on 8 September. It also includes the feasts of the Visitation on 2 July and the Conception of the Virgin on 8 December, observance of which continued to be controversial through the fifteenth century.[6]

The Glenorchy Psalter is of relevance to those interested in piety in Scotland since it also contains a Classical Gaelic poem, *Aingil Dé dom dhín*, written on to a flyleaf of the manuscript in *corr-litir*, the traditional hand for Classical Gaelic. The poem seeks the protection of an archangel for each day of the week.[7] The other side of the flyleaf containing the poem has the inscription 'Liber Coline Campbell of Glenurquhay eiusdem Glenurquhay', identified by David McRoberts as Colin Campbell, third laird of Glenorchy, *ob.* 1526.[8] The Glenorchy Psalter is an important source and the calendar

---

5   BL, MS Egerton 2899, known as the Glenorchy Psalter; David McRoberts, 'Addenda to catalogue of Scottish medieval liturgical books', *IR* 3 (1952), 131–5, at 132; *British Museum Catalogue of Additions to the Manuscripts 1911–1915*, 2 vols (London, 1925), I.411–13; Robin Flower, *Catalogue of Irish Manuscripts in the British Museum*, 2 vols (London, 1926), II.23–4. A number of images of the Glenorchy Psalter are available online as part of the British Library's Digital Catalogue of Illuminated Manuscripts at http://www.bl.uk/catalogues/illuminatedmanuscripts/welcome.htm

6   This was despite the rulings of the Council of Basel (not ecumenical) in 1439 and of Pope Sixtus IV in 1476. See Jaroslav Pelikan, *Mary through the Centuries* (New Haven, CT, 1996), 198–9.

7   For an edition of the poem, although not from this source, see Thomas P. O'Nolan, 'Imchlód Aingel', in *Miscellany Presented to Kuno Meyer*, eds Osborn Bergin and Carl Marstrander (Halle, 1912), 253–7.

8   McRoberts, 'Addenda to catalogue', 132.

provides evidence for the feasts of the Virgin from one area of the *Gàidhealtachd*.

Marian Gaelic Prose Texts and Prayer

Prose texts are a further source of evidence which can provide a more nuanced understanding of the importance of the Virgin during the later medieval period. The Gaelic manuscripts from the National Library of Scotland (NLS) in Edinburgh give us a glimpse of the kinds of Marian material which may have been circulating. One NLS manuscript, dated to 1467, contains a Gaelic translation of the thirteenth-century Pseudo-Anselm, *Dialogus Beatae Mariae et Anselmi de Passione Domini* (Dialogue of the Blessed Mary and Anselm on the Passion of the Lord).[9] The *Dialogus* is a meditative text in which Mary, prompted by Anselm's questions, narrates the events of the Passion. The text includes numerous references to the suffering of the Virgin, a motif which was to become increasingly important in later medieval devotion with the development of practices such as the veneration of the Seven Sorrows of the Virgin.[10] It is thought that the *Dialogus* was composed in Franciscan circles.[11] The following short excerpt from the Gaelic translation will serve as an example:

> Do ráidh Anselmus: Cinnus do rinnedar annsin reis?
> Do ráidh Muire: Inneosadsa sin duit, óir is truadh ro-toirseach hé re innisin, agus ní sgríbunn suibisgél dona suibisgéluibh hé. An uair tángudar gu Caluaire, gu hinadh césda mo micsi, an inadh adhuathmur urgranna ina(dh) mbídis coin agus bethadhaidh mharbha(dh) ar mbuain a seitheadha díbh agus ina curthai(dh) gadaidhi agus bithúnaidh chunn báis agus tar éis a corp do crochadh gu mbídh an t-inadh lán do mí-baladh agus do mí-dath dá n-éisi. Et do nochtudar mo macsa annsin ar mbuain a (i) édaidh co léir de agus arna feicsin damsa do bhághus leth-marb ann, agus gidedh do beanus in cibi[r]si .i. in bréid[ín] do bí umum ceann dím, agus do ceanglus agus do [sh]nighis áirne mo mic leis.

> (Anselm asked: What did they do to Him then?
> Mary said: That I will tell you as it is sorrowful and exceedingly lamentable to report and none of the gospels relate it. When they came to Calvary, to the cruci-

---

9 NLS, Adv. MS 72.1.1, fols 8a–13a. On this manuscript, see Martin MacGregor, 'Genealogies of the clans: contributions to the study of MS 1467', *IR* 51 (2000), 131–46. For an edition of the Gaelic *Dialogus* text, although largely based on another manuscript, see R. A. Q. Skerret, 'Fiarfaidhi San Anselmus', *Celtica* 7 (1966), 163–87. Another copy of the same translation with some additions is also found in NLS, Adv. MS 72.1.25, 1–6a. See the note on the *Dialogus* in Martin McNamara, *The Apocrypha in the Irish Church* (Dublin, 1984), 75–6. For the Latin text of the *Dialogus*, see *PL*, CLIX.cols 271–90.

10 For the influence of such texts on art, see Carol M. Schuler, 'The seven sorrows of the Virgin: popular culture and cultic imagery in pre-Reformation Europe', *Simiolus: Netherlands Quarterly for the History of Art* 21 (1992), 5–28.

11 Amy Neff, 'The "Dialogus Beatae Mariae et Anselmi de Passione Domini": toward an attribution', *Storiografia Francescana* 86 (1986), 105–8.

fixion site of my Son, the most terrible disgraceful of places, where dogs and other carcasses were thrown once their skins were removed and where thieves and criminals were put to death and once their corpses were hung the place filled with a vile stench and awful appearance afterwards. And they stripped my Son of all his clothes; and seeing this I was half-dead but nevertheless took the covering, that is, the veil from my head and I wrapped and covered my Son's loins with it.)[12]

This section of the *Dialogus* is significant, as it belongs to a common medieval tradition that the Virgin had swaddled the Infant at the Nativity with her veil, and used this same veil to cover his nakedness at the Crucifixion, 'a visual emblem linking the joyful maternity of the Virgin with her anguish at Calvary'.[13] A relic of the head veil of the Virgin was held in Assisi.[14] A colophon to the Gaelic *Dialogus* in the NLS manuscript informs us that the text was translated in Ireland, but transcribed by Dubhghall **Albanach** mac mhic Chathail (**Scottish** Dugald, son of the son of Cathal).[15] Therefore, the *Dialogus* is a meditational Marian text in Gaelic with some link to Scotland, depending on how we understand the by-name *Albanach*.[16]

Another *Albanach* worked on BL MS Egerton 93. The first section of this manuscript contains among other items the Tripartite Life of Patrick and the *Saltair Mhuire* (Mary's Psalter). John D. Miller explains the development of Mary's Psalter, or Our Lady's Psalter, and the rosary as stemming from the private recitation of the Psalter, in imitation of the canonical hours:

In the 'Marian psalm psalters', which originated around 1130, the antiphons that preceded each psalm and announced its theme were replaced by verses that interpreted each of the 150 psalms as a reference to Christ or Mary. Gradually the devotion was shortened to a recitation of the antiphons and, in place of the psalm proper, either a Paternoster or an Ave Maria. Without the psalm, the connection that the antiphon had to a specific theme was lost. As a result, the antiphons themselves came to be replaced by 150 verses in praise of the Virgin. Partly for ease of recita-

---

12 Skerret, 'Fiarfaidhi San Anselmus', 174–5, with my own translation. My translation differs slightly from the summary in English given by O'Dwyer, *Mary*, 156. Compare the corresponding section from the Latin original, *PL*, CLIX.col. 282, 'ANSELMUS: Quomodo fecerunt ei? MARIA: Audi, Anselme, quod modo referam nimis est lamentibile, et nullus evangelistarum scribit. Cum venissent ad locum Calvariae ignominiosissimum, ubi canes et alia morticina projiciebantur, nudaverunt Jesum unicum filium meum totaliter vestibus suis, et ego exanimis facta fui; tamen velamen capitis mei accipiens circumligavi lumbis suis.'

13 Gail McMurray Gibson, 'St. Margery: The Book of Margery Kempe', in *Equally in God's Image: Women in the Middle Ages,* eds Julia Bolton Holloway, Constance S. Wright and Joan Bechtold (New York, 1990), 144–63, at 149, and see 160 n. 28. See also Anne Derbes, *Picturing the Passion in Late Medieval Italy: Narrative Painting, Franciscan Ideologies, and the Levant* (Cambridge, 1996), 150–3.

14 McMurray Gibson, 'St. Margery', 148–9.

15 On possible Scottish Gaelic vernacular features in this text and for the identification of the scribe, see Colm Ó Baoill, 'Scotticisms in a manuscript of 1467', *Scottish Gaelic Studies* 15 (1988), 122–39.

16 It seems to be accepted that this Dubhghall was in fact Scottish but for some of the issues connected to the use of *Albanach* in personal names, see Matthew H. Hammond, 'The use of the name Scot in the central middle ages part I: Scot as a by-name', *The Journal of Scottish Name Studies* 1 (2007), 37–60.

tion, the Marian psalters were subdivided into three sets of 50 stanzas, each set of which was designated as a 'rosary'.[17]

The *Saltair Mhuire* in this case informs us that it is to be recited in honour of the Annunciation, Nativity and Assumption specifically.[18] It also tells us that Mary herself revealed that it was to be recited daily in this way, to an unidentified person.[19] St Dominic came to be popularly identified as a figure who received the revelation of the rosary, the Virgin having appeared to him and instructed him on its usage. It is thought that the narrative linking St Dominic to the rosary may have originated in the fifteenth century.[20] One of the antiphons given in Latin and then translated into Gaelic in this text refers, arrestingly, to Mary as *imperatrix inferni / banimpir ifírn* (Empress of Hell) and we shall return to this notion shortly.[21] A colophon following the Life of Patrick tells us that the first section of this manuscript, also containing the *Saltair Mhuire*, was written in 1477 by Domhnall **Albanach** Ó Troighthigh (**Scottish** Donald Ó Troighthigh).[22] Therefore, here we have a further Marian Gaelic text with some link to Scotland. There are very few examples of Marian Gaelic prose texts such as these surviving which we can claim to have any connection to Scotland. The few texts remaining give us some idea, however, that at least some Gaelic Scots were engaging with some of the most common features of later medieval christianity. These include, as we have seen, devotion to the rosary and the developing interest in the Co-Passion of the Virgin.

Marian sculpture

Stone sculpture also bears witness to the importance of the Virgin to medieval Gaels. Images of the Virgin and Child appear on the sixteenth-century font from St Maelrubha's Borline in Skye, and on the cross from Ardchattan Priory in Lorn from *ca* 1500, which also shows the words 'maria gracia ple*na*'.[23] The Virgin and Child again occupy a central place in the iconog-

---

[17] John D. Miller, *Beads and Prayers: The Rosary in History and Devotion* (London, 2002), 14.

[18] For an edition of this text of the *Saltair Mhuire*, see Brian Ó Cuív, 'Saltair Mhuire', *Éigse* 11 (1964–6), 116.

[19] *Ibid.*

[20] Miller, *Beads and Prayers*, 7–11; Sarah Jane Boss, 'Telling the beads: the practice and symbolism of the rosary', in *Mary: The Complete Resource*, ed. Sarah Jane Boss (Oxford, 2007), 385–94.

[21] Ó Cuív, 'Saltair Mhuire', 116. For the same antiphon, see *Religious Lyrics of the XVth Century*, ed. Carleton Brown (Oxford, 1939), 183.

[22] Ó Cuív, 'Saltair Mhuire', 116.

[23] For the Borline font, see K. A. Steer and J. W. M. Bannerman, *Late Medieval Monumental Sculpture in the West Highlands* (Edinburgh, 1977), 99–100. The image of the Virgin is not included in Plate 30 which shows the font; images can be found at the website of the RCAHMS (www.scran.ac.uk). For the Ardchattan Cross, see Steer and Bannerman, *Late Medieval Monumental Sculpture*, 134–9 and 73 (reconstruction drawing).

raphy of the tomb of Alasdair Crotach MacLeòid at St Clement's Church in Rodel, Harris.[24] We also have the record of a fascinating, although no longer surviving, representation from the tombstone of Prioress Anna Maclean of Iona who died *ca* 1543. We know from Thomas Pennant's eighteenth-century sketch that Anna's tomb effigy did at one time also show an image of the Virgin and Child, which 'mirrored' the image of Anna herself.[25] Mirrors and combs also accompany Anna on her effigy. The mirror was seen as a symbol of the Virgin, since the reference to the *speculum sine macula* (Wisdom 7: 26) was seen as prefiguring her.[26] The inscription on Anna's tombstone includes the supplication to the Virgin, *Santa Maria ora pro me*. The role of the Virgin in the salvation of souls will be discussed in detail below, in conjunction with poetry in Gaelic, and Anna's tombstone should be considered in this light. Madeleine Gray and Salvador Ryan bring attention to the notion that the appearance of the Virgin and Child on a tomb, 'acknowledges Mary's role in mitigating the severity of the Last Judgment. While she nurses Christ in her arms he is less likely to exercise the full severity of his role as judge.'[27] Work remains to be done on the reading of these images but Anna's tombstone testifies to the importance of the Virgin in the theology of salvation. So far we have considered Gaelic prose texts, calendars and sculpture from the area. While all of these sources can provide some fruitful evidence for devotion to the Virgin, they are, as noted, somewhat scarce. Therefore, it is to poetry that we must turn our attention for a fuller picture.

Marian Gaelic poetry

Martin MacGregor noted in an article on Church and culture in the late medieval Highlands that, 'For lay devotion at the aristocratic level, monu-mental sculpture can be supplemented by classical poetry as a source from which precious insights can be gleaned.'[28] Classical poetry, sometimes called bardic poetry, refers to the corpus of poems in syllabic metres composed in a Gaelic common to Ireland and Scotland, described as a 'codified high-

---

[24] Steer and Bannerman, *Late Medieval Monumental Sculpture*, 97–8 and Plates 31 and 32.

[25] For the remaining portion of the slab and the sketch, see *ibid.*, 118–19 and Plate 27. For recent comment on Anna's effigy, see Kimm Perkins-Curran, '"Quhat say ye now, my lady priores? How have ye usit your office, can ye ges": politics, power and realities of the office of a prioress in her community in late medieval Scotland', in *Monasteries and Society in the British Isles in the Later Middle Ages*, eds Janet Burton and Karen Stöber (Woodbridge, 2007), 124–41, at 136–9.

[26] Rubymaya Jaeck-Woodgate, 'Jacopo da Varagine's Virgin Mary as the "Mirror Without Blemish"', *Australian eJournal of Theology* 10 (2007), at http://dlibrary.acu.edu.au/research/theology/ejournal (accessed 24 June 2009).

[27] Madeleine Gray and Salvador Ryan, 'Mother of mercy: the Virgin Mary and the Last Judgment in Welsh and Irish tradition', in *Ireland and Wales in the Middle Ages*, eds Karen Jankulak and Jonathan M. Wooding (Dublin, 2007), 246–61, at 251.

[28] Martin MacGregor, 'Church and culture in the late medieval Highlands', in *The Church in the Highlands*, ed. James Kirk (Edinburgh, 1999), 1–36, at 3–4.

register literary language', during the period 1200–1600.[29] Therefore, one way to gain access to the ways in which the Virgin was conceptualised during our period in the *Gàidhealtachd* is from Gaelic poetry. There are a significant number of surviving classical poems on religious themes from both Ireland and Scotland.[30] In comparison to Ireland, the sources for this kind of material from Scotland are again somewhat scarce. One Scottish manuscript though, The Book of the Dean of Lismore (BDL), contains a number of religious poems.[31]

It is thought that BDL was compiled over a thirty-year period, 1512–42, by two brothers Seumas (the Dean) and Donnchadh MacGriogair.[32] They belonged to Fortingall in Perthshire. The manuscript contains mostly Gaelic poetry, and also some material in Scots and some in Latin. BDL is in some ways infamous due to its use of an orthography based on Scots, occasionally referred to as semi-phonetic, as opposed to traditional Gaelic orthography.[33] It also uses secretary hand rather than *corr-litir*. This use of a Scots orthography to represent Gaelic has meant that many poems from the manuscript remain to be deciphered and edited. The Gaelic poetry in BDL has recently been described by William Gillies as falling into four main categories: religious, court, heroic, and merry.[34] These poems are a mix of Irish and Scottish material and range in date from the thirteenth century to items composed during the lifetimes of the compilers at the beginning of the sixteenth century.[35]

---

29 Roibeard Ó Maolalaigh, 'Place-names as a resource for the historical linguist', in *The Uses of Place-Names*, ed. Simon Taylor (Edinburgh, 1998), 12–53, at 13. On the Gaelic classical poetry tradition in Scotland, see W. Gillies, 'Gaelic: the classical tradition', in *The History of Scottish Literature*, ed. Cairns Craig, 4 vols (Aberdeen, 1988), IV.245–61.

30 Gillies, 'Gaelic: the classical tradition', 255–6. See Marc Caball and Kaarina Hollo, 'The literature of later medieval Ireland, 1200–1600: from the Normans to the Tudors', in *The Cambridge History of Irish Literature*, eds Margaret Kelleher and Philip O'Leary, 2 vols (Cambridge, 2006), I.74–139, at 89–93. See also Salvador Ryan, 'A slighted source: rehabilitating Irish bardic religious poetry in historical discourse', *Cambrian Medieval Celtic Studies* 48 (2004), 75–99.

31 NLS, Adv. MS 72.1.37, known as the Book of the Dean of Lismore.

32 Donald E. Meek, 'The Scots-Gaelic scribes of late medieval Perthshire: an overview of the orthography and contents of the Book of the Dean of Lismore', in *Bryght Lanternis: Essays on the Language and Literature of Medieval and Renaissance Scotland*, eds J. Derrick McClure and Michael R. G. Spiller (Aberdeen, 1989), 387–404, at 389.

33 On the orthography issue, see Dòmhnall Eachann Meek, 'Gàidhlig is Gaylick anns na Meadhon Aoisean', in *Gaelic and Scotland/ Alba agus a' Ghàidhlig*, ed. William Gillies (Edinburgh, 1989), 131–45. For recent comment on what we should consider as 'traditional' Gaelic orthography in Scotland, see Aonghas MacCoinnich, 'Where and how was Gaelic written in late medieval and early modern Scotland? Orthographic practices and cultural identities', *Scottish Gaelic Studies* 24 (2008), 309–56.

34 William Gillies, 'Gaelic literature in the later middle ages: *The Book of the Dean* and beyond', in *The Edinburgh History of Scottish Literature*, eds Ian Brown et al., 3 vols (Edinburgh, 2002), I.219–25, at 220–1.

35 On the issue of poetry of Scottish as opposed to Irish provenance, see Martin MacGregor, 'Creation and compilation: *The Book of the Dean of Lismore* and literary culture in late medieval Gaelic Scotland', in *The Edinburgh History of Scottish Literature*, eds Brown et al., I.209–18, at 212. See also Martin MacGregor, 'The view from Fortingall: the worlds of the Book of the Dean of Lismore', *Scottish Gaelic Studies* 22 (2006), 35–85, at 62–4.

There are around twenty religious poems in BDL and they include a poem to St Katherine of Alexandria, poems based on *exempla*, a poem on the signs of Doomsday and a number of Marian poems among other things. It is our purpose here to discuss poetry from BDL concerning the Virgin. Although there are a number of Scottish Marian poems in the collection from the thirteenth and fourteenth centuries we will be focusing on material from the later period in particular. Three poems have been chosen from BDL, two of which contain significant sections concerning the Virgin and a third which is more focused on her.

Seacht saighde atá ar mo thí

One of the religious poems which makes reference to Mary, although is not exclusively about her, is *Seacht saighde atá ar mo thí* (Seven Arrows Pursue Me). In BDL the poem is attributed to Donnchadh Óg (Young Duncan), who to my knowledge has not yet been identified.[36] A later version of the same poem is also to be found in Donnchadh MacRath's seventeenth-century collection, the Fernaig Manuscript.[37] The seven arrows represent the Seven Deadly Sins, a not uncommon theme linked to Psalm 91: 5: 'Thou shalt not be afraid for the terror by night; nor for the arrow that flieth by day.'[38] The poet works through each sin, confessing his guilt in relation to each. For example, the fourth stanza deals with sloth:

> An treas saighead díobh atá
>   i n-altaibh mo chnámh a stigh:
> cha léig an leisge dá deoin
>   mise ar slighidh chóir ar bith.

> (The third shaft of them abides within the joints of my bones, even sloth that of its will lets me not enter on any good path whatever.)[39]

This stanza, then, reflects the idea that sloth was a sin of the flesh.[40] It is the seventh stanza which is particularly interesting for our purposes. It was edited and translated by W. J. Watson as follows:

---

36   *Scottish Verse from the Book of the Dean of Lismore*, ed. W. J. Watson (Edinburgh, 1937), 252–5. See also *Duanaire na Sracaire /Songbook of the Pillagers: Anthology of Medieval Gaelic Poetry*, eds Wilson McLeod and Meg Bateman (Edinburgh, 2007), 40–3.

37   *Làmh-Sgrìobhainn Mhic Rath*, ed. Calum MacPhàrlain (Dundee, 1923), 22–5.

38   Martin W. Bloomfield, *The Seven Deadly Sins* (Michigan, 1952), 109–10, 182, 212 and 383 n. 36. See also the recent collection of essays on the Sins in *The Seven Deadly Sins*, ed. Richard Newhauser (Leiden, 2007).

39   *Scottish Verse from Book of the Dean*, ed. Watson, 252–3.

40   Bloomfield, *The Seven Deadly Sins*, 213.

Dhíobh an seiseadh saighead gharg,
  chuireas fearg eadram is cách
Críost do chasg na n-urchar dhíom
  ó nach bhfaghaim díon go bráth

(Of them the sixth rude shaft is that which sets anger between me and
others; may Christ guard me from those casts, from which I find no
other shelter until doom.)[41]

In this stanza, on the sin of wrath, the poet appears to seek protection from
Christ. However, Watson points out in his notes to this poem that he has
emended the third line which is as follows in the manuscript, 'Murre chaska
ny' nvrchir reym'.[42] Since the line is unmetrical he has replaced *Muire* (Mary),
a word with two syllables, with *Críost* (Christ), only one syllable. The metre
of this poem is *rannaigheacht mhór*, meaning that there should be no more
than seven syllables in each line. However, it could be argued that the line
is only unmetrical if we edit the language omitting any vernacular Scottish
Gaelic features. Watson clearly saw features of the Scottish vernacular which
strayed from the classical norms as unacceptable; in this same poem he has
replaced *cuide ré* with *maille ré*.[43] MacGregor has recently recommended
that we recognise such occurrences of the vernacular as 'semi-bardic' verse.[44]
The reduction of the particle *do* to *a* is common in BDL and may have been
a feature of the poem as composed.[45] This would then allow us to elide two
vowels leaving us with seven syllables: *Muire a chasg na n-urchar dhíom.*
Mary then, despite the metrical problems, is clearly being invoked here in her
role as protectress. It is interesting that she appears in conjunction with this
particular deadly sin in the poem and not any of the others. The idea that the
Virgin is efficacious against anger is reminiscent of a section from a popular
thirteenth-century text, *Speculum Beatae Mariae Virginis.*[46] Mary is depicted
as effective against wrath since it is she who deflects the wrath of God from
man at Judgement:

Audiamus, quomodo benedicta sit Maria pro lenitate et mansuetudine contra iracun-
diam. Iracundi enim maledicti sunt, sicut scriptum est Genesis quadragesimo nono:
Maledictus furor eorum, quia pertinax, et indignatio eorum, quia dura. Contra hanc
irae maledictionem Maria obtinuit mansuetudinis benedictionem. Cuius re vera

---

[41] *Scottish Verse from Book of the Dean*, ed. Watson, 254–5. I have emended Watson's English
translation which has 'seventh' where it should have 'sixth'.

[42] *Ibid.*, 254 and 306.

[43] *Ibid.*, 306.

[44] MacGregor, 'Creation and compilation', 213.

[45] See, for example, Breandán Ó Buachalla, 'The relative particle Do', *Zeitschrift für Celtische
Philologie* 29 (1962–4), 106–13; Uilleam MacGill'Ìosa, 'Mo chreach-sa thàinig', *Rannsachadh
na Gàidhlig 2000*, eds Colm Ó Baoill and Nancy R. McGuire (Aberdeen, 2002), 45–59, at 54.

[46] For a brief introduction to the text, see Hilda Graef, *Mary: A History of Doctrine and Devotion*,
2 vols (New York, 1963), I.290–1.

mansuetudo tanta fuit, quod non solum propria ira caruit, sed etiam iram Domini ad mansuetudinem convertit.

(Hear how Mary is blessed for her meekness and gentleness against anger. For the angry are accursed, as it is written in Genesis: 'Cursed be their fury, for it was stubborn: and their wrath because it was cruel' (Gen. 49: 7). Against this curse of wrath, Mary obtained the blessing of meekness. For truly her meekness was such that not only had she no anger of her own, but she even turned the anger of God to meekness.)[47]

This image of the Virgin, meek, mild, submissive, and void of anger will be well known to most.[48]

Gearr go gcobhra Rí na ríogh

A further poem from BDL again illustrates this link of Mary with wrath. She is able to divert the wrath of God and ensure the salvation of humankind. The poem *Gearr go gcobhra Rí na ríogh* (The King of Kings will soon succour) has no published edition and these comments are based on the transliteration and translation to be found in the papers of Edmund Quiggin in NLS.[49] The poem is attributed to Roibéard Mac Laghmainn Ascaig (Robert Lamont of Asgog): the Lamont castle was at Asgog on the Cowal Peninsula.[50] The poem has eight stanzas and the last five appear to be advice on necessary good deeds such as the giving of tithes and charity to the poor. The poem begins however by explaining Mary's place in our salvation, 'Ar atach Mhuire i dtaoibh Críost ... maithidh don phobal a fhearg' (At the request of Mary by the side of Christ ... He forgives the people his wrath).

The Virgin's intercessory powers have various medieval manifestations across Europe; a good example is the motif, also found in the classical Gaelic poetry tradition, of the Virgin bearing her breast to Christ the Judge.[51] Mary is also commonly depicted across medieval Europe placing various objects such as the rosary or a candle into St Michael's scales during the Soul Weigh-

---

47 Conrad of Saxony, *Speculum Beatae Mariae Virginis*, Bibliotheca Franciscana Ascetica Medii Aevi 2 (Quaracchi, 1904), 217. English translation from Saint Bonaventure, *The Mirror of the Blessed Virgin Mary*, trans. Sr Mary Emmanuel, O.S.B (London, 1932), 152–3.

48 For more on this, see Marina Warner, *Alone of All Her Sex: The Myth and the Cult of the Virgin Mary* (New York, 1976), 177–91.

49 A transcription of the poem can be found in E. C. Quiggin, *Poems from the Book of the Dean of Lismore*, ed. J. Fraser (Cambridge, 1937), 17. For the transliterations and translation, see NLS, MS 14870, 340–4.

50 Hector McKechnie, *The Lamont Clan 1235–1935: Seven Centuries of Clan History from Record Evidence* (Edinburgh, 1938), 401–4. Cited by Ronnie Black, *Catalogue of the Classical Gaelic MSS in the National Library of Scotland* (forthcoming).

51 Salvador Ryan, 'The persuasive power of a mother's breast: the most desperate act of the Virgin Mary's Advocacy', *Studia Hibernica* 32 (2002–3), 59–74.

ing.[52] The message to the faithful of such motifs was that Marian devotional practices have a saving power.[53]

Ná léig mo mhealladh, a Mhuire

This message is also made explicit in our final BDL poem, *Ná léig mo mhealladh, a Mhuire*, introduced above. The twenty-five stanzas of the poem begin with nine which praise and explain the importance of the Virgin. For example, stanza 6 again provides us with further evidence of the intercessory power of the Virgin, of her deflecting the anger of God, 'ó tá fearg Dhé ris gach duine, ná hearb mé, a Mhuire, réd Mhac' (since God's anger is against every man, do not entrust me, O Mary, to your son).[54] However, this poem goes one step further and invokes Mary's own anger:

> Mar do léigfeadh lá dá éigin
> m'anam ré bás mar bhláth slat,
> gé tú riamh is cealg im chroidhe,
> do bhiadh fearg Mhoire ria Mac.

> (Although I have deceit continually in my heart, Mary's anger would be against her Son if He committed my body to death like the flower of the boughs.)[55]

The notion that the Virgin is capable of wrath, which she can direct towards her Son, is of course unlike the picture presented of the Virgin having no wrath of her own. From the texts discussed here it appears that Mary can intercede with God in a variety of ways, through having no personal anger, through petitioning him, and finally with her own anger. The poem shows how powerful Mary's intercession can be by telling the story of a man who regularly committed incest with his sister. We are told that:

> Do smuain an fear, fuar an t-inntleacht,
> ar eagal diomdha Dhé bhí
> páirt ré máthar Dhé gur dhéanta
> gur ghnáthaigh sé déarca dhí.

> (The man thought – it was a cold-blooded plan – that, for fear of the displeasure of the living God, he should seek favour with God's mother, so that he practised giving alms to her.)[56]

---

52 Andrew Breeze, 'The Virgin's rosary and St Michael's scales', *Studia Celtica* 24/25 (1989–90), 91–8.
53 Christine Peters, *Patterns of Piety: Women, Gender and Religion in Late Medieval and Reformation England* (Cambridge, 2003), 60–7.
54 Greene, 'Ná Léig mo mhealladh, a Mhuire', stanza 6.
55 *Ibid.*, stanza 23.
56 *Ibid.*, stanza 13.

On the man's death we learn that the Devil didn't dare hold the man in Hell and that the Virgin took him by force. The poem appears to say that she brought the man back to life, as there is mention of a second death after a subsequent life of piety. It was noted at the beginning of this chapter that Mary is referred to in the *Saltair Mhuire* from the BL as *imperatrix inferni / banimpir ifìrn* (Empress of Hell). This notion provides a context for the Virgin's action in *Ná léig mo mhealladh, a Mhuire* of forcibly wrestling the soul of her devotee from the Devil. The title 'Empress of Hell' is also to be found in a medieval English context. The English religious lyric *Owt of your slepe aryse and wake* contains the following stanza:

> Now man is brighter than the sonne;
> Now man in heven an hye shal wone;
> Blessed be God this game is begonne,
>   And his moder, Emperesse of Helle.
>   Nowel!
>   *Nowel, nowel, nowel,*
>   *Nowel, nowel, nowel!*[57]

A further example of the title 'Empress of Hell' occurs in conjunction with the extremely common medieval tale of Theophilus. Theophilus sold his soul to the Devil in return for promotion to a higher office in the Church. Through the intercession of Mary, who descends into Hell, he is released from his contract with the Devil.[58] In one English version of the tale Theophilus addresses Mary as 'Emperis of Hell' while pleading for mercy.[59] Kate Koppelman recommends that, 'modern scholars should attend to Mary's role as both Queen of Heaven and Empress of Hell in any effort to more fully understand her positioning as a devotional figure in the Middle Ages'.[60] Therefore, the three Gaelic poems discussed here testify to the fact that the figure of the Virgin was multi-faceted. She could be prayed to for protection against the sin of wrath as a result of her meekness, she could be called upon to calm the wrath of God and could also at times show her own wrath in order to save a soul, both in dealing with God and in her role as Empress of Hell. She is therefore crucial in the scheme of salvation presented by these texts.

---

[57] *Late Medieval English Lyrics and Carols 1400–1530*, ed. Thomas G. Duncan (London, 2000), 60.

[58] See Miri Rubin, *Gentile Tales: The Narrative Assault on Late Medieval Jews* (New Haven, CT and London, 1999), 7–8.

[59] Kate Koppelman, 'Devotional ambivalence: the Virgin Mary as "Empresse of Helle"', *Essays in Medieval Studies* 18 (2001), 67–82, at 74.

[60] *Ibid.*, 72.

Marian Excess?

Tales such as the tale of Theophilus, the incestuous man in our poem, and other similar tales of the sinful gaining mercy and other types of miraculous intervention through the intercession of the Virgin became extremely popular in the middle ages. What are we to make of such Marian devotion? First, let us take a look at a number of similar miracle tales and evidence for their popularity in medieval Scotland. We can then move to consider the thoughts of scholars on the issue. One of the most widespread examples of such Marian clemency is the tale of the thief Eppo. We read, in places such as the *Stella Maris* of John of Garland, that he was a wicked thief, who was nonetheless devoted to the Virgin. He was caught and strung up on the gallows. However, he hung there for three days held up by the Virgin until he was eventually freed.[61] One other common tale involved the Virgin taking the place of a nun who had fled her convent to meet her lover. The nun eventually returned and had not been missed.[62] In Scotland some of the most common Marian *exempla* appear in Walter Bower's *Scotichronicon*. He gives the tale of Theophilus, and also the story of a woman who arranged the murder of her son-in-law. She was ordered to be burnt:

> Sed prius ducta ad ecclesiam Beate Dei Genitricis Marie, peccatum suum coram Deo et hominibus ex ordine narravit, et sic meritis et precibus sanctissime Virginis Marie se ipsam fideliter commendavit.

> (But first she was brought to the church of St Mary the Mother of God, where she gave an ordered account of her transgression before God and men, and thus faithfully entrusted herself to the influence and prayers of the most holy Virgin Mary.)[63]

Thus, when the fire was lit it twice did no harm to the murderous woman. Again the importance of prayer to the Virgin is promoted in this tale. *Exempla* collections such as the *Speculum Laicorum* and the *Gesta Romanorum* provide plenty of examples of this kind of Marian clemency. These collections developed in conjunction with the mendicant orders.[64] We know that the mendicant orders were numerous in Scotland.[65] If we look at Perthshire, since BDL belongs to that locale, then we see that it was at Tullilum that the first Carmelite (Whitefriars) house in Scotland was founded in 1296.[66] In Perth

---

[61] *The Stella Maris of John of Garland*, ed. Evelyn Faye Wilson (Cambridge, MA, 1946), 152 and 209–10; Benedicta Ward, *Miracles and the Medieval Mind* (London, 1982), 156 and 163. For an edited prose Latin version, see Thomas Wright, *A Selection of Latin Stories from Manuscripts of the Thirteenth and Fourteenth Centuries* (London, 1842), 97–8.

[62] Ward, *Miracles and the Medieval Mind*, 163.

[63] *Chron. Bower*, IV.112–15 (Latin text and English translation). For the Theophilus story in Bower, see *Chron. Bower*, II.76–7.

[64] Carlo Delcorno, *Exemplum e Letteratura Tra Medioevo e Rinascimento* (Bologna, 1994), 30.

[65] David Ditchburn, *Scotland and Europe: The Medieval Kingdom and its Contacts with Christendom, 1214–1560* (East Linton, 2001), 47.

[66] *MRHS*, 138.

itself the Dominicans (Blackfriars) had a house from the thirteenth century and the Franciscans (Greyfriars) from the fifteenth century.[67] Stephen Boardman has recently highlighted the work of the Dominicans in Argyll from the thirteenth century.[68] Other than the *Scotichronicon* there is some evidence, both from manuscript and printed sources, that some of the *exempla* and *exempla* collections were well known in Scotland.[69] The canons at St Andrews had a printed copy of the *Gesta Romanorum* from Strasbourg and printed copies of the *Legenda Aurea* were owned by a significant number.[70] Our poems often appear to testify to the use of such *exempla* collections, at some point during the transmission of the tales. *Ná léig mo mhealladh, a Mhuire* introduces the tale of the incestuous man with the line, 'do dhearbh a leabhraibh lucht fis' (learned men have found it from books).[71] Therefore, it is clear that the more 'excessive' kinds of Marian miracles which appear in Gaelic poetry are part of a tradition which is greater than Gaelic Scotland.

Our final point for consideration is the stance scholars have taken over this kind of Marian devotion. Some recognise the long and prestigious history of such devotion to the Virgin. St Bernard of Clairvaux said the following in the twelfth century, 'Opus enim mediatore ad Mediatorem istum, nec alter nobilis utilior quam Maria' (Man needs a mediator with that Mediator, and there is no-one more efficacious than Mary).[72] It has been noted that such statements from St Bernard would of course have made 'an enormous impact'.[73] Some scholars however, such as Peter Whiteford, point the finger at *popular religion*. He says:

> Theologians strove to keep her mediation distinct from and subordinate to that of Christ, but popular belief cheerfully blurred the distinction. For in spite of the high lineage which these stories undoubtedly had, it is equally true that they had great appeal for the simple and unlettered people.... And just as their popularity can be related to the doctrinal and devotional developments found in writers of the calibre of Anselm of Canterbury and Bernard of Clairvaux, it can no doubt also be attributed to the superstition and credulity which are to be found in popular medieval religion.[74]

However, others do not agree with this assessment. Gabriela Signori notes that:

---

[67] *Ibid.*, 119.

[68] Stephen Boardman, *The Campbells 1250–1513* (Edinburgh, 2006), 118–20.

[69] John Durkan and Anthony Ross, *Early Scottish Libraries* (Glasgow, 1961), 92–4.

[70] See, for example, the library of Robert Stewart, bishop of Caithness: *ibid.*, 63.

[71] Greene, 'Ná Léig mo mhealladh, a Mhuire', stanza 11.

[72] Richard Baukham, 'The origins and growth of western Mariology', in *Chosen by God: Mary in Evangelical Perspective*, ed. David F. Wright (London, 1989), 141–60, at 156. The Latin text from *Library of Latin Texts Online* (CLCLT), http://www.brepolis.net/info/info_clt_en.html

[73] Graef, *Mary*, 239.

[74] *The Myracles of Our Lady: Ed. from Wynkyn de Worde's Edition*, ed. Peter Whiteford, Middle English Texts 23 (Heidelberg, 1990), 17.

Hymnical praises of the Virgin, enriched with biblical quotations and according the mother an equal status with her son, abound. This was at variance with theological notions, but was the result of contradicting views among the learned and did not, as often postulated, reflect the religious beliefs of the laity.[75]

As well as differing views on the origins and development of such Marian devotion, there appear to be different views taken of the miracles themselves. Some condemn the kinds of miracle stories we have seen as 'Mariological Excesses';[76] in fact, the poem *Ná Léig mo mhealladh, a Mhuire* has been summed up as 'an extravaganza of Marianism'.[77] One scholar recently published an edition of another Classical Gaelic religious poem, *Múin aithrighe dhamh, a Dhé*, attributed to the fifteenth-century poet Tadhg Óg Ó hUiginn. The poem deals with incest and infanticide, and in tracing the background of the motifs to the *Gesta Romanorum* the editor speaks of:

> the unlikely intervention of the Blessed Virgin Mary, which is quite awkwardly rationalized on the basis that, though the guilty woman in regularly confessing her sins concealed the sins of incest and murder, she nevertheless is described as having been very devoted to the Virgin Mary and having distributed alms for love of her.[78]

From what we have seen so far it may be that this rationalisation seems awkward to the modern reader but may not have seemed so to a medieval audience. It may be important to remember also that the Virgin is commonly linked with grave sins in these kinds of narratives. Sarah Kay has brought attention to this, noting that while most saints deal with 'humdrum needs' the Virgin 'specialises in lost lives and lost souls'.[79] For a medieval audience it seems that Mary would have been the obvious choice in such desperate circumstances as those involving incest and murder. Other commentators have tried to find a less critical view, such as the following from Eileen Power:

> If behind all the superficiality and irresponsibility of the miracles we look more closely at the Virgin of the middle ages, we shall perceive that she does represent the deepest and most essential side of the Christian religion, the insistence on faith, the power of love to blot away sin, above all the infinite mercy.[80]

---

75 Gabriela Signori, 'The miracle kitchen and its ingredients: a methodical and critical approach to Marian shrine wonders (10th to 13th century)', *Hagiographica* 3 (1996), 277–303, at 297.

76 Bauckham, 'The origins and growth', 154.

77 R. I. Black, 'Ó Muirgheasáin family', in *The Companion to Gaelic Scotland*, ed. Derick S. Thomson (Glasgow, 1983), 220.

78 Cathal Ó Háinle, 'Múin aithrighe dhamh, a Dhé revised', *Ériu* 54 (2004), 103–24, at 107.

79 Sarah Kay, *Courtly Contradictions: The Emergence of the Literary Object in the Twelfth Century* (Stanford, CA, 2001), 184.

80 Johannes Verolt, *Miracles of the Blessed Virgin Mary*, trans. C. C. Swinton Bland and intr. Eileen Power (London, 1928), xxxiv–v.

A further approach accepts the sensationalism of these Marian miracles but sees them as a means to an end. Carol M. Meale, writing on English Marian miracle poems, explains as follows:

> the devotional needs which were satisfied by the miracles can have been of no high order. Yet while they offer no profound spiritual insight, they do succeed in conveying important truths about religious practice.... The miraculous far from being an end in itself, is rather a means to an end, in demonstrating exemplary patterns of faith.[81]

Therefore, Meale's approach of looking past the uncomfortable elements in order to rehabilitate these miracle tales allows us to focus on the text as a teaching aid. Clearly, this was not lost on Walter Bower, in the 1440s, who introduced a number of Marian miracles and a discussion of the mystical significance of the word *ave* with the following, 'opere precium est referre aliqua que ad horas eius decantandas lectorem valeant incitare' (it is worth-while here to mention some things which might be effective in inducing the reader to sing her hours).[82]

A final approach would allow a metaphorical reading of the figure of the Virgin in such miracle tales. It was noted above that specific Marian devotional practices are often promoted by these texts and Kay notes that:

> This linking of the Virgin with ecclesiastical ritual suggests that Mary often has a metaphorical role in these stories, designating less a person than Mother Church. Those who are saved by her intervention usually have a record of devotion expressed through liturgical texts: hymns, anthems and psalms. The texts teach that adherence to the Church as an institution will ensure salvation for the sinner, however grievous his sin, provided he continues to practice her rites.[83]

Some may see the kinds of miracles discussed here as excessive or theologically unsound. However, they can still provide a window onto religious practice, or desired religious practice. Understanding the figure of the Virgin as a metaphor for the Church would also allow us to focus on the devotional practices recommended by the miracles.

An approach which does not solely dismiss these Marian miracle tales as 'excessive' but allows us to use them as evidence of (desired) religious practice is particularly useful for the study of piety in a culture for which other evidence is scarce. The selection of Gaelic poems mentioned here bear witness, if we take this approach, to prayer, almsgiving, renunciation of sin, the circulation of religious material and so on. Most strongly however, all of these later medieval Scottish poems testify to the fear of hell and hope of heaven. It has been noted that in the middle ages the fear of hell 'reached

---

[81] Carol M. Meale, 'The miracles of Our Lady: context and interpretation', in *Studies in the Vernon Manuscript*, ed. Derick Pearsall (Cambridge, 1990), 115–36, at 135.
[82] *Chron. Bower*, IV.124–5 (Latin text and English translation).
[83] Kay, *Courtly Contradictions*, 185–6.

a pitch of intensity bordering on obsession for many'.[84] This fear of hell is made clear and personal in each of our poems. As we have seen, the poem *Ná léig mo mhealladh, a Mhuire* contains the line, 'is eagal liom lá na hagra' (I fear the Day of Accusation). All of the poems mentioned here give the sense that this fear was acute, for the poets, and presumably for other members of their communities. The Blessed Virgin, as man's ultimate intercessor would have been the natural choice to allay these fears. Furthermore, the Virgin as ultimate intercessor, by whichever means, is a theme which links this later medieval Gaelic verse with sculpture from the area and devotional practices such as the *Saltair Mhuire*.

---

[84] Kenneth Hylson-Smith, *Christianity in England from Roman Times to the Reformation*, 3 vols (London, 2001), III.4.

8

SCOTTISH SAINTS' LEGENDS IN THE ABERDEEN BREVIARY

Alan Macquarrie

Breviarium Aberdonense (hereafter *BA*), published in Edinburgh in 1510 (NS), is the most important collection of information we have about Scottish saints' lives, as well as having the distinction of being Scotland's first full-scale printed book.[1] The *Propria Sanctorum* at the end of each of its two volumes contain prayers and *lectiones*, lessons or readings, to be read out during the office on each saint's feast day at Matins; in some cases these are interspersed with proper canticles, especially where the saint was patron of a cathedral or other important church. The readings are without exception short and do not constitute a complete *vita* or life of the saint in question; but in many cases they are demonstrably based on earlier and fuller materials. *BA* is by far our greatest collection of Scottish hagiography. For many saints it provides our only information, while for others it presents significant variants on traditions which are recorded elsewhere. Even in those instances where it does not provide lessons, it may have brief notes on the *cultus* of some saints together with a collect for their feast day. And in spite of its late date, *BA* is important because it records many earlier traditions which have otherwise been lost. Preliminary research into the question suggests that where *BA*'s compilers had earlier materials on which to draw, these are often twelfth-century or in many cases even earlier. As such, *BA* becomes one of our most important literary and historical sources for the Scottish church prior to the late twelfth century.

It is well known that James IV issued a licence for the establishment of a printing press in Edinburgh to Walter Chepman and Andrew Myllar, burgesses of Edinburgh, on 15 September 1507.[2] This specified that they were to publish 'the bukis of our lawis, actis of parliament, croniclis, mes bukis and portuus [that is, breviaries] efter the use of our realme, with additiouns and legendis of Scottis sanctis now gaderit to be ekit thairto'. The task of gathering the legendary of Scottish saints was assigned to William Elphin-

---

[1]   The Chepman and Myllar press had previously produced prints of poetry, but nothing on this scale. So we are justified in calling *BA* Scotland's first printed book.

[2]   *RSS*, I.223–4, no. 1546.

6. The device of Walter Chepman from fol. 146 of the *Breviarum Aberdonense* printed in 1509/10. © National Library of Scotland

144

stone, bishop of Aberdeen (*ob.* 1514). The first productions of the Chepman and Myllar press were prints of poetry, both Scots and English. Its most ambitious undertaking was *Breviarium Aberdonense*, printed in two octavo volumes using red and black ink; the first part, *Pars Hiemalis*, the offices of winter and spring, ran off the press in Edinburgh on 13 February 1510 (NS), and the *Pars Estivalis*, for summer and autumn, on 4 June 1510.[3] (Hereafter referred to as PH and PE.)

A splendid facsimile edition, edited by the Rev. William Blew and printed by J. Toovey of London, was published by the Bannatyne, Maitland and Spalding Clubs in 1854, which with its superb black-letter type in red and black ink must represent one of the great achievements of Victorian typesetting.[4] The comments that follow are not intended as a criticism of Blew or his achievement. Blew, a London Anglican clergyman, was a fine classicist and ecclesiologist, and his beautiful edition of *BA*, in which the things that he got right and the puzzles that he successfully solved vastly outnumber the relatively small number of mistakes that he made, is a remarkable achievement.[5]

The facsimile edition, for all its beauty, is not easy to use; it is quite bulky (much bigger, in fact, than the original octavo volumes), and has no table of contents, translation, critical apparatus or notes (the *Propria* does have an index, of sorts). Present-day scholars are, in effect, working with a medieval book. An additional problem is that the original edition contained many errors and misprints. Blew's edition silently corrects many of these, but it leaves others uncorrected, and in a number of cases it introduces new mistakes. Most of these are not serious, but in some cases Blew's silent editorial changes significantly alter the sense. Further, Blew was not familiar with Scottish place-names, and mis-transcribed several. The result is that scholars consulting the nineteenth-century edition cannot be certain that what they are looking at is an exact facsimile of the original printed book of 1510 (NS).

Even if it were, it would still be difficult to use. Knowledge of Latin is not as widespread as it once was, and even expert classicists are sometimes puzzled by the eccentric spelling, bizarre phraseology and clumsy grammar of *BA*'s medieval Latin, especially in the verse sections and where there are misprints and omitted words. Bishop Forbes's curious mixture of exact translations, paraphrases and summaries in the Appendix to his *Kalendars of Scottish Saints* possibly reflects the difficulties which even a very careful and accomplished scholar experienced in dealing with this text.[6]

Scholars from the time of Forbes onwards have recognised the importance of this source, and the fact that much of it is based on earlier and

---

3   Leslie J. Macfarlane, *William Elphinstone and the Kingdom of Scotland, 1431–1514* (Aberdeen, 1985), 237.

4   *Aberdeen Breviarium.*

5   A. F. Pollard, 'Blew, William John (1808–1894)', rev. H. C. G. Matthew, *ODNB*, http://www.oxforddnb.com/view/article/2642 (accessed 24 June 2009).

6   Forbes, *Kalendars*, Appendix, 262 ff.

more complete texts; most notable in this context is its extensive use by W. J. Watson in his great *Celtic Place-Names of Scotland*.[7] But apart from the work of J. D. Galbraith and Alexander Boyle,[8] there has been little attempt in recent years to analyse the collection systematically or to identify its sources in place or time.

Problems of sources

The task of giving Scotland a large-scale national hagiography, which had previously been approached haphazardly, was taken in hand by William Elphinstone, bishop of Aberdeen, at the promptings of King James IV. The book is modelled on the English *Sarum Breviary*, but with important modifications: a large number of English local saints are excluded from the Calendar and their places are taken by Scottish saints, while other English feasts are downgraded in rank and Scottish ones elevated. There seems to have been a conscious attempt to spread the net over the whole of Scotland, to include saints from every diocese and to have a sprinkling of obscure and little-known local saints as well as national heroes such as St Ninian and St Margaret. Saints of the northeast, such as St Machar of Aberdeen, find a prominent place in *BA*, but his day was not required to be celebrated as a major feast except in the diocese of Aberdeen.

The sources used by *BA* were various. The historian Hector Boece tells us that Bishop Elphinstone made a collection of legends of saints 'sought out in many places' in a single volume, presumably preparatory to drawing up the propers of saints in the *Breviary*.[9] This Legendary has not survived. In some cases the source is clear enough: for example, the lessons for St Ninian (15 September; PE, fols 107r–110r) are drawn, rather slavishly, from the Preface and Chapter 1 of the *Vita Niniani* attributed to Ailred.[10] Another example of slavish copying is found in the office for St Brendan (16 May; PH, fols 98v–99r), part of which is drawn almost verbatim from chapters 2–4 of the popular *Navigatio Sancti Brendani*.[11] The narration, down to Brendan's visit with St Enda and his trip to Brandon Mountain in Co. Kerry, are faithfully

---

7 W. J. Watson, *The History of the Celtic Place-Names of Scotland* (Edinburgh, 1926; repr. 1989) [hereafter Watson, *CPNS*].

8 James D. Galbraith, 'The Sources of the Aberdeen Breviary' (University of Aberdeen, unpublished M. Litt. thesis, 1970); Alexander Boyle, 'Some saints' lives in the Breviary of Aberdeen', *Analecta Bollandiana* 94 (1976), 95–106; *idem*, 'Notes on Scottish saints', *IR* 32 (1981), 59–82.

9 Hector Boece, *Murthlacensium et Aberdonensium Episcoporum Vitae*, ed. Thomas Maitland, Bannatyne Club (Edinburgh, 1825), 68.

10 In Alexander Penrose Forbes, *Lives of SS Ninian and Kentigern*, Historians of Scotland 5 (Edinburgh, 1874), 137–57.

11 Carl Selmer, *Navigatio Sancti Brendani Abbatis from Early Latin Manuscripts* (Notre Dame, IN, 1959); many English translations, including by J. F. Webb and D. H. Farmer, *The Age of Bede* (Harmondsworth, 1983).

reproduced in *BA*; the story breaks off, rather unsatisfactorily, just as Brendan is about to embark on his voyage.

It is not always clear, however, whether the compilers of *BA* used a well known existing *vita* of a saint. For example, the lessons for St Fursey (16 January; PH, fols 32r–33v) mention a 'little book of his life', but this does not necessarily mean that the compilers used it. In fact, the lessons are drawn entirely from Bede's *Historia Ecclesiastica*.[12] In the case of St Kessog (10 March; PH, fols 66v–67r), venerated around Loch Lomond and at Auchterarder and elsewhere, the compilers seem to have had access to a *vita* originating at Luss on Loch Lomond, from which they extracted one miraculous episode from Kessog's boyhood, and a reference to his burial at Luss. This *vita* seems to have contained a garbled allusion to a practice of fostering the sons of sub-kings at the court of the over-king of Munster, which, if it is an allusion to the Eóganacht, is suggestive of considerable antiquity; but by the time it entered *BA*, the story was being interpreted in terms of late medieval chivalrous feasting.

An example of the complexity of the source problems of *BA* can be found in its material for the lessons for St Kentigern (13 January; PH, fols 27v–30v). These appear to derive not directly from Jocelin of Furness's *Vita Kentigerni*, but from one of its sources, the little volume described by Jocelin as *codiculum stilo Scottico dictatum*, 'written in a Gaelic style'; they are closely related to the canticles in the Sprouston Breviary.[13] There may be points where *BA* has preserved its 'Scotic' original more faithfully than Jocelin has done. For instance, *BA* describes how St Kentigern used to levitate at the *Sursum Corda* while saying mass: *Et cum 'Sursum corda' decanteret, corpus eius in aere a terra elevabatur*. Jocelin says only that while holding up his hands at the *Sursum corda*, exhorting others to do likewise, he raised his own (heart) to the Lord (*Dum enim elevatis in modum crucis manibus, 'Sursum corda' diceret, ad quod ceteros ammonuit, suum habebat ad Dominum*). Jocelin may here have suppressed or misunderstood a fantastic detail in his original, for his version is tame by comparison.[14]

For compiling its lessons for St Columba (9 June; PH, fols 102v–104v), *BA* appears to have used a later medieval abbreviation of Adomnán's *Vita Columbae* rather than *Vita Columbae* itself, although this was known in Scotland and was turned into Latin verses by a later sixteenth-century

---

12 *Bede's Ecclesiastical History of the English People*, eds Bertram Colgrave and R. A. B. Mynors (Oxford, 1969), 268 ff.

13 A new edition in the *Musica Scotica* series, edited by G.-M. Hair and B. Knott-Sharpe, is in preparation. Recorded as *Scottish Medieval Plainchant: The Miracles of St Kentigern*, Alan Tavener and Cappella Nova (Gaudeamus, 1997). The text is edited in Forbes, *Lives of SS Ninian and Kentigern*.

14 Alan Macquarrie, *The Saints of Scotland* (Edinburgh, 1997), 126.

commendator of Iona.[15] On the other hand, the three hymns for St Columba show evidence of being connected with a twelfth-century Irish *Betha* or *Life* composed in the north of Ireland, probably at Derry.[16] Likewise, in compiling an office for St Adomnán himself (24 September; PE, fols 114v–115r), *BA* has had access to a source which shows evidence of having been composed on Iona, possibly as early as the eighth century, which was also used in the tenth-century Irish *Betha Adamnáin*.[17] How this tradition survived and reached sixteenth-century Aberdeen is not clear; *BA* mentions the dedication to Adomnán at Forvie in Buchan, but does not assert that the kirk of Forvie was the source of the lessons.

It may be that the offices for Columba and Adomnán are not the only materials of Iona origin which are incorporated into *BA*. In view of Boece's statement that Elphinstone sought out ancient Scottish histories, 'especially in the Western Isles where are preserved the tombs of our former kings and the ancient monuments of our race',[18] we may by careful study be able to identify other offices which *BA* acquired from Iona. Possibly there was an 'Iona Breviary' or 'Iona Legendary' which was a component of the *propria sanctorum* in *BA*.

In the case of St Serf (1 July; PE, fols 15r–16v), the compilers of *BA* appear to have used a *Life* very closely related to the *vita* bound with Jocelin's *Vita Kentigerni* in a (probably) Glasgow MS now preserved in Dublin, and to the *vita* preserved at Loch Leven and incorporated by Prior Wyntoun into his *Cronykil*.[19] But the compilers claimed that St Serf was a Scot and a contemporary of St Palladius, while at the same time they knew of 'another St Serf, an Israelite by nationality, who at the time of the abbot St Adomnán shone with many miracles in the island of Portmoak' (that is, Loch Leven in Fife). For St Margaret of Scotland (16 November; PE, fols 162r–163r), the compilers have used Turgot's *Vita Margaretae*, but with very little direct quotation.[20] The account of the translation of St Margaret's relics at Dunfermline in 1250 (19 June; PE, fol. 1r–v) is connected with the account in Bower's *Scotichronicon*.[21]

---

15 *Adomnán's Life of Columba*, eds Alan Orr Anderson and Marjorie Ogilvie Anderson, 2nd edn (Oxford, 1991); Roderici Maclenii Hectorogenis Scotigathaelici Ionitae, *De Intuitu Prophetico D. Columbae Ionidos Liber* (Rome, 1549); cf. Richard Sharpe, 'The life of St Columba in latin verse by Roderick Maclean (1549)', *IR* 42 (1991), 111–32.

16 Máire Herbert, *Iona, Kells and Derry: the History and Hagiography of the Monastic Familia of Columba* (Oxford, 1988), 211–86.

17 *Betha Adamnáin: the Life of St Adamnán*, eds Máire Herbert and Pádraig Ó Riain, Irish Texts Society (London, 1988).

18 Boece, *Vitae*, ed. Maitland, 68.

19 Alan Macquarrie, '*Vita Sancti Servani*: the life of St Serf', *IR* 44 (1993), 122–52.

20 *Vita Margaretae Reginae*, in *Symeonis Dunelmensis Opera et Collectanea*, ed. John Hodgson Hinde, Surtees Society (Durham, 1868).

21 *Chron. Bower*, V.296–8.

A number of offices in *BA* are drawn from Bede's *Historia Ecclesiastica*, for example, Oswald (5 August; PE, fols 55r–56v), Aidan (31 August; PE, fols 95v–96v), Fursey (16 January; PH, fols 32r–33v) and Etheldreda (23 June; PE, fols 2v–3r), and quote extensively from that work, verbatim or nearly so.[22] The Lessons for St Cuthbert (20 March; PH, fols 76v–77r) are drawn from Bede's *Vita Sancti Cuthberti*, but with the exception of one passage (Lesson 5), Bede's words are severely abbreviated. Cuthbert's vision of the soul of St Aidan being borne to heaven, recounted in the office for St Aidan, comes from a source which mixes together words from Bede's *Vita Sancti Cuthberti* and from the anonymous *Life of St Cuthbert*.[23]

BA includes a good deal of local legend and tradition. For example, the lessons for St Patrick (17 March; PH, fols 70v–72r) allude to his supposed birth at Old Kilpatrick on the Clyde near Dumbarton, and also to traditions relating to 'St Patrick's Well' and 'St Patrick's Stone' near the kirkyard. These were important places of pilgrimage in the middle ages. Some Irish pilgrimage sites mentioned in the lessons, such as Croagh Patrick and 'St Patrick's Purgatory' in Lough Derg, are relatively late additions to the Patrician 'dossier'. The tradition linking Patrick's birth with Old Kilpatrick is found in the *Tripartite Life* of *ca* 900, but not in the *Book of Armagh* of about one hundred years earlier; this has implications for the dating of *kil-* names with dedications to Irish saints in Strathclyde.

There is a tendency in *BA* to claim saints as Scots who were in fact Irish. A good example here is St Finnbarr (26 September; PE, fol. 115r–v), venerated at Dornoch in Sutherland, the medieval cathedral of the diocese of Caithness, and at Kilbarr on Barra. *BA* makes him son of a Caithness nobleman related to the (otherwise unknown) local king Tigernach. There are *vitae* of St Finbar of Cork in Irish and Latin, in which Tigernach is a king in south Munster; the wording in *BA* looks closer to the Old Irish version, but because it is so short it is not possible to be certain.[24]

On the other hand, some claims of Scottishness in earlier sources are ignored. St Constantine (11 March; PH, fol. 67r–v), to whom there are important dedications at Kilchousland in Kintyre and at Govan, is claimed by Jocelin of Furness as a son of King Rhydderch of Glasgow, granted to his queen in old age in response to St Kentigern's prayers; but *BA* ignores this tradition and links him with the (British) royal house of Cornwall, stating that he became a monk in Ireland, then a missionary in Scotland, associated with Columba and Kentigern, and was martyred in Kintyre. *BA*'s compilers seem

---

[22] *Bede's Ecclesiastical History*, eds Colgrave and Mynors. *passim.*

[23] *Two Lives of St Cuthbert*, ed. and trans. Bertram Colgrave (Cambridge, 1940).

[24] *Vita Sancti Barri episcopi Corcagie*, in *Vitae Sanctorum Hiberniae*, ed. Charles Plummer, 2 vols (Oxford, 1910), I.65–74; *Betha Bhairre ó Chorcaigh*, in *Bethada Náem nÉrenn: Live of Irish Saints*, ed. Charles Plummer, 2 vols (Oxford, 1922), I.11–22; II.11–21.

to have had access here to a Kintyre tradition, and to have ignored Glasgow Cathedral's twelfth-century aggrandizement.

It is noteworthy that no saint included in *BA* is claimed to be a Pict. Some of them certainly or probably were Pictish: Adrian, Boniface, Drostan, Ethernan, Ethernasc, Fergus, Fittick, Gartnait (for Gervadius read Gernadius [9 November; PE, fol. 148r–v]), Lolan, Nechtan (Nathalanus), Serf, Talorcan, and possibly a few others, were certainly or probably Pictish. But at some point they have undergone a process of 'depictification', and have become Irishmen, Scots, Pannonians (that is, fellow-countrymen of St Martin of Tours), Gauls, or exotic visitors from the eastern Mediterranean. St Fittick's dedication at Torry by Aberdeen has become linked with St Photinus of Lyon (23 December; PH, fols 23r–24r), a second-century martyr whose death was described by Eusebius.[25] There may have been a conscious Gaelicisation of the church in Pictland about the tenth century, with native Pictish churchmen being 'rebranded' for political reasons.

A few continental saints make their way into *BA* with claims of Scottishness. The office for St Fiacre (30 August; PE, fols 93v–95v) may have come originally from Meaux. His popularity in late medieval Scotland may partly derive from his involvement in the death, from *la maladie de saint Fiacre*, of the detested King Henry V of England, which was gleefully reported in a number of Scottish chronicles.[26] The lessons for St Fursey of Péronne (16 January; PH, fols 32r–33v), however, are drawn from Bede's *Historia Ecclesiastica* rather than any continental source.[27] The office for St Rumbald of Mechlin (1 July; PE, fols 16v–17v) comes from that city, mentioning his relics there.[28] St Levin (12 November; PE, fols 157v–158v), 'greatly venerated in the town of *Gandava* [Ghent]', appears to have been an Englishman called Leofwyn who died at Deventer in the Netherlands, *ca* 770. Like St Willibrord of Utrecht (6 November; PE, fols 146v–147v), another English missionary to the Frisians, he had no discernable connection with Scotland, but *BA* attributes Scottish ancestry to both. Another example of a continental saint being expropriated to Scotland is St Kennera (29 October; PE, fols 133v–134v). In casting around for a legend for the saint of Kirkinner in Galloway, the compilers have lighted on a sermon for the feast day of St Cunera of Rhenen in the Netherlands, which associates her with St Ursula

---

[25] Eusebius, *The History of the Church*, ed. and trans. G. A. Williamson (Harmondsworth, 1965), 198; Boyle, 'Some saints' lives', 99–100.

[26] *Chron. Bower*, VIII.122–4; cf. *The Book of Pluscarden*, ed. Felix J. H. Skene, Historians of Scotland 10 (Edinburgh, 1880), 357–9.

[27] *Bede's Ecclesiastical History*, eds Colgrave and Mynors, 268 ff.

[28] *Acta Sanctorum*, eds Johannes Bollandus et al., 68 vols (Antwerp and Brussels, 1643–1940), *Iulii*, I.169 ff.

and the 11,000 virgins of Cologne.[29] The inclusion of these Netherlandish saints may reflect commercial and intellectual links in the later middle ages.

Some saints are so obscure that it is impossible to speak with any confidence of their origins. It is not certain that St Romanus (23 October; PE, fol. 132r), historically a seventh-century bishop of Rouen, should be considered among the Scottish saints at all; but Forbes says that St Rowan or Romhan was commemorated at Monzievaird, where his bell was kept.[30]

Hymns, responsories and antiphons

For most of the saints whom it includes, *BA* provides a prayer and set of lessons (three, six, or nine), with instructions for the use of common hymns, responsories and antiphons. In the case of a small number of native saints, patrons of cathedral churches or otherwise of great importance, it presents proper hymns, responsories and antiphons for Vespers, Matins and Lauds as well. These are Kentigern (Glasgow Cathedral), Columba (Iona Abbey and Dunkeld Cathedral), Blane (Dunblane Cathedral), Machar (Aberdeen Cathedral), Moluag (Lismore), Magnus (Orkney) and Ninian (Whithorn); see also the remarks about St Fiacre below. Some patrons of cathedrals (for example, St Finnbarr of Dornoch) do not receive such elaborate treatment; probably this reflects the availability of sources to the compilers. In general, the proper verses show signs of originating at the cathedral church where the saint was venerated (or in the case of Columba, Iona Abbey). The office for the patronal festival of St Andrew's Cathedral makes no mention of Scottish connections.

These verses present interesting problems. They show a rich variety of metres and styles, ranging from rhyming and unrhyming hexameters to Sapphic metre, and syllabic verse with different rhyming and syllabic patterns. The responsories in particular were intended for quite elaborate melismatic settings (that is, with several notes to each syllable), with repeated sections and (at the end of each Nocturn) the *Gloria Patri*. The office for St Ninian, unique among the Scottish offices, also has a *prosa*, twelve lines of rhyming verse of fifteen syllables each, which would have been sung with a single note to each syllable. This came at the end of Matins just before Lauds (where some offices prescribe the hymn *Te Deum laudamus*).

The poems are not all of high quality, and some of them verge on the banal and repetitive. Often words are compressed to fit the metre, and sometimes this is carried to extremes which would not meet the approval of classical scholars. The rules of grammar are stretched to, and sometimes beyond,

---

[29] *Acta Sanctorum, Iunii*, III.55–69, at 59–60; Boyle, 'Notes on Scottish saints', 62; Boyle, 'Some saints' lives', 105–6.
[30] Forbes, *Kalendars*, 442.

extremes. Some verses describe a miracle in very cryptic and allusive style, which is difficult to follow especially if the miracle to which allusion is made is not found in a prose lesson or in any other source. This problem is especially acute in the offices for St Blane (10 August; PE, fols 86v–87v and 173v–174v)[31] and St Moluag (25 June; PE, fols 5v–8r), where there is no obvious identifiable source.

An exception to the above remarks is found in the office for St Fiacre, where stylistically the sung sections are mostly unlike the bulk of the poetry in the offices for local saints in *BA*, and are in effect passages of prose. Since the lessons concern the foundation of Fiacre's monastery at Meaux, that place will be the ultimate origin of this material, which would explain the different treatment of the sung sections of the office.

Some of the verses are important, and all are worthy of study. The hymns for St Columba, as has been mentioned, show an interesting connection with the twelfth-century Middle Irish *Life of Columba*. The presence of one of the hymns for St Columba in the fourteenth-century *Inchcolm Antiphoner* confirms that some at least of these hymns are earlier than the sixteenth century; in fact, probably they all are. The verses for St Kentigern appear to have a different source from the prose lessons in the same office. The verses for St Blane show that his name, Bláán, latinised as Blaanus, was still a disyllable in the medieval period. There are many allusions to miracles or stories from a *vita* which are not mentioned in prose lessons or other sources. So the verse sections are an important supplement to our knowledge about the *cultus* of certain saints.

The verse sections remind us of one important point which might otherwise be forgotten: all of this material was intended to be performed in church as part of an act of worship. Sadly, *BA* contains no indications of the music to which the material was to be sung: at the time of its publication music printing was still in its infancy.[32] Manuscripts such as the *Inchcolm Antiphoner* and *Sprouston Breviary* help to fill some of the gaps in our knowledge.[33] It might be possible for musicologists to reconstruct some of the music for the offices in *BA* from these sources and the general corpus of Western music contained in the Sarum rite and the *Liber Usualis*.[34] In the meantime, the poetry in *BA* reminds us how much of this material was intended to be sung.

---

[31] Alan Macquarrie, 'The Office for St Blane (10 August) in the Aberdeen Breviary', *IR* 52 (2001), 111–31.

[32] Percy A. Scholes, *Oxford Companion to Music* (Oxford, 1939), s.v. Printing of Music; Willi Apel, *Harvard Dictionary of Music*, 2nd edn (Cambridge, MA, 1969), s.v. Printing of Music. The earliest printing of music in Scotland was by Robert Leprevick of Edinburgh in 1564; Scholes, *Oxford Companion*, 752.

[33] Isobel Woods, '"Our awin Scottis use": chant usage in medieval Scotland', *Journal of the Royal Musical Association* 112 (1986–7), 21–37; John Purser, *Scotland's Music* (Edinburgh, 1992), 37–56.

[34] Monks of Solemnes, *Liber Usualis* (Tournai, 1953).

Latin prose style in BA

Although much more detailed study is required, it is worth making a few tentative preliminary observations about the Latin prose style in *BA*.

In general, there is some quite ambitious and florid 'renaissance' language in the most generalised offices, while the more specific, narrative or circumstantial ones tend to use simpler prose. A good example of florid prose is in the lessons for St Modan (4 February; PH, fols 51r–52r), which provide no circumstantial detail, apart from a statement that Modan converted the area round Falkirk, 'on the west side of the River Forth or Scottish Sea', before retiring to Rosneath. These attempt to explain the name Modan as *modos odens uanos*, 'hating vain ways', a far remove from its Gaelic origins.[35] Other examples of sets of Lessons with florid ambitious prose and little or no circumstantial detail are to be found in the offices for SS Ethernan (2 December; PH, fols 6v–7v), Manirus (18 December; PH, fols 19v–20v) (which similarly has a fanciful Latin derivation for the saint's name: *manendo rure*, 'by remaining in the country'), Marnan (1 March; PH, fols 60r–61r) and Kevoca (13 March; PH, fols 68v–69r). The last-named has changed gender as well as having lost almost all circumstantial detail: Caomhóc or Cóemhóc was originally a man's name, but she is venerated as a female at St Quivox in Ayrshire.[36] Lessons 3 and 7–9 in the office of St Mayhota (23 December; fols 21v ff.) show similar characteristics, and are particularly corrupt and difficult to make sense of, with several missing words, confused word order, and seemingly ungrammatical constructions. These examples may all be from the hand of a single author whose ambition to write florid prose may have exceeded the compositors' ability to understand it. The precentor of Aberdeen at the time was Archibald Lindsay, and one might speculate that he had a part in drawing together these offices.[37]

There are a few examples of quotations from classical writers: Forbes detects an echo from Terence in the office for St Lolan.[38] Printed editions of the plays of Terence became available from the 1470s. Among the most important stylistic influences are the Vulgate, which is freely quoted and adapted, and Sulpicius's *Vita Sancti Martini*. A number of offices for saints for which Bede's *Historia Ecclesiastica* is the principal source (for example, Oswald, Aidan, Fursey, Etheldreda) quote extensively from that work, verbatim or nearly so, and show characteristics of Bede's distinctive Latin style. For example, in the office for St Oswald the word *cepit* with an infinitive is used four times, and *ceperunt* once, in the course of some 750 words. A few of the legends show distinctive characteristics: that for St Kennera, mentioned

---

[35] Watson, *CPNS*, 289–90, argued that his name was originally M'Aedhán.
[36] *Ibid.*, 189–90; Forbes, *Kalendars*, 374–5.
[37] Macfarlane, *Elphinstone*, 207–8, 240.
[38] Forbes, *Kalendars*, 379.

above (29 October) is a little unusual, being a well-constructed short story with some elegant turns of phrase. The Lessons for St Brigit (1 February; PH, fols 45v–46v), by contrast, are a catalogue of fantastic miracles briefly told in unadorned language, characteristic of her hagiographic tradition. The offices for St Patrick (17 March; PH, fols 70v–72r) and St Boniface (16 March; PH, fols 69r–70v) conclude with lists of statistics. The Lessons for St Colmóc (6 June; PH, fols 100v–102r) have a very Irish flavour, with allusions to various Irish kings and to a band of travelling poets.

There are some examples of unusual words. For example, the legal term *certioratus*, 'having been informed', makes several appearances, although it is rare in non-legal contexts: Sulpicius Severus, author of the very influential *Vita Sancti Martini*, was a lawyer by training. Genuinely esoteric words, however, are fairly rare. The odd spelling *probleumata* in the office for St Adomnán might be thought of as a 'graecified' spelling (perhaps influenced by προβούλευμα, 'preliminary decree'). *Uranica*, 'heavenly', in the office for St Columba (from 'ουρανός) is also unusual. St Munn (21 October; PE, fols 131r–132r) is said to have been visited by a heavenly *paranimphus*, 'companion' (παράνυμφος = bridesmaid). There are few other examples. These three examples certainly or possibly have Iona connections, but that may not be significant. They are perhaps more likely to be attempts at 'renaissance' Latin by a later medieval editor, rather than traces of esoteric language in the source. Where *BA* has *probleumata*, *Betha Adamnáin* uses *ceist*, an Irish loan-word from Latin *quaestio*, which might suggest that that was what was in the Latin original.[39] In describing Columba's heavenly visions, Adomnán usually uses *angelicae apparationes*, or similar words.[40] The *vitae* of Fintan Munnu, from which the office for St Munn is derived, are in mostly rather plain unadorned language, and use the common word *angelus* at this point.[41]

There is, however, no single characteristic style which permeates the whole. The prose of the offices gives the impression of having been drawn together from a wide range of sources with a number of different characteristics.[42]

The text abounds in misprints, missing words, and spelling mistakes. It is not always clear whether some of these are eccentric medieval spellings or simple misprints. On the whole, though, spelling is conventional rather than eccentric. Missing words are sometimes difficult to detect, more so in

---

[39] *Betha Adamnáin*, eds Herbert and Ó Riain, 48–9; dative plural *cestaib(h)*.

[40] *Adomnán's Life of Columba*, eds Anderson and Anderson, 6, 182, and Book 3, *passim*.

[41] *Vitae Sanctorum Hiberniae ex codice olim Salmanticensi nunc Bruxellensi*, ed. W. W. Heist, Société des Bollandistes (Brussels, 1965), 198–209, at 206–7; *Vitae Sanctorum Hiberniae*, ed. Plummer, II.226–40, at 235–6.

[42] This conclusion differs somewhat from that of Boyle: 'A linguistic analysis of the text would seem to show that … there is not such a diversity of either style or treatment … as to convince us that they were simply printed without either being edited or re-written.' Boyle, 'Some saints' lives', 97.

the prose lessons than in the verse sections, where syllable-counting easily reveals omissions. Sometimes peculiarities of word order may be the result of a compositor's error: an entire sentence is misplaced in the office for St Levin, clearly by a compositor's mistake, and the inversion of two clauses in the office for St Maelrubai (27 August; PE, fols 89v–91r) probably has the same cause.

Conclusions

It might seem that the remarks above raise more questions than they answer. A new edition of the Scottish saints' legends in *BA* is a major *desideratum* in Scottish church history and hagiography, and is actively in preparation as the five hundredth anniversary of its first publication approaches. It is hoped that such an edition, with more reliable text, translations and notes, will make for greater convenience for study and will help to open up this source for scholarship in the future.

Appendix

Saints claimed to be Scottish or in some way connected with Scotland in the Aberdeen Breviary

Part I: Saints of Winter (and Spring)		*Pars Hiemalis*
St Ethernan, bishop and confessor	2 December	fol. 6v
St Drostan, abbot	14 December	fol. 19r
St Manirus, bishop and confessor	18 December	fol. 19v
St Ethernasc, bishop and confessor	22 December	fol. 21v
St Mayhota, virgin	23 December	fol. 21v
St Caran, bishop and confessor	23 December	fol. 23r
St Photinus, bishop and martyr	23 December	fol. 23r
St Kentigerna, matron, mother of Abbot Fillan	7 January	fol. 24v
St Nechtan, bishop and confessor	8 January	fol. 25v
St Fillan, abbot and confessor	9 January	fol. 26v
St Kentigern, bishop and confessor	13 January	fol. 27v
St Fursey, abbot	16 January	fol. 32r
St Winnin, bishop and confessor	21 January	fol. 38r
St Voloc, bishop and confessor	29 January	fol. 44v
St Glassie, bishop and confessor	30 January	fol. 45v
St Modoc, bishop and confessor	31 January	fol. 45v
St Brigid, virgin	1 February	fol. 45v
St Modan, abbot and confessor	4 February	fol. 51r
St Ronan, bishop	10 February	fol. 54v
St Finnan, bishop and confessor	17 February	fol. 55v

St Colmán, bishop and confessor	18 February	fol. 56r
St Monan, confessor	1 March	fol. 59v
St Marnan, bishop and confessor	1 March	fol. 60r
St Adrian and companions, martyrs	4 March	fol. 62v
St Baldred, bishop and confessor	6 March	fol. 63r
St Duthac, bishop and confessor	8 March	fol. 65r
St Kessog, bishop and confessor	10 March	fol. 66v
St Constantine, king and martyr	11 March	fol. 67r
St Kevoca, virgin	13 March	fol. 68v
St Boniface, bishop and confessor	16 March	fol. 69r
St Patrick, bishop and confessor	17 March	fol. 70v
St Finian, bishop and confessor	18 March	fol. 72r
St Cuthbert, bishop and confessor	20 March	fol. 76v
St Rule, abbot	29 March	fol. 82r
St Gilbert, bishop and confessor	1 April	fol. 83r
St Magnus, martyr	16 April	fol. 87r
St Donnan, abbot	17 April	fol. 87r
St Asaph, bishop and confessor	1 May	fol. 92r
Translation of St Andrew, apostle	9 May	fol. 96r
St Comgall, abbot and confessor	12 May	fol. 97v
St Brendan, abbot and confessor	16 May	fol. 98v
St Colmóc, bishop and confessor	6 June	fol. 100v
St Columba, abbot and confessor	9 June	fol. 102v
St Ternan, bishop and confessor	12 June	fol. 105v

Part II: Saints of Summer (and Autumn)		*Pars Estiualis*
Translation of Queen Margaret of Scotland	19 June	fol. 1r
St Etheldreda, virgin	23 June	fol. 2v
St Moluag, bishop and confessor	25 June	fol. 5v
St Serf, bishop and confessor	1 July	fol. 15r
St Rumbald, bishop and martyr	1 July	fol. 16v
St Palladius, bishop and confessor, apostle of the Scots	4 July	fol. 24r
St Tenew, matron, mother of St Kentigern	15 July	fol. 34v
St Oswald, king and martyr	5 August	fol. 45r
St Blane, bishop and confessor	10 August	fol. 76v, 173v
St Ebba, virgin	23 August	fol. 87r
St Irchard, bishop and confessor	24 August	fol. 89r
St Maelrubai, abbot and martyr	27 August	fol. 89v
St Fiacre, abbot and confessor	30 August	fol. 93v
St Aidan, bishop and confessor	31 August	fol. 95v
Translation of St Cuthbert, bishop	4 September	fol. 97r
St Mirren, bishop and confessor	15 September	fol. 106r
St Ninian, bishop and confessor	15 September	fol. 107r
St Lolan, bishop and confessor	23 September	fol. 113v

St Adomnán, abbot and confessor	24 September	fol. 114v
St Finnbarr, bishop and confessor	26 September	fol. 115r
St Machan, bishop and confessor	28 September	fol. 116v
St Conval, confessor	28 September	fol. 117r
St Triduana, virgin	8 October	fol. 122v
St Kenneth, abbot	11 October	fol. 125r
St Comgan, abbot	13 October	fol. 126r
SS Finnchán and Finndoch, virgins	13 October	fol. 126v
St Etheldreda, [virgin]	16 October	fol. 128r
St Colmán, bishop and confessor	16 October	fol. 128r
St Rule, abbot	17 October	fol. 128r
St Munn, abbot	21 October	fol. 131r
St Marnock, bishop and confessor	25 October	fol. 132r
St Bean, bishop and confessor	26 October	fol. 132v
St Kennera, virgin and martyr	29 October	fol. 133v
St Talorcan, bishop and confessor	30 October	fol. 134r
St Begha, virgin	31 October	fol. 136r
SS Baya and Maura, virgins	3 November	fol. 145v
St Englacius, abbot	3 November	fol. 146r
St Willibrord, bishop and confessor	6 November	fol. 146v
St Moroc, bishop and confessor	8 November	fol. 147v
St Gartnait, confessor	9 November	fol. 148r
St Machar, bishop and confessor	12 November	fol. 154v
St Levin, bishop and martyr	12 November	fol. 157v
St Devenick, bishop and confessor	13 November	fol. 160v
St Modan, bishop and confessor	14 November	fol. 161r
St Machutus, bishop and confessor	15 November	fol. 161v
St Margaret, queen of Scotland	16 November	fol. 162r
St Fergus, bishop and confessor	18 November	fol. 173v
St Maiden, virgin	19 November	fol. 153v

9

MOTHERS AND THEIR SONS:
MARY AND JESUS IN SCOTLAND, 1450–1560

Audrey-Beth Fitch

In the past few decades there has been a great deal of interest expressed in the history of the family in medieval Europe, particularly the emotional bonds between parents and children. Analysing royal families is one place to start exploring familial bonds. Lois Huneycutt has begun the process for Scottish history by studying St Margaret of Scotland (*ob.* 1093) and her children.[1] Investigating the portrayal of the relationship between the Blessed Virgin Mary and Jesus is another route to understanding affective familial relations. Scots were children of Mary and siblings of Jesus, believing that a fuller understanding of Mary and Jesus's relationship brought them closer to salvation. They were taught that Mary and Jesus shared a close emotional bond forged through a lifetime of interaction. Jesus began life as a nursing infant clinging to His mother's arms, and ended it as a voluntary sacrifice for human sin. His ascension into heaven, and Mary's later assumption, did not break this tie. Mother and son remained close, working to rescue humanity from sin. Lay people were taught about the Trinity, but tended to distinguish between Jesus and God; Mary was believed to have allied herself with the Son rather than the Father. This mother-son alliance gave humanity hope for salvation, for Mary's determination to help people at Judgement was matched by her influence over Jesus. Whether as human son or resurrected king, Jesus appeared willing to forgive sinners at His mother's request.[2]

While in principle women were deprived of authority publicly and privately, in practice they followed Mary's example, exerting influence through sons whom they had nurtured materially and spiritually. In Scotland, there is little direct discussion of maternal influence prior to the Reformation, but there are hints about the ideals governing filial relationships. Mary's pious, nurturing,

---

[1] Lois L. Huneycutt, 'The idea of the perfect princess: the life of Saint Margaret in the reign of Matilda II, 1100–1118', *Anglo-Norman Studies* 12 (1989), 81–97, and her 'Images of queenship in the high middle ages', *The Haskins Society Journal* 1 (1989), 61–71, at 70.

[2] Marina Warner, *Alone of All Her Sex: The Myth and Cult of the Virgin Mary* (London, 1976; rev. 2000).

compassionate, forgiving, protective, and mediating characteristics were shared to a large degree by Jesus, suggesting a pedagogical role, and clerics urged queens to set an example to their families.[3] Writers celebrated mothers who directed the spiritual education of children, encouraged husbands to act with justice and mercy, defended the helpless, and aided the poor by dispensing alms.[4] Scotland's late medieval kings appear to have shared their mothers' pious outlook. Like their mothers they regularly attended religious services, valued personal prayer, made pilgrimages, distributed alms, and supported the Church through gifts and foundations.

John Major (1467–1550), author of *A History of Greater Britain* (1521), deemed David I (1124–53), son of St Margaret of Scotland, a worthy royal exemplar to Scotland's late medieval kings. The king had a great 'regard for religion'; he cultivated personal piety and urged others to follow his lead, particularly his family and courtiers. He was an 'observant Christian' who regularly attended church services, remained chaste after his wife's death, and trained his children in virtue by word and example. He expelled people from court who exhibited too many vices, kept a 'cloister of religious persons' there, and supported the Church by founding and endowing numerous abbeys. Finally, he was concerned about justice and fair treatment of the poor, character traits John Major attributed to the king's temperance, fortitude and clemency.[5]

St Margaret of Scotland, the king's strong-willed mother, was an acknowledged saint, canonised in the mid-thirteenth century. Illuminations depicting her are to be found in late medieval prayer books,[6] and her reputation was enhanced through visual comparisons to the Blessed Virgin Mary. In the burgh seal of Queensferry (1529), a haloed and crowned St Margaret stands on a curved boat holding her gospel book and a sceptre surmounted by a fleur-de-lys.[7] This depiction echoes the ubiquitous image of the queen of heaven standing on a crescent moon. St Margaret's biographer and confessor Turgot (*ob.* 1115) constructed St Margaret as a saint and queenly ideal[8] by emphasising her lifelong pursuit of holiness and adherence to the rules of the

---

3 Huneycutt, 'Images of queenship', 66–8; Late medieval depictions of St Anne often showed her in the act of teaching her daughter Mary to read. See Michael Camille, *Mirror in Parchment, the Luttrell Psalter and the Making of Medieval England* (London, 1998), 161–2; M. T. Clanchy, *From Memory to Written Record, England 1066–1307*, 2nd edn (Oxford, 1993), 13; Pamela Sheingorn, '"The Wise Mother": the image of St. Anne teaching the Virgin Mary', *Gesta* 32 (1993), 69–80.

4 Huneycutt, 'Images of queenship', 67, and Turgot, *Saint Margaret*, ed. and intro. Iain Macdonald (Edinburgh, 1993), 28–9, 31–2, 43–4, 46.

5 John Major, *A History of Greater Britain, as well as England as Scotland (1521)*, ed. and trans. Archibald Constable, SHS (Edinburgh, 1892), 135, 138–9, 141–2.

6 For example, NLS, MS 10271, Blackadder Prayer Book, fol. 101r.

7 R. M. Urquhart, *Scottish Burgh and County Heraldry* (London, 1973), 179–80.

8 Huneycutt, 'Perfect princess', 88–9.

'ars moriendi'.[9] Turgot reports that she died as a good christian, first hearing mass in the oratory, then receiving the last rites. She expressed contrition for her sins, prayed continuously, and kissed and held the Black Cross. In his description of St Margaret's death, Turgot represents the ideal mother-son bond as a close and emotional one. When the future King David enters the sickroom to tell St Margaret that his father and brother are dead, he finds her at death's door. Turgot reports: 'What must then have been his distress? What his agony of soul? He stood there in a strait, with everything against him; whither to turn he knew not . . . the loss of his dearest mother, whom he saw lying almost dead before his eyes, pierced his heart with the sharpest pain.'[10] A successful practitioner of the 'ars moriendi' manages to resist the temptation of demons, in particular the temptation to despair; the queen did not despair as she lay dying. Her response to hearing news of the deaths of her husband and eldest son was not to rail against God and thus succumb to the wiles of the devil. Rather, she praised God for having given her an opportunity to cleanse sin by enduring the pain this knowledge gave her.[11]

St Margaret was also represented as having deeply influenced her husband King Malcolm III (1058–93) in religious matters. According to Turgot she encouraged the king to cultivate personal piety through prayer and service to the poor, and to express his religiosity by founding churches and exercising royal authority in a just manner.[12] Furthermore, with regard to her children, in particular her son David and daughter Edith or Matilda, she is presented as having been as great a model as Mary was for Jesus. David spent his early years with her, and later joined his pious sister at the court of her English husband Henry I. About 1100, Queen Matilda asked Turgot to write a *vita* of her mother, and thereafter the queen is reputed to have lived her life in a manner remarkably similar to that of her mother. Queen Matilda 'mothered' the kingdom and set an example for her children by intervening in state affairs, supporting the Church, aiding the poor, directing the spiritual educa-tion of her children, and displaying personal piety.[13]

St Margaret's relationship with her children was close not only because of natural bonds of affection, but also because she was concerned for their spir-itual welfare. Apart from founding a church of the Holy Trinity to ensure their earthly and heavenly prosperity,[14] she also directed their religious education.

> She would often call them to her, and, as far as their age would allow, instruct them concerning Christ and the faith of Christ, and carefully endeavour to admonish them to always fear Him ... that they might acknowledge their Maker in the faith

---

[9] Turgot, *Saint Margaret*, ed. Macdonald, 43, 50.
[10] *Ibid.*, 58–9.
[11] *Ibid.*, 60–1.
[12] *Ibid.*, 31, 35–6; Major, *History*, ed. Constable, 130, 132; *Chron. Bower*, III.71–5.
[13] Huneycutt, 'Perfect princess', 84, 87–91, 97; Iain Macdonald, 'Introduction', in Turgot, *Saint Margaret*, ed. Macdonald, 13. Cf. *Chron. Bower*, III.123.
[14] Turgot, *Saint Margaret*, ed. Macdonald, 25.

that works through love ... and loving Him attain to the glory of the heavenly kingdom.[15]

The queen's concern for her children's education continued as she lay dying. She asked Turgot not only to pray for her soul and celebrate mass on her behalf, but also to 'take some care of my sons and daughters, pour out your affection upon them, above all things teach them to fear and love God, and never cease from instructing them'.[16] The queen's daughter Matilda also accepted this role of spiritual guide.[17]

Like her son David and daughter Matilda, St Margaret was often portrayed as assuming responsibility for religious matters beyond her family. At court, she was said to have delighted in good works, urged the worthy to greater feats of goodness, and admonished the wicked. Turgot claims that she tried to influence ecclesiastical policy, expressing outrage that some Scots avoided taking Communion at Easter. A 'most devoted servant and mother' for Jesus' sake', she waited on the poor, notably small children, during Advent and Lent, washing their feet and distributing food.[18] Following her mother's example, at Easter-time in 1105 Queen Matilda washed the feet of lepers. She invited her brother David to join her, but he rejected her offer.[19] Although his own father had joined his mother in serving the poor, King David may have believed that this activity was more appropriate to mothers than fathers. Turgot did describe feeding the poor as the activity of 'a most devoted servant and mother'.[20]

Regardless of the historical accuracy of Turgot's *vita* of St Margaret, it did serve as an advisory text for her daughter, and reflects contemporary notions of ideal queenship. The image of Margaret as pious christian, mother and queen, a very 'pattern of the virtues', survived into the late medieval period.[21] Given the norms of late medieval society, it is entirely likely that Major's contemporaries accepted that Margaret's religious values and priorities had formed David I's character and outlook, just as contemporary queens influenced their own offspring. Certainly David's well-attested concern for personal piety and the spiritual welfare of family, court and country paralleled that of his mother.

John Major used David I's career to demonstrate that it was possible and desirable for kings to follow in their mothers' footsteps by living spiritually laudable lives.[22] Most late medieval royal sons may have failed to replicate

---

[15] *Ibid.*, 28–9.

[16] *Ibid.*, 55–6.

[17] Huneycutt, 'Images of queenship', 68 and 70.

[18] Turgot, *Saint Margaret*, ed. Macdonald, 24–5, 27, 34–5, 37–8, 47–9.

[19] John of Tynemouth, *Life of St. Margaret*, cited in Huneycutt, 'Perfect princess', 92.

[20] Turgot, *Saint Margaret*, ed. Macdonald, 48–9; Major, *History*, ed. Constable, 130.

[21] Huneycutt, 'Images of queenship', 67, Turgot, *Saint Margaret*, ed. Macdonald, 27, and image of Margaret the Queen, in NLS, MS 10271, Blackadder Prayer Book, fol. 101r.

[22] Major, *History*, ed. Constable, 130.

David's adherence to maternal example, but the evidence suggests that the notion of following a mother's lead in spiritual matters remained a powerful ideal and, perhaps, in some measure a social reality. In so doing, kings could portray themselves as heeding the advice of women who had nurtured them as children, guided them in adolescence, and worried about them in adulthood. According to James IV (1488–1513), his grandmother Mary of Gueldres (*ob.* 1463, m. 1449) set an impressive example of religiosity. The queen introduced the Observant Franciscans to Scotland[23] and undertook several ecclesiastical building projects. Generous with alms and reputedly personally devout, James III (1460–88) apparently inherited his mother's sensibilities. He continued work on Holy Trinity collegiate church, which his mother had begun, although it may have been the brainchild of his father James II (1437–60).[24] James III also founded the collegiate church of Restalrig and a chapel to house the relics of St Triduana.[25] According to Hector Boece (*ca* 1465–1536), the king expressed personal devotion by crying and praying at images of Jesus or Mary.[26]

James III's wife Margaret of Denmark (*ca* 1457–86, m. 1469) was described in an Italian *vita* as 'most gentle, forbearing and devoted, and extremely religious' and very willing to intercede for others.[27] She also was reputedly kind to the poor.[28] She joined her husband as a 'cordial friend' to the Observant Franciscans,[29] and made a pilgrimage with him to St Ninian's, Whithorn, in July 1474, probably to give thanks for the birth of their son James.[30] James testified to his wife's sanctity and virtue in a letter to her brother Hans after her death, suggesting that she had set an excellent example for their children:

> She is immortal through her virtue. She lived in great sanctity and devotion, and is now translated from this mortal life of misery to immortality and eternal joy ... He will give thanks that his children grew up under such a mother.[31]

Even if Margaret's qualities were embellished for the sake of her brother, the letter gives some indication of the anticipated influence of a queen on

---

[23] 'James IV to Julius II, 1 February 1507', in *James IV Letters*, 55.
[24] Norman Macdougall, *James III. A Political Study* (Edinburgh, 1982), 62.
[25] For which, see Alastair A. MacDonald, 'The chapel of Restalrig: royal folly or venerable shrine?', in *A Palace in the Wild: Essays on Vernacular Culture and Humanism in Late-medieval and Renaissance Scotland*, eds L. A. J. R. Houwen, A. A. MacDonald and S. L. Mapstone (Leuven, 2000), 27–59, and Helen Brown, 'Saint Triduana of Restalrig? Locating a saint and her cult in late medieval Lothian and beyond', in *Images of Medieval Sanctity: Essays in Honour of Gary Dickson*, ed. Debra Higgs Strickland (Leiden, 2007), 45–70.
[26] Ranald Nicholson, *Scotland. The Later Middle Ages* (Edinburgh, 1974), 470–1.
[27] S. B. Chandler, 'An Italian Life of Margaret, Queen of James III', *SHR* 32 (1952), 52–7.
[28] See, for example, her almsgiving in 1474. *TA*, I.72.
[29] 'James IV to Julius II, 1 February 1507', in *James IV Letters*, 55.
[30] Macdougall, *James III*, 110. James III tried to convince the papacy to canonise Margaret after her death in 1486. *Ibid.*, 139.
[31] NAS, RH2/8/35, James III to John King of Denmark and Norway, after July 1486, fols 26–7, pp. 18–19.

her royal offspring. Moreover, Margaret's son James IV does seem to have followed in his mother's footsteps, particularly in terms of personal piety. This is perhaps not surprising since he was brought up in Margaret's household at Stirling, and remained there after her death in July 1486.[32] Described by contemporaries as extremely pious, truthful and humane, James's charitable activities were even broader in scope than his mother's.[33] Bishop John Leslie (?1527–96) celebrated his piety. He argued that he had ruled in a 'religious fashion',[34] a claim similar to that made by John Major for David I.[35] More than devout, King James was 'inflamed' with religious spirit, providing an excellent example to his subjects of that 'burning love' for Jesus which honoured Him by its intensity and cleansed them for Communion.[36] The king, according to Leslie, feared God, was well read in the Bible, and strictly observed Church ritual, devoutly hearing mass and other divine services. He built churches, located relics, visited cloisters, and donated numerous ornaments, chalices and other gifts to churches and monasteries. Named 'protector of the Christian faith', he insisted that prelates be respected. In particular, he was the 'devoted son and defender' of the Observant Franciscans. It has been suggested that the king's fear of Judgement may have been exacerbated by his guilt over his father's death. James's piety may have been exaggerated by sixteenth-century commentators, but there can be little doubt that he was a conventionally, some might say ostentatiously, devout monarch.[37]

James V would later claim that he saw his grandmother, Margaret of Denmark, as his great religious exemplar, although as this assertion was made in a letter to her brother King Frederick of Denmark in 1532, it should be treated with some caution. In the letter James attributes his love for the Observant Franciscan order to his great-grandfather John (*sic*) late King of Denmark, but even more so to his grandmother. He also acknowledges that she was his father's inspiration, and that it was public knowledge that Margaret of Denmark gave James IV his 'strong sense of duty to God'.[38]

James IV's wife Margaret Tudor (1487–1541, m. 1503) also seems to have been devout in an entirely orthodox way, crediting her recovery from childbirth to her husband's piety and the aid of St Ninian, and joining him on

---

[32] Macdougall, *James III*, 218.

[33] For example, John Leslie, *The Historie of Scotland*, ed. E. G. Cody, STS, 2 vols (Edinburgh, 1895), II.107, 123; 'Letter of Don Pedro de Ayala to Ferdinand and Isabella', in *Early Travellers in Scotland*, ed. P. Hume Brown (Edinburgh, 1891), 41.

[34] Leslie, *Historie*, ed. Cody, II.147.

[35] Major, *History*, ed. Constable, 138.

[36] Leslie, *Historie*, ed. Cody, II.107, 147; For the 'burning love', see 'Off ye birnyng lufe and gret effectioun yat we suld haue to resaue our saluiour Iesu Crist', in *Devotional Pieces in Verse and Prose*, ed. J. A.W. Bennett, STS (Edinburgh, 1955), 250, lines 347–8.

[37] Norman Macdougall, *James IV* (East Linton, 1997).

[38] 'Letter to Frederick I, 25 December 1532', in *James V Letters*, 231. The letter seems to have misidentified John (who was actually James' great-uncle, Hans) as the Scottish king's great-grandfather (who was Christian I, John's father).

pilgrimage to Whithorn after giving birth. Her husband had already made one journey on foot, believing that only God could save the queen as she lay ill in childbirth.[39] Their son James V grew to be a staunch defender of traditional christianity, deeply involved in national anti-heresy campaigns.[40] His personal piety and orthodoxy were indisputable, his traditional outlook reflected in his commitment to alms-giving. For example, from September 1540 to September 1541 he donated £270 in alms.[41]

Intercession is an area where queenly influence over kings could be publicly demonstrated. As prominent intercessors on behalf of erring subjects, queens demonstrated to husbands and sons that power and authority should be tempered with mercy. Mary, the supreme intercessor, also had set an example to her son, and her intercessory activities legitimised those of earthly queens. Following Mary's example made queenly intercession more likely to succeed. That is, a humble demeanour, entreaty rather than demand, tears and a kneeling attitude, were most helpful in bringing a reduced sentence in the afterlife. Mary's humility was central to Jesus's success in pacifying God the Father.[42] A variety of Annunciation scenes depicted Mary as a humble maiden, eyes downcast and kneeling in prayer.[43]

There is plenty of evidence that the Marian intercessory model was familiar to queens. The Coronation of the Virgin, hands joined and arms upraised, was adopted as a common queenly image. English queens interceded for royal pardons as part of their coronation ceremony,[44] and the foreign queens Margaret Tudor, Margaret of Denmark and Joan Beaufort (*ca* 1400–45, m. 1424) took seriously their intercessory roles. Margaret Tudor prayed earnestly on behalf of her rebellious second husband, Archibald, sixth earl of Angus (*ca* 1489–1557),[45] and Margaret of Denmark intervened on behalf of John, fourth Lord of the Isles (*ob.* 1503), against whom James III had gone to war in 1476. The king stripped him of the title earl of Ross and annexed that territory to the Crown, but rehabilitated him somewhat by making him a lord of Parliament; this honour was officially presented as a consequence of

---

[39] Leslie, *Historie*, ed. Cody, II.123.

[40] *Ibid.*, 226–7; *APS*, II.370.

[41] *TA*, VII.473.

[42] For example, Walter Kennedy, 'Closter of crist riche Recent flour delyss', in *The Asloan Manuscript*, ed. W. A. Craigie, STS, 2 vols (Edinburgh, 1925), II.272–8, at 275, lines 65–70.

[43] For example, BL Arundel Manuscript 285, fols 193v, 213v; Edinburgh, NMS, Beaton Panel; David Caldwell, 'The Beaton Panels – Scottish Carvings of the 1520s or 1530s', in *Medieval Art and Architecture in the Diocese of St Andrews*, ed. John Higgitt, British Archaeological Association Transactions 14 (Tring, 1994), 175, plate XXVII. See also 'Ros Mary: Ane Ballat of Our Lady', in *The Poems of William Dunbar*, ed. William Mackay Mackenzie (Edinburgh, 1932), 175–7, at 176, lines 47–50, 67–8. This poem was formerly commonly attributed to Dunbar, but is not now generally accepted as his work.

[44] John Carmi Parsons, 'The Queen's intercession in thirteenth-century England', in *Power of the Weak. Studies on Medieval Women*, eds Jennifer Carpenter and Sally-Beth MacLean (Urbana, 1995), 155–6.

[45] Leslie, *Historie*, ed. Cody, II.180.

the queen's intercession as well as the earl's submission.[46] Joan Beaufort had performed a similar role for John's father, Alexander, third Lord of the Isles (*ob.* 1449) in 1429 after the latter had launched a destructive attack on the royal burgh of Inverness. Forced to submit to the king in a stage-managed ceremony before the High Altar of Holyrood Abbey the earl, 'clad only in his shirt and drawers' and on his knees' begged James I's forgiveness while 'the queen and the more important lords of the kingdom interceded for him'. Alexander was warded in Tantallon castle instead of being executed.[47]

Some young princes watched their mothers intercede with kingly fathers, while others heard later about activities which had taken place before they were born. Once they ascended the throne, royal sons responded positively to their mothers' intercessory requests. In 1524 Margaret Tudor persuaded her son to leave Stirling castle for Edinburgh, and a few years later the king responded positively to her entreaties on behalf of her third husband Sir Henry Stewart, who was entrenched in Edinburgh castle with his brother James and a war band. Learning that her son was at the gates, the queen had them opened, went forward and prayed on her knees for her son to spare her husband and his brother. She refused to rise until he agreed to be merciful.[48]

Due to the poor survival of evidence it is difficult to ascertain the degree of influence late medieval Scottish queens exerted over sons. However, there is plenty of scope for explorations of Mary and Jesus's relationship. This in turn might offer insight into the ideals governing royal relationships. Mary's motherhood was a source of great joy and comfort to all the devout of Western Europe in the late middle ages. The Incarnation had made salvation possible, and Mary's high status in heaven made her a successful intercessor. Her intercession was needed because, despite the assurances of theologians, Jesus's sacrifice on the Cross was regarded as insufficient atonement for human sin. As mother of Jesus, Mary was in an excellent position to gain His forgiveness on behalf of humanity, and together Mary and Jesus interceded with God on behalf of supplicants. Yet Mary's intercession was associated with Jesus rather than God the Father, for mothers were understood to wield greater influence over sons than husbands. Mary's influence over Jesus is represented visually in depictions of Jesus sitting in Judgement after the Second Coming. A painted panel in a burial vault in the Guthrie family's burial aisle in Guthrie, Angus, depicts Jesus sitting on a rainbow. Mary and St John kneel before Him, interceding for the dead as they rise from the grave and pass before Him.[49] A missal of Sarum Use produced in Scotland in the sixteenth century suggests a liturgical basis for this belief in Mary's influence over Jesus. In the missal, Mary is referred to as 'Our Lady

---

[46] *APS*, II.113, cited in Macdougall, *James III*, 123.
[47] *Chron. Bower*, VIII.262–3.
[48] Leslie, *Historie*, ed. Cody, II.198, 216.
[49] Michael Apted, *The Painted Ceilings of Scotland 1550–1650* (Edinburgh, 1966), 2.

Queen of Heaven', ever 'intact' mother of God who suckled baby Jesus and interceded for humanity when he grew to adulthood.[50]

As an archetypal mother, Mary was assigned certain maternal traits. Scottish evidence characterises her as pious, nurturing, compassionate, forgiving, protective, and mediating. Although these traits were expressed most clearly within the context of her relationship to Jesus, Scots also could count on her unflagging concern and intercession, particularly on the Day of Judgement. Pleas for intercession were based upon a belief that Jesus and Mary would grant each other's requests because of the love they shared. Supplicants were urged to call on Mary's intercession in her son's name. In 'Ros Mary: Ane Ballat of Our Lady', William Dunbar pleads with Mary to ask Jesus to defend him from Satan and accept him into heaven.[51] The refrain '*O mater Ihesu salue maria*' emphasises the filial relationship, reminding listeners that Mary's intercessory power derives in large part from her bond with Jesus.

Walter Kennedy also reminds Mary that she should assist humanity for the sake of her suffering son.[52] Kennedy's hope for salvation depended entirely on Mary's ability to gain her son's favour. He asks Mary to plead with Jesus to help him cleanse inward sin for the sake of the blood He shed on humanity's behalf. On the off chance that Jesus was not sufficiently aware of his debt to His mother, and therefore inclined to ignore her pleas, the poet advises Mary to show Jesus the breasts that nurtured Him.[53]

Ideas about Mary informed ideas about queenly motherhood. It was accepted that queens, like Mary, were committed to the welfare of sons. St Margaret's greatest concern was said to be the spiritual welfare of her children, and even a queen's political machinations could be viewed as acceptable as long as they were undertaken to advance a son's prospects.[54] When the widowed Joan Beaufort carried off the young James II from Edinburgh castle, the governor supposedly lauded this 'noble woman, our souerane mother' for having risked her life for the welfare of her son and the realm.[55]

Mary and Jesus offered advice and encouragement to people as they attempted to live holy lives, and to cleanse sin through penance, prayer, support for religious foundations and involvement in Church ritual. Scots were confident that the emotional bond between Mary and Jesus would lead to successful intercession, because Mary and Jesus were merciful as well as

---

50 NAS, RH12/28, Scottish Missal, sixteenth-century.
51 'Ros Mary', 176, lines 49–56.
52 Kennedy, 'Closter of crist', 274, lines 45–8.
53 *Ibid.*, 273, lines 12–14; 275, lines 65–72.
54 For general discussion, see Fiona Downie, *She is but a Woman: Queenship in Scotland, 1424–1463* (Edinburgh, 2006).
55 Robert Lindesay of Pitscottie, *The Cronicles of Scotland*, ed. John Graham Dalyell, 2 vols (Edinburgh, 1814), I.6–9.

powerful.[56] In an anonymous sixteenth-century paean to Mary, she is asked to help sinners forsake their sinful, unclean lives, and beseech Jesus to grant them sufficient time before death to amend their lives.[57] In the same century too, in his foundation charter of the collegiate kirk of Biggar, Malcolm, third Lord Fleming, Great Chamberlain of Scotland (*ca* 1494–1547) asked that 'Jesus Christ with the help of the ever blessed Virgin Mary His Mother' keep Cardinal Beaton (?1494–1546), then Chancellor, Cardinal, and Archbishop of St Andrews, prosperous 'for the performance of your devotions, for the happy guidance of the church, and for the honour of your pastoral office (1546)'.[58]

Mothers were expected to be unfailingly supportive of wayward children, but some people worried that Mary might forsake or punish them. In the orison '*Sancta Maria Mater Dei Regina Celi et Terre*', Jesus is asked to defend the supplicant and all good christians from the anger of his 'maist haly mothir' as well as Himself. In the orison '*O Illustrissima et excellentissima*' Mary is asked to support supplicants despite their wicked sins. The supplicant also reminds her that she is mother not only to Jesus, but to all creatures, implying that she is obligated to forgive them their transgressions.[59] When he founded the hospital of St Martha in 1474, James Douglas, first earl of Morton, declared that he hoped the foundation would convince not only God to forgive him his sins, but also Mary. To this end, each afternoon hospital inmates were to pray devoutly on their knees, first the *Pater Noster*, then the *Ave Maria*. An augmentation of the foundation in 1486 placed more emphasis on Mary's maternal influence. Instead of 'blessed genetrix, perpetual Virgin Mary our lady' she was hailed as the 'most glorious Virgin Mary his [omnipotent God's] most pious mother'.[60]

The bonding process between Jesus and Mary began at birth, although by the fifteenth century christians believed that Mary's role as nurturer lasted throughout His lifetime.[61] Late fifteenth-century theologian John of Ireland reminded readers that Mary had not only borne Jesus, but had nursed, cared for, and clothed Him,[62] and the *Catechism* of 1551–2 insisted that 'we ar all dettouris to ye blissit virgin nixt eftir Christ', because Mary conceived,

56 David F. Wright, 'Mary in the Reformers', in *Chosen by God: Mary in Evangelical Perspective*, ed. D. F. Wright (London, 1989), 161–83, at 162.

57 Anonymous, 'Ane Ballat of Our Lady', in *The Asloan Manuscript*, ed. Craigie, II.245–6, at 246, lines 13–22; Kennedy, 'Closter of crist', 275, lines 65–9.

58 Foundation charter of Biggar collegiate church, cited by David S. Rutherford, *Biggar St. Mary's. A Medieval College Kirk* (Biggar, 1945), 36.

59 'Ane deuoit orisoun till our Lady in Inglis callit sancta maria mater dei regna celi et terre', in *Devotional Pieces*, ed. Bennett, 283–4, at 283, lines 158–9; 'O Illustrissima et excellentissima', in *ibid.*, at 282, lines 102–3.

60 *Registrum Honoris de Morton. Ancient Charters*, eds Thomas Thomson, Alexander Macdonald and Cosmo Innes, Bannatyne Club, 2 vols (Edinburgh, 1853), II.236, 241.

61 Edwin Mullins, *The Painted Witch. Female Body: Male Art* (London, 1985), 157–62.

62 John of Ireland, *The Meroure of Wyssdome*, ed. Charles Macpherson, STS, 2 vols (Edinburgh, 1926), I.147, lines 9–10.

bore and nourished humanity's Saviour, and 'lyk a diligent mother had cure of him'.[63] Visual images of Mary holding Jesus as a baby are extremely common.[64] In a large painting in Fowlis Easter collegiate church, Mary stands tenderly nursing Jesus. Next to her is a young, triumphant Jesus after the Resurrection.[65] In devotional work BL Arundel MS 285, produced in the 1540s, Mary appears almost exclusively in relation to Jesus. Eleven wood-cuts depict Mary and Jesus together; in nine of them Jesus is an infant. To emphasise Jesus's humanity, three woodcuts place His grandmother St Anne alongside Mary and Jesus. In one Jesus sits on his grandmother's lap; in another He appears to be rambunctiously jumping from Mary to Anne.[66]

The laity responded to imagery focusing on this filial relationship by founding chaplainries, altars and prebendaries celebrating the Nativity and Mary's motherhood. Altars of the Three Oriental Kings and the Three Kings and the Blessed Virgin Mary were founded in Dundee and Haddington, respectively,[67] and the community of Peebles dedicated a prebendary to St Mary in Childbirth when it transformed its parish church into a collegiate church in 1541.[68] The importance of Marian and other imagery in cultivating traditional religiosity was recognised by both the established Church and Protestant reformers.[69]

Mary's nurturing role continued up to the Crucifixion. She had sacrificed her son to God just as Jesus had sacrificed Himself, although her martyrdom was emotional rather than physical.[70] Maternal love, as well as devotion to God's plan, had brought her to Jerusalem and Calvary and led her to keep vigil at her son's tomb. Her reward was seeing Jesus soon after the Resurrection.[71] The long devotional prayers 'The Thre Rois Garlandis' and 'The Lang Rosair' in BL Arundel MS 285 emphasise Mary's compassion and love for

---

[63] John Hamilton, *The Catechism Set Forth by Archbishop Hamilton Printed at St. Andrews – 1551 Together with The Two-Penny Faith 1559*, ed. Alex F. Mitchell (Edinburgh, 1882), fol. clxxxxii.

[64] For example, in 1505 the Chapel Royal in Stirling castle contained an image of Mary holding Jesus in her arms. James Murray Mackinlay, *Ancient Church Dedications in Scotland, vol. I: Scriptural Dedications* (Edinburgh, 1910), 81.

[65] Fowlis Easter church, Angus. See M. R. Apted and W. N. Robertson, 'Late fifteenth century paintings from Guthrie and Foulis Easter', *PSAS* 95 (1961–2), 262–79; Audrey-Beth Fitch, *The Search for Salvation: Lay Faith in Scotland 1480–1560* (Edinburgh, 2009), plate 22.

[66] BL Arundel MS 285, fols 182r, 185r, 190v, 208v. Cf. Huneycutt, 'Images of queenship', 64.

[67] *The Scottish Grey Friars*, ed. William Moir Bryce, 2 vols (Edinburgh, 1909), II.131; NAS, RH1/2/339, altar of the Three Kings, Haddington, 20 October 1522.

[68] *MHRS*, 226.

[69] *Statutes of the Scottish Church 1225–1559*, ed. David Patrick (Edinburgh, 1907), 174; James Kirk, 'Iconoclasm and reform', *Records of the Scottish Church History Society* 24 (1992), 366–83, at 366.

[70] Richard Bauckham, 'The origins and growth of western Mariology', in *Chosen by God*, ed. Wright, 141–60, at 157.

[71] Elaine Storkey, 'The significance of Mary for feminist theology', in *Chosen by God*, ed. Wright, 184–99, at 197–8.

the adult Jesus.[72] A powerful *Pietà* woodcut stands across from the first verse of the Second Garland of 'The Thre Rois Garlandis'. Mary is a powerful, nurturing, middle-aged mother, much larger than the young, crucified Jesus, who is draped across her knees. Stabbing into Mary's neck and head are seven swords, representing the seven dolours of the Virgin, all relating to the life and Passion of Jesus.[73]

There is no better testimony to the emotional bond between Mary and Jesus than the complex Crucifixion painting (*ca* 1480) in Fowlis Easter collegiate church. This large canvas would have made a deep impression on the laity, for it was fully visible during long Latin services. Colourful, emotional and moving, Mary is depicted as a tearful mother standing at the foot of the Cross. The knight Longinus thrusts a spear into Jesus's side while Mary, head averted, turns away slightly, as if unable to bear any longer the sight of His suffering. Horsed knights in medieval dress congregate around the Cross, and in the background is a medieval city. By choosing the visual idiom of late medieval Scotland, the painter made real and present the suffering of Jesus and His mother to redeem human sin.[74]

Usually Mary was depicted as a strong, if grief-stricken, maternal figure, but scenes of maternal collapse emphasised her human suffering. A swooning St Mary of Pity, supported by others in her grief, is carved on a Crucifixion retable in St Michael's parish church, Linlithgow.[75] Jesus recognised His mother's suffering. In 'Ane Deuoit Remembrance of ye Passioun of Crist', Jesus addresses humanity as friends and brothers, asking them to empathise with His physical suffering and value His sacrifice, but also to picture His mother's terrible agony as she watched His ordeal: 'Behald my mother swonyng for grevance, / Apoun ye croce quhen scho sawe me dey.'[76]

Writers and artists linked Passion imagery to rose and rosary imagery to highlight Jesus and Mary's emotional bond and common intercessory aim. Supplicants asked Mary to intercede with Jesus for the sake of her maternal grief and commitment to the work of the Cross, and Jesus was exhorted to mediate for and forgive humanity for the sake of his mother's grief. Through the rosary, Mary helped people overcome sin and obtain God's mercy. The *Catechism* explains that God listens to the prayers of people who honour Mary, particularly those who say the *Ave Maria*. Apart from impressing God, the *Ave Maria* leads Mary to intercede with her son on behalf of suppli-

---

[72] She was 'mothir & lady of piete', in 'The Lang Rosair'. See *Devotional Pieces*, ed. Bennett, 322–34, at 332, lines 302–7.

[73] BL Arundel MS 285, fol. 204v; 'The Thre Rois Garlandis', in *Devotional Pieces*, ed. Bennett, 299–321, at 307.

[74] Fowlis Easter church. See Fitch, *Search for Salvation*, plate 2.

[75] James S. Richardson, 'Fragments of altar retables of late mediaeval date in Scotland', *PSAS* 62 (1927–8), 197–224, at 213.

[76] 'Ane Deuoit Remembrance of ye Passioun of Crist', in *Devotional Pieces*, ed. Bennett, 270–4, at 270, lines 1–8; 272, lines 91–6 and 95–6; 273–4, lines 137–44.

cants.[77] In 'Closter of crist', Walter Kennedy argues that the rosary helps humanity overcome sin and gains Mary and Jesus's protection and intercession. Others agreed, expressing their views through tomb decoration. The effigy of George, second Lord Seton (b. after 1459, *ob.* 1507), founder of the collegiate church of Seton (1493), clasps a rosary; his spouse's tomb is decorated with roses.[78]

A woodcut depicting the afterlife in a compilation of parliamentary acts dating to 1541 reinforces the notion that Mary's aid is necessary to profit fully from the Crucifixion. The heavenly scene, peopled by the holy family, saints and angels, is surmounted by an image of Jesus on a rose-festooned Cross and enclosed by a circlet of roses. The living kneel on the ground outside the circle, clasping rosaries as they pray.[79] Marian and Passion imagery also play a prominent role in the Paisley Abbey altar retables (late fifteenth century),[80] and Beaton Panels.[81] Combinations of Marian and Passion imagery on baptismal fonts is of particular note, for Original Sin is cleansed through holy water. Fowlis Easter's late medieval font is decorated with scenes from the life and Passion of Jesus, and roses form a decorative border along the base; the font of St John's church, Aberdeen, is decorated with a crowned Gothic 'M' along with rose and Passion symbolism (*ca* 1525).[82]

There are many notable examples of combined Passion and rose or rosary imagery, but most remarkable are the poems of William Dunbar, devotional prayers in BL Arundel MS 285,[83] and the Fetternear Banner. Dunbar's 'Of the Passioun of Christ' begins with the protagonist's entry to an oratory, where he kneels down 'befor ye michti king of glorye' to offer up a *Pater Noster*, 'Havand his passioun in memorye'. He appears to be kneeling before an image of Jesus intending to pray. However, he begins by saluting Mary with a hymn, claiming he does so because 'till his [Jesus'] moder I did Inclyne'.[84] Thoughts of Jesus's Passion naturally gave rise to thoughts about Mary, and it was quite natural to combine praise and prayers to Mary with meditation on the Passion.

The rosary of prayers in 'The Lang Rosair' provides a focal point for lay meditation and guidelines for cultivating personal holiness. It prefaces

---

77 Hamilton, *Catechism*, ed. Mitchell, fol. clxxxxii.
78 For example, Kennedy, 'Closter of crist', 274–5, lines 57–64; Seton collegiate church, East Lothian.
79 *The New Acts and Constitutionis of parliament made be Iames the Fift kyng of Scottis, 1540*, fol. 27v; David MacGibbon and Thomas Ross, *The Ecclesiastical Architecture of Scotland*, 3 vols (Edinburgh, 1896), III.193; Fitch, *Search for Salvation*, frontispiece.
80 Deposition from the Cross and the Entombment. Below the latter is a border of roses.
81 NMS; Caldwell, 'Beaton panels', 174–5, 176.
82 Fowlis Easter church; MacGibbon and Ross, *Ecclesiastical Architecture*, III.193–6; Charles Carter, 'The *Arma Christi* in Scotland', *PSAS* 90 (1956–7), 116–29, at 123.
83 'The Lang Rosair' and 'The Thre Rois Garlandis'.
84 William Dunbar, 'Of the Passioun of Christ', in *The Asloan Manuscript*, ed. Craigie, II.242–5, at 242, lines 4–7.

requests for Mary's prayers with descriptions of the life and Passion of Jesus; after each verse the supplicant recites the *Ave Maria* to obtain Mary's intercession. Priestly counsel also would have been along these lines, for the *Catechism* argues that saying the *Ave Maria* moves Mary to intercede for supplicants with 'hir sonne'.[85]

'The Thre Rois Garlandis', a long series of prayers in BL Arundel MS 285, has no known extant Latin or vernacular antecedent, so may offer a useful insight into contemporary Scottish views of Mary and Jesus's relationship at the time of the Crucifixion. The rubric states that supplicants must meditate on the Passion of Jesus to be sinless, virtuous, and victorious over enemies, enjoy a happy life spiritually and materially, and experience a 'gracius end' followed by entry into heaven.[86] By linking Marian prayers to the Passion narrative, supplicants maximise Mary's intercessory power. Each 'garland' is filled with images of the Passion, along with prayers applicable to the supplicant's own spiritual life, and is followed by an *Ave Maria*, implying that praying to Mary makes Jesus more willing to listen to a supplicant's requests.[87]

The Fetternear banner (*ca* 1520), belonging to Edinburgh's confraternity of the Holy Blood, depicts a crucified Jesus dripping with blood, standing in front of the Cross, a reminder that He suffered greatly to save humanity from eternal death. Above this scene is an image which confirms the close relationship of Mary and Jesus, and encourages viewers to cultivate a personal relationship with Jesus. A thoughtful, expectant layman looks up at the face of Jesus, who looks down in sober attentiveness. Surrounding these scenes is a rosary, five white beads separating each large red rose. This image encouraged supplicants to believe that they would benefit from Jesus's Passion and win His favour by expressing devotion to Mary through the rosary.[88]

Religious foundations focusing on the Crucifixion reminded community members of Mary and Jesus's emotional bond and mutual suffering, and aided named souls. Spiritual benefit derived from the sacrifice of Jesus in the mass, as well as the prayers of titular saints and those of clerics and lay people attending services. In 1520, David Menzies of Aberdeen founded a mass of the Passion at the altar of St Mary of Pity in St Nicholas Church.[89] By making his foundation on 24 December, the eve of the Nativity, he celebrated Mary's role as delighted mother of the infant Jesus as well as grieving mother of the crucified Christ. 'The Thre Rois Garlandis' echoes Menzies's belief

85 'The Lang Rosair', 329, lines 217–23 and *passim*; Hamilton, *Catechism*, ed. Mitchell, fol. clxxxxi.
86 'The Thre Rois Garlandis', 299, lines 1–14, and editor's note (*Devotional Pieces*, ed. Bennett, xxii–xxiii).
87 *Ibid.*, 299–321, *passim*.
88 NMS; Carter, '*Arma Christi*', 125; Fitch, *Search for Salvation*, plate 23.
89 *Cartularium Ecclesiae Sancti Nicholai Aberdonensis*, ed. James Cooper, New Spalding Club, 2 vols (Aberdeen, 1888–92), II.117–18.

in Jesus and Mary's loving bond and the spiritual power of Mary's compassionate grief and Jesus's suffering humanity. The author suggests that Jesus is likely to listen to His mother:

> For quhais [whose] lufe, sweit Lady, I ask at the [th]at you cum to me in [th]e hour of my dede, and tak my saule in [th]i virgin handis and offer it to [th]i sueit sone Iesus, that bocht me apoun [th]e croce with his precius blud and dede.[90]

To further emphasise the human dimension of the Crucifixion, and by extension the role it played in deepening the bond between Jesus and Mary, late medieval Scots commissioned representations of 'Passion symbols' referred to as '*arma Christi*'. Body parts and torture implements associated with Jesus's suffering at the Crucifixion, such as the nails, crown of thorns, spear, flaming heart, hands and feet of Jesus, were carved in a variety of locations, including doorways, exterior walls and buttresses, corbels, ceiling bosses, tomb recesses, and baptismal fonts.[91] *Arma Christi* imagery reminded people that the spiritual value of the Crucifixion depended upon Jesus's physical suffering, and that meditation on the Passion was necessary to spiritual success.

Theologians called on people to trust God as a loving, nurturing father,[92] but it was primarily to the suffering, brotherly Jesus[93] that the laity turned for succour, along with His influential mother. Conceptions of God, Jesus and Mary changed in the later middle ages. In the century prior to the Reformation, the term 'omnipotent God' gave way in religious foundations to the phrase the 'Holy and Indivisible Trinity', often followed by the phrase 'most glorious, ever virgin, mother of our lord Jesus Christ'.[94] In some respects, Mary had become conjoined to the Trinity, her bodily assumption into heaven bringing a material element to the 'quaternity'. By 1553 the deity in the Perth hammermen play was described as 'Trinity' rather than 'God',[95] and the 'Blessed Virgin Mary', vessel of God's will, had become the mother of our lord Jesus Christ, saviour. Jesus increasingly was described as Mary's son, thereby separating Him from the 'God' of the Trinity. Paternal 'archetypes' had made God a remote and forbidding figure, but the Incarnation had made Jesus a loving 'brother' to humanity and son of the compassionate

---

90 'The Thre Rois Garlandis', 321, lines 608–11.
91 St Mary's collegiate church, Haddington; Seton collegiate church, East Lothian; MacGibbon and Ross, *Ecclesiastical Architecture*, III.226 Fig. 1146; Falkland Palace; Carter, '*Arma Christi*', 126; Glasgow Cathedral; St Giles Kirk, Edinburgh; See Fitch, *Search for Salvation*, plate 25; Caldwell, 'Beaton panels', 175, 180, plate XXVII.
92 Hamilton, *Catechism*, ed. Mitchell, fol. xcxviii.
93 'Ane Deuoit Remembrance', 270, lines 1–8; 274, line 143.
94 1543 obit foundation in Haddington, in *Scottish Grey Friars*, ed. Bryce, II.41–2. Cf. 1499 foundation in Paisley parish church in *Charters and Documents Relating to the Burgh of Paisley (1163–1665)*, ed. W. M. Metcalfe (Paisley, 1902), 56.
95 *The Perth Hammermen Book*, ed. Colin A. Hunt (Perth, 1889), 78.

and welcoming Mary.[96] An illustration in the Arbuthnott Missal (*ca* 1491), commissioned for the parish church of St Ternan's, Arbuthnott, draws a startling contrast between Jesus and God. Jesus is a small, thin, vulnerable young man, whereas God is a large, middle-aged king on a throne, holding Jesus across His lap.[97]

The incorporation of Mary into the Trinity received literary, artistic and dedicatory treatment. In 'Ros Mary: Ane Ballat of Our Lady', Mary was described as the 'temple of the Trinity'.[98] Visual representations of the Trinity tend to depict Jesus as a baby on Mary's lap, as a young man with flowing hair and thin body hanging on a Cross, or as the crucified Christ lying across Mary's lap after the Deposition.[99] Annunciation or other Marian imagery appears nearby or is entwined with images of God and/or Jesus. For example, Mary appears next to a triumphant Jesus after the Resurrection in a painting in Fowlis Easter collegiate church.[100] When James III founded a church within the bounds of the parish church of Restalrig, and petitioned for it to be raised to collegiate status in 1487, he dedicated it to the Holy and Indivisible Trinity and St Mary the Virgin.[101]

The laity's hopes for salvation were based upon a belief that Jesus was distinct from God, and that Mary and Jesus's close and loving relationship was spiritually effective and guaranteed Jesus's goodwill. In his Prologue to the first book of the *Aeneid*, Gavin Douglas emphasised Mary and Jesus's human relationship. He asked Mary and the Trinity for protection, and sought salvation through the crucified Christ and His mother, queen of heaven.

> In personys thre, equale of a substans,
> On the I call and Mary Virgyn myld;
> …
> In Criste is all my traste and hevynnys queyn.
> …
> For the sweit liquor of thy pappis quhite
> Fosterit that prynce, that hevynly Orpheus,
> Grond of all gude, our Saluyour Ihesus.[102]

96 Jacques Pohier, *God in Fragments*, trans. John Bowden (London, 1985), *passim*; Bauckham, 'The origins and growth of western Mariology', 147.
97 Paisley Museum, Arbuthnott Missal, 25. Available online at: http://www.bl.uk/ttp2/hiddentreasures. html.
98 'Ros Mary', 175, line 19.
99 BL Arundel MS 285, fol. 183v; Arbuthnott Prayer Book; Thomas Lewington, 'The Crucifixion', in *The Book Intytulid the Art of Good Lywyng and Good Deyng* (Paris, 1503), fol. 13(e₄); Fowlis Easter church.
100 Fowlis Easter church.
101 *MRHS*, 224.
102 Gavin Douglas, 'The Proloug of the First Buke', in *The Aeneid of Virgil Translated into Scottish Verse by Gawin Douglas Bishop of Dunkeld*, ed. George Dundas, Bannatyne Club, 2 vols (Edinburgh, 1839), I.3–20, at 18, lines 16–17, 20–3, 26–8.

People's sense of spiritual inadequacy and belief in the insufficiency of the Crucifixion meant that they needed Mary's maternal authority and influence to assist them in their struggle against evil inward and outward, and to intercede with God. In contrast to Jesus, a vulnerable baby or suffering young man, Mary was a good match for the stern God of Judgement Day. She was a powerful young mother, protective older mother, celestial queen, and defeater of demons.[103]

Further, Mary was excellently placed to reconcile God with humanity. The image of the afterlife in the Acts of the Parliaments of 1541 places Mary, as crowned queen of heaven, to the right of a resplendent God. As both wife of God and mother of Jesus, whom she holds on her lap, she has full access to the royal ear.[104] Earthly queens also acted as agents of reconciliation. Mary of Guise, for example, sought Mary's assistance after the death of James V. She passed on foot to the shrine of Our Lady of Loreto, an extremely popular foundation established in Musselburgh by 1536, and remained there in prayer for twenty days, hoping to achieve peace between England and the Scottish nobility.[105] In *The Richt Vay to the Kingdome of Heuine* (1533), reformer John Gau exhorted the laity not to trust Mary, but rather Jesus Christ, 'our lord and saluiour and mediatur betuix wss and the fader'.[106] This comment revealed annoyance at lay belief in Mary's intercession, but also the emerging distinction between God and Jesus. The privileging of Jesus and Mary's relationship increased as the period progressed, emerging in testaments, poetry, chaplainry and church dedications, missals, and prayer books.[107]

Crediting Mary as well as Jesus with successful intercessory activities further separated God the Father from Jesus the Son. Mary comforted and interceded for people day and night, in life and in death,[108] and most of all protected and defended them on the Day of Judgement. In a bas-relief in Roslin Chapel, a protective Mary shepherds a quaking layman away from a horned devil, her arm flung across his shoulders.[109] Burial near a Marian altar or statue improved access to Marian intercession, and placement of a Marian image, altar or chaplainry near the high altar linked Marian intercession to the Crucifixion; in personal terms, it brought mother and son into greater proximity. Seton family members chose to be buried close to a Marian side

---

103   Kennedy, 'Closter of crist', 275, lines 59–62.
104   *The New Acts and Constitutionis of parliament made be Iames the Fift kyng of Scottis, 1540,* fol. 27v.
105   *A Diurnal of Remarkable Occurrents that have Passed within the Country of Scotland,* ed. T. Thomson, Maitland Club (Edinburgh, 1833), 30.
106   John Gau, 'The Richt Way to the Kingdome of Hevine', in *The Bannatyne Miscellany*, ed. David Laing, Bannatyne Club, 3 vols (Edinburgh, 1827–55), II.357–8.
107   For example, NAS, CC20/4/1, Register of Testaments, Commissariot of St Andrews, 1549–1551 (unfoliated). Testaments from 1544, 1547 and 1548 referred to Mary as 'most glorious Virgin Mary' or 'Blessed and ever virgin Mary'; Douglas, 'Proloug of the First Buke', 18, lines 11–14.
108   'Obsecro', in *Devotional Pieces*, ed. Bennett, 290–3, at 292, lines 75–83.
109   Roslin Chapel, Midlothian. See Fitch, *Search for Salvation*, plate 12.

altar and choir in their collegiate church.[110] From the synod of Merton in 1305 it had become standard practice to have a statue of Mary at the high altar along with that of the titular saint. For example, a Marian statue stood next to St Andrew at the high altar in St Andrews Cathedral.[111]

Tree of Jesse imagery reinforced the notion that Mary was co-redeemer with Jesus. At some point between the 1520s and late 1530s, David Beaton, then commendator of Arbroath (1524), commissioned a series of carved wooden panels. One of these 'Beaton panels' places Mary and the baby Jesus together at the top of the tree of Jesse, the apostles on branches below. Thus eternal life came through Jesus and Mary, and only secondarily through apostolic prayer.[112] 'Ros Mary: Ane Ballat of Our Lady' describes Mary as 'genetrix, of Jesse germynat',[113] and 'The Lang Rosair' insists that she is crucial to salvation, the very 'tre of lif'.[114] Tree of Jesse imagery also appears in the stained glass windows of St Bride's church, Douglas, Lanarkshire,[115] and on the binding of a 1506 Missal, where it is combined with Passion imagery.[116]

In the century prior to the Reformation, devotion to the Blessed Virgin Mary and Jesus Christ was well advanced. People still honoured saints and the fatherly, middle-aged God, but most turned to the compassionate and merciful Mother Mary and her Son Jesus for models of morality, religious devotion, and filial bonding. By understanding their emotional bond, Scots hoped to succeed on earth as well as in heaven, and in particular, to gain Mary and Jesus's intercessory assistance. Further, the late medieval emphases on the Crucifixion, humanity of Jesus and Trinity made transparent the nature of their relationship, particularly in literary and visual media. While in principle Jesus was God, in practice the laity distinguished between the two. This facilitated Jesus's transformation from passive, sacrificial victim to active and loving Son of Mary. Mary and Jesus were willing to follow each other's advice because of their great love for each other, and together they confronted omnipotent God, the stern Judge, on humanity's behalf. While Scottish understanding of the relationship between Jesus and Mary can, in historical terms, only have been an ideal, the maternal devotion and filial affection they expressed must have resonated with late medieval Scots, for they were willing to stake their spiritual future on the power of this mother-son bond.

---

[110] Seton collegiate church. MacGibbon and Ross, *Ecclesiastical Architecture*, III.229.

[111] David McRoberts, 'The Glorious House of St. Andrews', *IR* 25 (1974), 102–3, citing D. Wilkins, *Concilia Magnae Britanniae*, II.280; *St A. Lib.*, 406.

[112] Caldwell, 'Beaton panels', 175, 180, plate XXVII.

[113] 'Ros Mary', 175, line 36.

[114] 'The Lang Rosair', 332, line 291.

[115] F. C. Eeles, 'Mediaeval stained glass recently recovered from the ruins of Holyrood Abbey Church', *PSAS* 49 (1914–15), 81–91, at 87.

[116] Carter, '*Arma Christi*', 126.

10

THE 'McROBERTS THESIS' AND PATTERNS OF SANCTITY IN LATE MEDIEVAL SCOTLAND

David Ditchburn

In 1968 *The Innes Review* published an article by David McRoberts which was (to use a word often overused in recent years) seminal.[1] Its influence is visible in much, indeed in almost everything, that has been written since 1968 about the Church and about religion in later medieval Scotland. The thesis which it presented was relatively straightforward. McRoberts argued that the fifteenth century witnessed a new and what he called 'nationalist' trend in Scottish religious observation. There were several dimensions to this development – but it was especially apparent, McRoberts argued, in the veneration of saints. Before the fifteenth century the Church had neglected Scotland's early saints; thereafter leading clergymen began to look anew at these forgotten worthies. In the earlier part of the century Prior James Haldenstone of St Andrews had coordinated a campaign to have St Duthac officially canonised. Elsewhere there were efforts to relocate the relics and to promote the cults of St Kentigern (at Glasgow and Culross), St Ninian (at Whithorn) and St Triduana (at Restalrig). We find the chronicler Walter Bower lauding St Columba and Archbishop Schevez of St Andrews mounting a search for the relics of St Palladius. This 'devotional nationalism' reached its culmination, according to McRoberts, in the early sixteenth century with the work of Bishop William Elphinstone and a team of collaborators in Old Aberdeen, who produced a new martyrology and a new breviary. In this work the feast days of almost one hundred saints in some way connected with Scotland were identified, so that they could be henceforth celebrated in Scottish churches.[2] And that this was a national endeavour (rather than just an Aberdonian idiosyncrasy) was underlined by the licence which in 1507 James IV granted to the Edinburgh burgesses Walter Chepman and Andrew Myllar,

---

[1] David McRoberts, 'The Scottish Church and nationalism in the fifteenth century', *IR* 19 (1968), 3–14: the quotation which follows comes from p. 6.

[2] Alan Macquarrie, 'Scottish saints' legends in the Aberdeen Breviary', in this volume, appendix. See too James D. Galbraith, 'The Sources of the Aberdeen Breviary' (University of Aberdeen, unpublished M. Litt. thesis, 1970), 139.

to print, amongst other things, liturgical books adorned with 'additions and legends of Scottish saints'.[3]

Over forty years on, although its broad outlines remain intact, a moderate revisionism has been applied to the rougher edges of the 'McRoberts thesis'. Michael Penman, for instance, has suggested that the national saints were far from overlooked in the fourteenth century.[4] A still more pronounced trend has been to temper 'devotional nationalism' with a dose of internationalism. In advancing his nationalist thesis McRoberts ignored cults focused on Christ, his family and early followers and even Mary rated not a mention from the *Monsignor*. McRoberts was, of course, aware of continental influences on Scottish religious practices and in other publications he had done much to illuminate these foreign linkages.[5] These paved the way, indeed, for the subsequent discussion of the international cults by Donald Galbraith and Leslie Macfarlane and more recently still (and with a slightly different approach) by Alasdair A. MacDonald, Audrey-Beth Fitch and Mark Hall.[6] While not explicitly dissenting from the McRoberts thesis, all of these scholars have, however, drawn attention to the prevalence of christocentric and Marian devotions in the later middle ages, a trend evident across christendom and illuminated most famously in Scotland by the crucifixion depicted on the Fetternear Banner, now in the National Museum of Scotland.[7]

It was not just on the processional banner of the Edinburgh merchant guild that the Passion assumed its central devotional position. An earlier royal attachment to the Passion is perhaps suggested by the fragment of the True Cross, gifted to Alexander III (1249–86) by a French king, possibly Louis IX (1226–70) who had purchased large segments of the Cross in the 1230s.[8]

---

3   *RSS*, I.no. 1546; Leslie J. Macfarlane, *William Elphinstone and the Kingdom of Scotland, 1431–1514: The Struggle for Order* (Aberdeen, 1985), 236–7; Norman Macdougall, *James IV* (East Linton, 1997), 218.

4   M. A. Penman, 'Christian days and knights: the religious devotions and court of David II of Scotland, 1329–71', *Historical Research* 75 (2002), 249–72.

5   See especially David McRoberts, 'Notes on Scoto-Flemish artistic contacts', *IR* 10 (1959), 91–6; *idem*, 'Scottish pilgrims to the Holy Land', *IR* 20 (1969), 80–106; *idem*, 'The rosary in Scotland', *IR* 23 (1972), 81–6.

6   Galbraith, 'Sources', esp. 52–133; Macfarlane, *William Elphinstone*, 232, 243; A. A. MacDonald, 'Passion devotion in late-medieval Scotland', in *The Broken Body: Passion Devotion in Late-medieval Culture*, eds A. A. MacDonald, H. N. B. Ridderbos and R. M. Schlusemann (Groningen, 1998), 109–31; Audrey-Beth Fitch, 'Maternal mediators: saintly ideals and secular realities in late medieval Scotland', *IR* 57 (2006), 1–35; *eadem*, 'Popular piety in Scotland prior to the Reformation: death, purity and the Blessed Virgin Mary', in *Symposium on Popular Religion and Society*, Association of Scottish Historical Studies (1991), 1–21; M. A. Hall, 'Of holy men and heroes: the cult of saints in medieval Perthshire, *IR* 56 (2005), 61–88. See too Audrey-Beth Fitch, 'Mothers and their sons: Mary and Jesus in Scotland, 1450–1560' and Mark A. Hall, 'Wo/men only? Marian devotion in medieval Perth', in this volume.

7   David McRoberts, 'The Fetternear banner [I]', *IR* 7 (1956), 69–96.

8   TNA, E101/370/3; *CDS*, V.no. 494; Holger A. Klein, 'Eastern objects and western desires: relics and reliquaries between Byzantium and the West', *Dumbarton Oaks Papers* 58 (2004), 283–314, at 307–8.

Later Scottish kings expressed their devotion for Christ in a desire to visit personally, vicariously or posthumously the Holy Land and presumably also its principal shrine, the Holy Sepulchre.[9] Royal dispositions aside, churches and other buildings in Scotland were decorated with Passion imagery, which also featured strongly in contemporary literature.[10] The new Christ-focused cults, such as the Five Wounds, the Name of Jesus and the Crown of Thorns, began to be celebrated in Scottish churches.[11] Similarly, the cults of Corpus Christi and the Holy Blood were introduced to Scotland. The former, which had originated in the diocese of Liège during the thirteenth century, became a universal observance in the early fourteenth century, probably at the instigation of Pope John XXII (1316–34). Although its introduction to Scotland was perhaps retarded by the thorny relationship which the pope enjoyed with Robert I (1306–29), copies of the canon law collection *Clementines*, in which the festival was promulgated, eventually reached Scotland.[12] Indeed, the feast was apparently known of in Scotland by 1327.[13] By at least the fifteenth century it was celebrated in processions and plays which were perhaps modelled on examples from northern England, where Corpus Christi was also widely observed.[14] By contrast, Flemish, rather than English, influences almost certainly explain the appearance of the cult of the Holy Blood in Scotland. It was popular in towns and merchants were its vector; Flanders and Zeeland were Scotland's most important trading partners; and Bruges staged an annual procession in commemoration of the Holy Blood which had allegedly been brought to Flanders following the Second Crusade.[15] But there

9   *ER*, V.156, 179; Lille, Archives Départementales du Nord [ADN], B2030, fol. 319r; Macdougall, *James IV*, 199–205.

10 Priscilla Bawcutt, 'Religious verse in medieval Scotland', in *A Companion to Medieval Scottish Poetry*, eds Priscilla Bawcutt and Janet Hadley Williams (Cambridge, 2006), 119–31, at 124–8; Charles Carter, 'The *Arma Christi* in Scotland', *PSAS* 90 (1956–7), 116–29; A. A. MacDonald, 'The chapel of Restalrig: royal folly or venerable shrine?', in *A Palace in the Wild: Essays on Vernacular Culture and Humanism in Late-medieval and Renaissance Scotland*, eds L. A. J. R. Houwen, A. A. MacDonald and S. L. Mapstone (Leuven, 2000), 27–59, at 37; James S. Richardson, 'Fragments of altar retables of late mediaeval date in Scotland', *PSAS* 62 (1927–8), 197–224.

11 Macfarlane, *William Elphinstone*, 232, 243.

12 Miri Rubin, *Corpus Christi: The Eucharist in Late Medieval Culture* (Cambridge, 1991), 164–85; *Abdn. Reg.*, II.130–1.

13 *ER*, I.60, 482, 525–6.

14 Anna Jean Mill, *Mediaeval Plays in Scotland* (Edinburgh, 1927), 61–73; P. J. P. Goldberg, 'Performing the word of God: Corpus Christi drama in the northern province', in *Life and Thought in the Northern Church, c.1100–c.1700*, ed. Diana Wood, Studies in Church History (Woodbridge, 1999), 145–70.

15 C. Verschelde, 'Les matines brugeoises et la procession du St Sang', *Annales de la Société d'Émulation de Bruges* 31 (1880), 119–24; N. Huyghebaert, 'Iperius et la translation de la relique du Saint Sang à Bruges', *Annales de la Société d'Émulation de Bruges* 100 (1963), 110–87; Alexander Stevenson, 'Medieval Scottish associations with Bruges', in *Freedom and Authority: Scotland, c.1050–1650*, eds Terry Brotherstone and David Ditchburn (East Linton, 2000), 93–107, at 104–5; Andrew Brown, 'Civic ritual: Bruges and the counts of Flanders in the later middle ages', *English Historical Review* 112 (1997), 277–99, esp. 280–2, 292. More generally, see Rubin,

was a domestic stimulus to christocentric devotion too, most notably perhaps in pilgrimage to centres such as Crail, Montrose and Peebles. All three towns hosted shrines associated with Christ or the Cross. Crail's pilgrimage remains (to me at least) obscure; but Montrose reportedly attracted significant numbers of local pilgrims on holy days, even although its miracles were not (by the fifteenth century) considered contemporary. By contrast, frequent miracles were still reported in sixteenth-century Peebles, where a cross and the remnants of a supposed martyr had been discovered in the thirteenth century. In a fashion which remains unclear (but which was perhaps the result of simple misunderstanding and confusion), Peebles also came to be associated with the True Cross. Regular royal visits in the fifteenth and sixteenth centuries, and perhaps before, helped to ensure that the town and its church of the Holy Cross remained one of the most significant of Scottish pilgrim destinations both before (and more surprisingly after) the Reformation.[16]

The prominence accorded to Christ in devotional practices was paralleled by a flourishing interest in his family and friends. It is well known that Marian cults also assumed a growing significance across christendom and in this volume Sìm R. Innes demonstrates that the Virgin's influence was pronounced, even in an area remote from Rome and often regarded pejoratively as peripheral to the Latin West.[17] Elsewhere in Scotland churches, chapels and altars were routinely dedicated to the Virgin, their number including the parish churches of St Mary *ad Nivem* in Old Aberdeen and Ladykirk in Upsettlington, both of which date to the 1490s; the chapel of St Mary's College, as the university of Aberdeen was called upon its foundation in 1495; and the altar of *S Maria libera nos a penis inferni*, established at Dunkeld Cathedral.[18] Marian feasts were also quickly integrated into the Church calendar and Marian prayers became fashionable in Scotland as elsewhere. She became a popular subject of literary consideration, in the

---

Corpus Christi, esp. ch. 3; Caroline Walker Bynum, *Wonderful Blood: Theology and Practice in Late Medieval Northern Germany and Beyond* (Philadelphia, 2007).

[16] For Crail, see *The Works of Sir David Lindsay of the Mount, 1490–1555*, ed. Douglas Hamer, STS, 4 vols (Edinburgh, 1931–6), I.270. For Montrose, see *CSSR 1433–1447*, eds A. I. Dunlop and David MacLauchlan (Glasgow, 1983), nos 1328–9; and on Peebles: John of Fordun, *Chronicle of the Scottish Nation*, ed. W. F. Skene, 2 vols (repr. Lampeter, 1993), II.294–5; *Chron. Bower*, V.335; *Foreign Correspondence with Marie de Lorraine, Queen of Scotland*, ed. Marguerite Wood, SHS, 2 vols (Edinburgh, 1923–5), I.no. 50; Robert Lindesay of Pitscottie, *The Historie and Cronicles of Scotland*, ed. Æ. J. G. Mackay, STS, 3 vols (Edinburgh, 1899–1911), II.151; F. A. Greenhill, 'Notes on Scottish incised slabs (ii)', *PSAS* 80 (1945–6), 43–61, at 50–61. Peebles also featured regularly on the itineraries of James V: NAS, E31/3–8, *passim*; E32/2–8, *passim*.

[17] See above, Sìm R. Innes, '*Is eagal liom lá na hagra*: devotion to the Virgin in the later medieval Gaidhealtachd'. The broadest ranging surveys of Marian cults remain Marina Warner, *Alone of All Her Sex: The Myth and the Cult of the Virgin Mary* (London, 1976; rev. 2000); and Jaroslav Pelikan, *Mary through the Centuries: Her Place in the History of Culture* (London, 1996).

[18] *Records of Old Aberdeen*, ed. A. M. Munroe, New Spalding Club, 2 vols (Aberdeen, 1899–1909), II.266–75; *Fasti Aberdonenses, 1494–1854*, ed. C. Innes, Spalding Club (Aberdeen, 1854) [*Abdn. Fasti*], 13, 31; Macfarlane, *William Elphinstone*, 314–17; Charles Burns, 'Curious altar-dedication at Dunkeld', *IR* 9 (1958), 215–16.

poetry of William Dunbar, Robert Henryson, Walter Kennedy and others; her image appeared on seals and in sculpture: indeed, King's College Aberdeen, possessed at least four Marian statues.[19] And, of course, there was also pilgrimage traffic. Whitekirk, in East Lothian, was seemingly the most popular Marian pilgrimage centre in Scotland; and by 1470 it was still allegedly attracting substantial numbers 'on account of frequent miracles'.[20] But there were other Marian shrines too. Marian miracles had enticed 'a multitude of the faithful' to Dumfries by 1475, and to Fetteresso (in Kincardineshire) by 1510.[21] Others were attracted to her Nazareth home which 'surpassing the feats of modern engineering' miraculously replicated itself across christendom.[22] In 1526 an image of the Loretto was obtained from Flanders by the Edinburgh goldsmiths and soon afterwards two replicas of the house also appeared: Perth acquired an otherwise obscure Loretto in 1528 and a second was established at Musselburgh in 1533. That the latter attracted such excited opprobrium from humanists and Protestants alike suggests its considerable popularity with the lower orders of society.[23]

Mary was by no means the only 'international saint' to win a devoted following in Scotland. Her relations also won acclaim, albeit more slowly and less remarkably than she did. The cults of Joseph and of his father-in-law, Joachim, were, of course, notoriously slow to gain popularity but Joseph at least was favoured and encouraged by, among others, the Franciscans and a Franciscan pope, Sixtus IV (1471–84).[24] Joseph's inclusion in the Aberdeen Breviary presumably reflects an awareness of these continental developments on the part of the breviary's compilers. Their interest in Joseph was not, however, unique in Scotland. Although it remains questionable whether Joseph's feast day (19 March) was observed by (the ironically childless) David II (1329–71), Joseph had certainly acquired a limited Scottish

---

[19] For example, *The Poems of William Dunbar*, ed. James Kinsley (Oxford, 1979), 4–7; *The Poems and Fables of Robert Henryson*, ed. H. Harvey Wood, 2nd edn (Edinburgh, 1958), 197–201; Ian C. Cunningham, 'Two poems on the Virgin (National Library of Scotland, Adv. MS 18.5.14)', *Edinburgh Bibliographical Society Transactions* 5 (1988), 32–40; Walter de Gray Birch, *History of Scottish Seals*, 2 vols (Stirling, 1905–7), II.*passim*; Francis C. Eeles, *King's College Chapel Aberdeen* (Edinburgh, 1956), 37–8.

[20] *Papal Letters to Scotland of Clement VII of Avignon, 1378–1394*, eds Charles Burns, A. I. Dunlop and I. B. Cowan, SHS (Edinburgh, 1976), 112; *CSSR 1447–71*, ed. James Kirk et al. (Edinburgh, 1997), no. 1427; J. B. Paul, 'Whitekirk church and its history', *Transactions of the Scottish Ecclesiological Society* 6 (1920–1), 119–24.

[21] *CSSR*, V, no. 244; *James IV Letters*, no. 334.

[22] Louis A. Barbé, 'Loretto', in *idem*, *In Byways of Scottish History* (London, 1924), 141.

[23] *Edinburgh Goldsmiths' Minutes, 1525–1700*, eds Jean Munro and Henry Steuart Fothringham, Scottish Record Society (Edinburgh, 2006), nos A2, A6; David Ditchburn, '"Saints at the door don't make miracles"? The contrasting fortunes of Scottish pilgrimage, *c.*1450–1550', in *Sixteenth-century Scotland: Essays in Honour of Michael Lynch*, eds Julian Goodare and Alasdair A. MacDonald (Leiden, 2008), 69–98, at 79, 96–7, in which I ought to have thanked the Cardinal Penitentiary for permission to quote the Roman archival references cited.

[24] Paul Payan, *Joseph: Une image de la paternité dans l'Occident médiéval* (Paris, 2006), esp. chs 12–13.

following, usually in association with the Virgin, before the early sixteenth century.[25] By then the cult of Mary's mother, Anne, was also firmly established in Scotland, though its development had perhaps been retarded by the Schism: the Roman pope, Urban VI, whose writ did not extend to Scotland, seems to have been especially attached to Anne's cult and active in its promotion in England. Nevertheless, Anne's cult flourished across fifteenth-century christendom and by the early sixteenth century altars dedicated to Anne had been established in Aberdeen, Ayr, Edinburgh, Paisley and elsewhere too.[26] Hymn-singers sung her praises (along with those of her less well known husband, Joachim); and her image, if not quite so prevalent as that of her daughter, nonetheless adorned Books of Hours, a tapestry in King's College Aberdeen and, presumably, the altars which were dedicated in her name.[27]

Aside from the rediscovered national saints and the saints associated with Christ's immediate family, other biblical cults and early christian martyrs also acquired a following in Scotland. Eila Williamson has drawn attention to the growth of the cult of the Three Kings, while Audrey-Beth Fitch has discussed the following acquired by the female martyr-saints.[28] The feast days of all of the disciples – save, of course, Judas Iscariot – were accorded their proper place in the Aberdeen Breviary, which in this respect followed in the main closely upon Sarum precedents. Altars, chapels and fairs throughout the country were dedicated to Peter, James the Greater, John the Evangelist, and occasionally also to the less well known disciples, Philip, James the Lesser, Bartholomew, Matthew, Simon, Jude, and Thomas.[29] Of all the apostles Andrew was, of course, particularly prominent because of his personal association with the nation. No other disciple had bequeathed so many relics

---

25 Penman, 'Christian days', 271; Galbraith, 'Sources', 122, 124–5; Henry Laing, *Descriptive Catalogue of Impressions from Ancient Scottish Seals*, Bannatyne Club (Edinburgh, 1850), no. 896 for a depiction of Joseph and Mary on the seal of Bishop Kinninmoth of Aberdeen (1357–82); *CDS*, IV.no. 1409 (for his depiction, along with the Virgin, on a seal of the abbot of Jedburgh in 1473).

26 For example, *Aberdeen Friars, Red, Black, White Grey: Preliminary Calendar of Illustrative Documents*, ed. P. J. Anderson (Aberdeen, 1909), 55; *Abdn. Reg.*, I.282; *RMS*, II.no. 1320; *RSS*, II.nos 1303, 3798; *TA*, II.253, 263, 260; IV.190. See too 'Anne' references in 'Survey of dedications to saints in medieval Scotland': http://www.shca.ed.ac.uk/Research/saints/; and for a general survey of her cult in northwestern Europe, Ton Brandenbarg, 'Saint Anne: a holy grandmother and her children', in *Sanctity and Motherhood: Essays on Holy Mothers in the Middle Ages*, ed. Anneke B. Mulder-Bakker (New York, 1995), 31–65.

27 George Hay and David McRoberts, 'Rossdhu church and its book of hours', *IR* 16 (1965), 3–17, at 7; Eeles, *King's College Chapel*, 23; Galbraith, 'Sources', 122.

28 Eila Williamson, 'The cult of the Three Kings of Cologne in Scotland', in *Saints' Cults in the Celtic World*, eds Steve Boardman, John Reuben Davies and Eila Williamson (Woodbridge, 2009), 160–79; Audrey-Beth Fitch, 'Power through purity: the Virgin martyrs and women's salvation in pre-Reformation Scotland', in *Women in Scotland, c.1100–c.1750*, eds Elizabeth Ewan and Maureen M. Meikle (East Linton, 1999), 16–28. See too Priscilla Bawcutt, 'Two cases of mistaken identity: Sir David Lindsay's St Syith and St Margaret', *IR* 52 (2001), 189–94; P. A. Wilson, 'The cult of St Martin in the British Isles', *IR* 19 (1968), 129–43.

29 See relevant entries in 'Survey of dedications to saints in medieval Scotland'; David McRoberts, 'A sixteenth-century picture of St Bartholomew from Perth', *IR* 10 (1959), 281–6.

to Scotland; and his three fingers, arm bone, tooth and kneecap became the focus of an early and significant pilgrimage traffic.[30] In the absence of a king, Andrew's cross had also come to adorn the seal of the Guardians in the later thirteenth century and in diplomatic intercourse with the papal *curia* great play was made of the fraternal link between Andrew and Peter, Scotland and Rome.[31] He was, in short, 'the protector of the kingdom'.[32] Yet, there are hints that by the later middle ages it was necessary to bolster Andrew's influence. From the fifteenth century the Virgin began to intrude onto the seals of bishops of St Andrews; and on those of bishops and archbishops who became (or aspired to become) cardinals, Andrew was joined by SS Peter and Paul.[33] Besides, as far as the Stewart monarchy was concerned, Andrew stood in the shadows by contrast with its own favourite apostle, James the Greater. Stewart family interest in St James can be dated to at least the mid-thirteenth century when Alexander Stewart planned to undertake a pilgrimage to the shrine of St James, at Santiago de Compostela in Galicia. We cannot be certain that he went but it has been suggested that the frequency with which later Stewarts were christened James dates from this episode.[34] And we know too that by the fifteenth century several prominent members of the royal family honoured James in prayer, pilgrimage and gift.[35]

The devotional interests of the royal family were, then, cosmopolitan and diverse – ranging from the cults surrounding Christ, Andrew and James to Robert II's apparent fondness for SS Brendan and Brioc, whose cults were associated with the king's ancestral estates in Bute.[36] This breadth of devotional attachments was fully in keeping with the practices of other fifteenth-century rulers. In 1446–7, to take a financial year at random, Philip the Good, duke of Burgundy, marked several major religious festivals with monetary offerings. These donations were made on the moveable feasts of Easter, Ascension Day, Whit and Trinity as well as on 24 June (St John the

---

[30] *Chron. Bower*, I.313–17; Peter Yeoman, *Pilgrimage in Medieval Scotland* (London, 1999), 53–70.

[31] John Horne Stevenson and Marguerite Wood, *Scottish Heraldic Seals*, 3 vols (Glasgow, 1940), I.5; Birch, *Scottish Seals*, I.32–3 and plate 14; *Anglo-Scottish Relations, 1174–1328: Some Selected Documents*, ed. E. L. G. Stones (London, 1965), 171. See too *Chron. Bower*, VI.149.

[32] *Chron. Bower*, VI.291, 413.

[33] Birch, *Scottish Seals*, II.19–26.

[34] Geoffrey Barrow and Ann Royan, 'James, fifth Stewart of Scotland, 1260(?)–1309', in *Essays on the Nobility of Medieval Scotland*, ed. Keith Stringer (Edinburgh, 1985), 166–94, at 166. Someone (I apologise, I cannot remember who!) suggested to me that Stewart interest in Compostela may date to the christian recapture of Lisbon in 1147: we know that Scots participated in this event (Alan Macquarrie, *Scotland and the Crusades, 1095–1560* (Edinburgh, 1985), 18–19); that some of the crusaders who did so visited Compostela before reaching Lisbon (Jonathan Phillips, *The Second Crusade: Extending the Frontiers of Christendom* (New Haven, CT, 2007), 144–5); and that Walter son of Alan [Stewart] (who in 1163 founded the Jacobean-dedicated monastery of Paisley (G. W. S. Barrow, *The Anglo-Norman Era in Scottish History* (Oxford, 1980), 67), can not be traced around this time.

[35] Ditchburn, 'Saints at the door', esp. 87–90.

[36] Stephen Boardman, *The Early Stewart Kings: Robert II and Robert III, 1371–1406* (East Linton, 1996), 94.

Baptist's Day), 29 June (SS Peter and Paul), 15 August (Assumption of the Virgin), 8 September (Nativity of the Virgin), 1 and 2 November (All Saints and All Souls), 30 November (St Andrew), 8 December (Conception of the Virgin), 25 December (Christmas), 6 January (Three Kings) and 2 February (Purification of the Virgin).[37] All of these occasions might well have been commemorated in a similar fashion by Scottish kings. Indeed, a particularly full record of offerings made by James IV survives for 1504–6 during which almost all of the dates upon which Duke Philip made offerings were also marked by King James – St Andrew's Day being a noticeable exception.[38] But the similarities go further for just as King James made donations to both national cults and international cults with national connections (such as, in 1504–6, to the relic collections and/or pilgrimage centres at Beauly, Dunfermline, Peebles, Whitekirk and Whithorn) so too did the duke – in his case, in 1446–7, to the relics at St Omer and to the shrine of Our Lady at Halle, near Brussels.

There is, then, a considerable body of evidence to set beside that adduced by McRoberts and which dilutes the impression which he presented of an unqualified 'devotional nationalism'. Much of this evidence relates, however, to the uppermost echelons of the ruling elites, both secular and temporal, and especially to the royal family. We should not automatically assume that other sections of society imitated the inclinations of their unusually peripatetic and cosmopolitan social superiors. Helen Brown's path-breaking analysis of the devotional habits of the Hays of Yester does, nevertheless, suggest that the popularity of the great international saints was not a royal peculiarity. It extended to baronial families, in Lothian at least.[39] What, then, of other sections of society?

Although it is especially difficult to identify the religious inclinations of the great mass of the rural poor, the popularity of particular forenames perhaps offers one insight into the matter. Historians of different countries across the Latin West have noted a pronounced christianisation of forenames from the eleventh century and later, as secular society came to abandon traditional forenames in favour of saints' names.[40] Some have gone further and explained the growing popularity of particular forenames – such as Christopher and George – in terms of the growing popularity of the synonymous cults.[41] Hitherto

[37] ADN, B1991, fols 239v–242r.

[38] *TA*, III.56–77.

[39] Helen Brown delivered her sadly unpublished paper at a conference on the cult of saints in medieval Scotland, organised by Steve Boardman and held at the NMS, in September 2007.

[40] Robert Bartlett, *The Making of Europe: Conquest, Colonization and Cultural Change, 950–1350* (Harmondsworth, 1994), 270–80; David Herlihy, 'Tuscan names, 1200–1530', *Renaissance Quarterly* 41 (1988), 561–82; Benjamin Z. Kedar, *Merchants in Crisis: Genoese and Venetian Men of Affairs and the Fourteenth-century Depression* (New Haven, CT, 1976), 97–102.

[41] Steve Boardman, 'The cult of St George in Scotland', in *Saints' Cults in the Celtic World*, eds Boardman, Davies and Williamson, 146–59; Virginia Davies, 'The popularity of late medieval personal names as reflected in English ordination lists, 1350–1540', in *Studies on the Personal*

little analysis has been undertaken of peasant names in Scotland.[42] Many peasant names are, however, listed in the records of the subsidy imposed on aliens in England from 1440. Almost all of the aliens recorded in the north-ernmost counties of England were Scottish. Most were probably itinerant agricultural labourers and servants. Of over two hundred Scotsmen recorded in Cumberland and Westmorland in 1440, the most common name, by a long margin, was John (34%), followed by Thomas (12%), the non-saintly names of William (12%) and Robert (8%), and then Patrick (5%). Among the 175 women recorded, Joanne (29%) dominated, followed by Margaret (13%), and Mariota (11%).[43]

Although the sample dates from one or two generations before that which produced the Aberdeen Breviary, and although the names may have been anglicised by the English record-keepers, the almost complete absence of names akin to those of the rediscovered national saints is striking. Even Andrews were sparse. Among women, Mary too was rare. Instead, the names of 1440 resemble patterns evident among other sections of society not just in England and Ireland, but also in continental Europe, where the dominance of John, the disciple whom 'Jesus loved', is discernible as far apart as Italy, Paris and Breslau/Wrocław.[44] Yet, if this suggests similar saintly attachments at work in naming patterns right across later medieval christendom, we must be careful not to identify saintly reverence as necessarily the sole, or even as the most immediate, influence behind naming patterns. The choice of a saint's name for a child might reflect family tradition. More likely still, in England at least, godparents and *their* names were overwhelmingly the single most influential determinant of later medieval naming patterns.[45] It is, then, difficult to establish how, if at all, naming patterns and saintly attachments were related – though there is no indication from the Cumbrian sample that peasants were so enthused by the saintly attachments of their social superiors that they decided to name their children after the saints favoured by the elite in society.

Name in Later Medieval England and Wales, eds Dave Postles and Joel T. Rosenthal (Kalamazoo, MI, 2006), 103–14, at 107–8.

[42] See, however, Matthew Hammond, 'Ethnicity, personal names and the nature of Scottish Europe-anization', in *Thirteenth Century England XI*, eds Björn Weiler et al. (Woodbridge, 2007), 82–93, at 91–2.

[43] TNA, E179/90/27; E179/195/33.

[44] John 13:23; Joel T. Rosenthal, 'Names and naming patterns in medieval England', in *Studies on the Personal Name*, eds Postles and Rosenthal, 1–28, at 5; Davis, 'The popularity of late medieval personal names', 106; Freya Verstraten, 'Naming practices among the Irish secular nobility in the high middle ages', *JMH* 32 (2006), 43–53, at 51; Herlihy, 'Tuscan names', 573; Benjamin Z. Kedar, 'Nom de saints et mentalité populaire à Gênes au XIV siècle', *Le Moyen Age* 73 (1967), 431–46, at 436. (In Tuscany John's popularity was second to Anthony, while in Breslau John came second to Nicholas.)

[45] Michael Bennett, 'Spiritual kinship and the baptismal name in traditional European society', in *Studies on the Personal Name*, eds Postles and Rosenthal, 115–46; Philip Niles, 'Baptism and the naming of children in late medieval England', in *ibid.*, 147–57.

We are, of course, much better informed about the townspeople than about the peasants of medieval Scotland. The database 'Survey of Dedications to Saints in Medieval Scotland' points to twenty-two saints with a following of some sort in Edinburgh between 1200 and 1500 and to thirty-seven saints with a following in the same town between 1200 and 1560. Edinburgh's medieval records are now notoriously scant, so these figures are likely to constitute a highly conservative estimate of what may be defined as the town's 'total hagiographic programme'.[46] Edinburgh's saintly attachments compare with 115 saintly cults recorded between *ca* 1200 and *ca* 1500 in the much better documented Italian city of Perugia, whose medieval population peaked at perhaps 20–40,000. Given that Edinburgh's population reached perhaps 12,500 by the mid-sixteenth century, the extent of its saintly attachments is not unimpressive.[47] Such an approach to patterns of sanctity is, however, problematic, for as Gary Dickson has argued with regard to Perugia, it ignores the relative significance of cults, the differing needs and identities which different saints serviced and the differing clientele of saints.

These variations and nuances in saintly attachment can, to some extent, be explored among particular sections of urban society in Scotland. Among, for instance, the merchants and mariners who traded abroad both James and Andrew acquired a significant following. In Dieppe the Scottish altar was located within a church dedicated to James; and at Regensburg and in Bruges we find Scottish altars dedicated to Andrew, whose feast day was also observed by another group of migrants, the Scottish students at the universities of Orléans and Paris in France.[48] Both James and Andrew figure on the centrepiece of the Scottish altar at Elsinore, in Denmark, now preserved in the National Museum in Copenhagen.[49] Yet, here the two apostles flanked St Ninian; and elsewhere – certainly in Copenhagen, in Bergen-op-Zoom, at two further dedications in Bruges and perhaps at Roscoff – we know that Ninian, rather than James or Andrew, was the principal saint patronised by

[46] Gary Dickson, 'The 115 cults of the saints in later medieval and Renaissance Perugia: a demographic overview of a civic pantheon', *Renaissance Studies* 12 (1998), 6–25.

[47] For population sizes, see Michael Lynch, 'The social and economic structure of the larger towns, 1450–1600', in *The Scottish Medieval Town*, eds Michael Lynch, Michael Spearman and Geoffrey Stell (Edinburgh, 1988), 261–86, at 279; *Atlas of Medieval Europe*, eds David Ditchburn, Simon MacLean and Angus MacKay, 2nd edn (Abingdon, 2007), 157.

[48] Michel Mollat, *Le commerce maritime normand à la fin du moyen age* (Paris, 1952), 171; Ludwig Hammermayer, 'Deutsche Schottenklöster, Schottische Reformation, Katholische Reform und Gegenreformation in West- und Mitteleuropa (1560–1580)', *Zeitschrift für Bayerische Landesgeschichte* 26 (1963), 131–255, at 174; Stevenson, 'Medieval Scottish associations', 98–9; D. E. R. Watt, 'Scottish student life abroad in the fourteenth century', *SHR* 59 (1980), 3–21, at 7. See too 'The Scottish nation at the university of Orléans, 1336–1538', ed. J. Kirkpatrick, in *Miscellany of the Scottish History Society* vol. II (1904), 47–102, at 60.

[49] George Hay, 'A Scottish altarpiece in Copenhagen', *IR* 7 (1956), 5–10, at 6; Thomas Riis, *Should Auld Acquaintance be Forgot: Scottish-Danish Relations, c.1450–1707*, 2 vols (Odense, 1988), I.196–7.

the emigrant Scottish communities.[50] This may seem odd; but Ninian was in these continental environments largely unique in a way in which Andrew and James were not. James enjoyed a strong following throughout northern Europe and beyond;[51] and Andrew's cult was extremely popular throughout the Netherlands, France, Switzerland and indeed in Italy, where his relics (so far as we know) were largely ignored by Scottish pilgrims.[52] By contrast, much greater Scottish distinction cloaked Ninian – and only in Regensburg, where Scots contested possession of the town's *Schottenkloster* with Irishmen, was it prudent to sideline Ninian in favour of Andrew. Ninian enjoyed some following in Ireland and he was perhaps not terribly supportive of Scottish plans in Regensburg.[53]

Affection for the distinctively native Ninian among that section of Scottish society which was most open to continental influence would seem to support the modified McRoberts thesis which seeks to meld the national and international in devotional practice. And yet, a very different indication of saintly devotions in these maritime communities is afforded by the names which were given to ships. The names of vessels were routinely recorded by English customs officials in the early sixteenth century and the customs accounts of Hull and Lynn include a sufficiently large number of Scottish vessels for some conclusions regarding nomenclature to be drawn. These must, however, remain tentative since the analysis is not without methodological problems. We cannot, of course, be certain that clerks always recorded ship names accurately or fully: at least some ships, such as the '*Sainct-Pierre* dit *Le Mothon*' of Penmarche, recorded at Bordeaux in 1497, clearly had more than one name.[54] More seriously, perhaps, many vessels were recorded by customs officials more than once – both as they entered and left port and then again if they appeared in subsequent years. All have been included in the analysis which follows even although this obviously distorts the overall picture. This

50 Hay, 'Scottish altarpiece', 5; Riis, *Should Auld Acquaintance be Forgot*, I.240–1; Stevenson, 'Medieval Scottish associations', 98, 100; *idem*, 'Notice of an early sixteenth-century Scottish colony at Bergen-op-Zoom and an altar once dedicated to St Ninian', *IR* 26 (1975), 50–2, at 50.

51 See, for example, *Der Jakobuskult in Süddeutschland: Kultgeschichte in regionaler und europäischer Perspektive*, eds Klaus Herbers and Dieter R. Bauer (Tübingen, 1995), which includes contributions on the Asturias, 'Britain' and the Low Countries and Switzerland as well as southern Germany; Christian Krötzl, 'Om nordbornas vallfarter till Santiago de Compostela', *Historisk Tidskrift för Finland* 72 (1987), 189–200; *idem*, 'Wege und Pilger aus Skandinavien nach Santiago de Compostela', in *Europäische Wege der Santiago-Pilgerfahrt*, ed. Robert Plötz (Tübingen, 1990), 157–69; Constance M. Storrs, 'Jacobean pilgrims from England from the early twelfth to late fifteenth century' (University of London, unpublished M.A. thesis, 1964).

52 See, however, *RSS*, I.no. 1606. The most recent surveys of the Andrean cult are Ursula Hall, *The Cross of St Andrew* (Edinburgh, 2006); Charlotte Denoël, *Saint André: Culte et iconographie en France (V–XVe siècles)* (Paris, 2004).

53 *James V Letters*, 66, 363. I am very grateful to Katharine Simms and Anne Buckley for drawing my attention to other evidence regarding Ninian's following in Ireland. See, for example, James F. Kenney, *The Sources for the Early History of Ireland: Ecclesiastical* (New York, 1929), 159–60.

54 Jacques Bernard, *Navires et gens de mer à Bordeaux (vers 1400–vers 1550)*, 3 vols (Paris, 1968), III.60.

is, however, almost unavoidable since insufficiently detailed information was recorded by the customs clerks to distinguish beyond all doubt between incoming and outgoing ships, especially over the *longue durée*. We have, then, a broad impression rather than a precise account of naming patterns.

The first point that emerges from this study is that comparatively few Scottish ships bore non-religious or secular names. There were, certainly, exceptions – such as the duke of Albany's *Tay*, which had sailed to Compostela in 1409.[55] And after the Reformation non-religious designations became common. Of about seventy Scottish vessels recorded at Hull between 1577 and 1585, overtly secular names such as *Falcon*, *Lyon*, and *Mayflower*, accounted for just under a quarter of the ships, to which we may perhaps add about another sixth, since it seems unlikely that ships named *Robert* and *Jennitt* commemorated saints.[56] But, in the sample of over two hundred Scottish ships recorded in the customs returns of Hull and Lynn between *ca* 1511 and *ca* 1542, fewer than 5% carried secular names, such as *Swan* or *Lyon*. It follows that the overwhelming majority of recorded ships bore what seems to have been a religious name. Religion, and the intercessionary power of saints in particular, offered protection in dangerous and stormy waters. What we might call the 'heavenly names' (such as *Trinity* with 12%, and *God's Grace* with 5%), and the 'angelic names' (with about 10% and including Michael and Gabriel) were fairly common, and marginally more so as a group than the ships named after biblical saints, such as Mary, Anne, Peter, James, Andrew, and so on – though, with only six sightings to his name, James was a rarity. Andrew, with only three recorded vessels, was even more so though he increased significantly in popularity after the Reformation (rising from just over 1% in the pre-Reformation sample to 10% in the post-Reformation sample from Hull). In the earlier cohort, however, the biggest group of ships was named after the non-biblical saints, especially *Katherine*, *Clement* and, with 17% of all names, *Nicholas*.

With one exception it is difficult to detect local peculiarities in the naming habits applied to vessels in different Scottish ports. Among the small number of dedications to Clement in Scotland were chapels at the seaside settlements of Footdee (near Aberdeen) and Dundee and altars in Edinburgh and Perth.[57]

---

[55] *Rotuli Scotiae in Turri Londinensi et in Domo Capitulari Westmonasteriensi assevati*, eds D. Macpherson et al., 2 vols (London, 1814–19), II.193; *Calendar of Signet Letters of Henry IV and Henry V, 1399–1422*, ed. J. L. Kirby (London, 1978), no. 741. See too *Ledger of Andrew Halyburton*, ed. Cosmo Innes (Edinburgh, 1867), *passim*: ship names have been extracted by Alexander William Kerr Stevenson, 'Trade between Scotland and the Low Countries in the Later Middle Ages' (University of Aberdeen, unpublished Ph.D. thesis, 1982), Appendix, Table 6/2.

[56] Hull, City Archive, BRB/2 (unfoliated). I am extremely grateful to Helen Good for providing me with a copy of this record.

[57] See references to Clement in 'Survey of dedications to saints in medieval Scotland': http://www. shca.ed.ac.uk/Research/saints/. Despite the anglocentric title, Clement's cult across christendom is discussed in Barbara E. Crawford, *The Churches Dedicated to St Clement in Medieval England* (Axioma, 2008).

But vessels named *Clement* came not from Aberdeen and Dundee, but from Dysart, Kirkcaldy, and Montrose, where there were no such recorded ecclesiastical dedications. St Nicholas is especially associated with Aberdeen, where the parish church is dedicated in his name; but he was, of course, also the patron of mariners; and altars and chapels were commonly dedicated to Nicholas in ports all along the east coast of Scotland and, of course, abroad.[58] Nicholas, indeed, acted as something of a bond between maritime communities and vessels bearing his name came from Dysart, Kirkcaldy, and St Monans and Leith, as well as from Aberdeen.[59]

By contrast, there is little evidence of ships named after local cults, in this sample at least. So – from Leith no *James* or *Anthony*, even although there were chapels dedicated to both saints there; and no *Machar* from Aberdeen.[60] Indeed, there was not one Scottish/Irish saint's name to note in this sample.[61] The exception to this pattern of comparative uniformity in naming patterns is, however, Dundee, from where almost half of the secular-named ships derive. Dundee was also, in this sample at least, unusual in its choice of saintly names: all the *Jameses* came from Dundee, together with the only instances of *Frances* and *Bonaventure*. The last two names suggest Franciscan attachments. It is perhaps only a coincidence but in 1536, at much the same time as the sample was being recorded, the bailies of Dundee were looking for two men suspected of hanging an image of St Francis.[62] Was this a town where anticlericalism and religious affiliation were already strongly marked – both for and against the old Church? Were these divisions reflected in the naming of the town's ships?

If, with the possible exception of early sixteenth-century Dundee, there was little local distinction to the ship names bestowed in Scottish ports, neither were Scottish naming patterns significantly different from those found elsewhere in christendom. There was, however, some variation in the popularity of different names and different types of name from country to country. As in Scotland, secular names, though not rare in the thirteenth century, had largely disappeared from Genoese vessels after 1300.[63] Very

---

58 For 'Nicholas' references (connected inter alia with Aberdeen, Arbroath, Berwick, Dundee, Leith, Perth, St Andrews and Stirling) see 'Survey of dedications to saints in medieval Scotland': http://www.shca.ed.ac.uk/Research/saints/. See too Karl Meisen, *Nikolauskult und Nikolausbrauch in Abendlande: Eine kultgeographisch Volkskundliche Untersuchung* (repr. Düsseldorf, 1981).

59 TNA, E122/60/3; E122/64/2; E122/64/5–6, E122/64/10; E122/64/15–16; E122/205/2–3; E122/99/16; E122/99/18–19; E122/99/23–24; E122/99/26–27. See too *The Customs Accounts of Hull, 1453–1490*, ed. Wendy R. Childs, Yorkshire Archaeological Society (Leeds, 1986) [*Hull Customs*], 89, 93, for a North Berwick ship of this name; and *The Customs Accounts of Newcastle upon Tyne, 1454–1500*, ed. J. F. Wade, Surtees Society (Durham, 1995) [*Newcastle Customs*], 279 for a *Nicholas* from Kinghorn.

60 For earlier examples, see, however, *Hull Customs*, 81, 83, 92, 100, 111; and *Newcastle Customs*, 105, for an *Anthony* of Leith.

61 See, however, *Hull Customs*, 7, for the fifteenth-century *Serf* of Dysart.

62 *TA*, VI.307.

63 Kedar, *Merchants in Crisis*, 102.

Figure 1. Ship names noted in Hull and Lynn's Custom Records, *ca* 1511–42

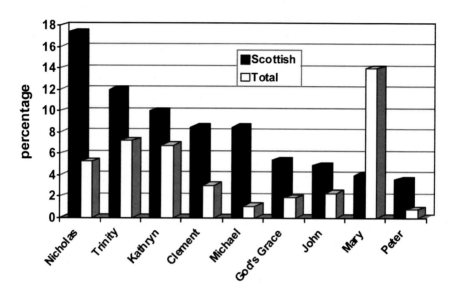

Figure 2. Ship names noted in Hull and Lynn's Custom Records, *ca* 1511–42

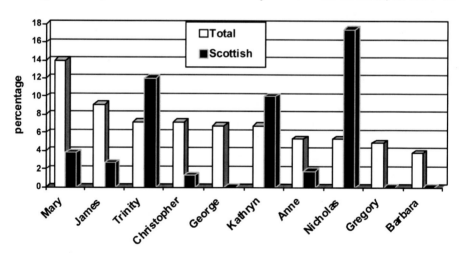

few overtly secular names can be noted among the French ships recorded at Bordeaux between the 1470s and 1510s, though there were, in this latter cohort, several Breton vessels which took their names from Breton saints, such as Guenael and Tremorus.[64] In southern Europe it was not unusual for a single vessel to carry the names of two or even three saints; even two names was a rarity in Scotland. In Figure 1 the top ten Scottish ship names from the early sixteenth-century Hull and Lynn customs accounts are indicated side by side with the percentage of these names among all 265 ships from North Sea and Baltic ports recorded in four randomly selected Lynn accounts, from between 1513 and 1542. All of the most popular Scottish names were also to be found among other ships from around the North Sea and Baltic recorded in Lynn and – with the exception of *God's Grace* – among the French cohort at Bordeaux. It is, however, noticeable that except for Mary the other Scottish favourites were proportionately more common on Scottish vessels than they were on vessels from other countries. This is confirmed in Figure 2 which firstly ranks the most frequent names in the European-wide sample of 265 ships and then the equivalent frequency with which these names were found in the Scottish sample from Hull and Lynn. Mary's lack of popularity in Scotland by comparison with other countries is further confirmed by the Genoese and Bordeaux evidence: between 1375 and 1414 Mary was the single most popular name among Kedar's sample of Genoese ships; and in the 1470s and in the 1490s Mary accounted for about a quarter of all French ships, though she had fallen back to just over 14% by 1510.[65] As for other European favourites, in the Hull/Lynn sample there was not a single Scottish *Barbara, Gregory,* or *George.* Each of these saints had, of course, some following in Scotland. Barbara was one of the saints depicted on the Scottish altar at Elsinore and there were other altars dedicated to her in Aberdeen and Dundee. Perhaps particularly popular with women, she appeared in Books of Hours and in sculpture – and from other evidence we know that even the occasional ship bore her name.[66] Meanwhile, there were altars dedicated to Gregory – for instance, at Dumfries and Dundee – and his mass and image became increasingly familiar.[67] George's absence from Scottish ship names in the sixteenth century may reflect the fact that by at least the 1540s 'wearing the red cross' had become an increasingly common synonym for 'enemy'.[68]

---

[64] Bernard, *Navires,* III.12, 24, 28, 30, 34, 36, 52.

[65] Kedar, *Merchants in Crisis,* 104; Bernard, *Navires,* III.12–26, 28–84, 272–92.

[66] Hay, 'Scottish altarpiece', 7; *RSS,* II.no. 1017; *RMS,* III.no. 578; Mark Dilworth, 'Book of Hours of Mary of Guise', *IR* 19 (1968), 77-80, at 79; Bawcutt, 'Two cases', 193–4; *Extracts from the Council Register of the Burgh of Aberdeen,* ed. John Stuart, Spalding Club, 2 vols (Aberdeen, 1844–8), I.417; Eeles, *King's College Chapel,* 37; E. P. D. Torrie, *Medieval Dundee: A Town and its People* (Dundee, 1990), 95.

[67] *RMS,* II.3335; Alexander Maxwell, *Old Dundee* (Edinburgh and Dundee, 1891), 36; McRoberts, 'Fetternear banner', 75.

[68] *RSS,* III.nos 999, 1074, 1115.

On the other hand, we may note that one of the Scottish 'Johns', a Leith vessel, was not the Evangelist, but rather the surprisingly anglophile *St John of Beverley* – a saint deleted by Elphinstone's collaborators but reinstated by hand into the Glamis copy of the Aberdeen Breviary.[69] The anglophobia detected by McRoberts was not, then, universal.

In some ways this excursion into both personal and ship names makes the task of summing up complicated. There are clearly contradictions to the evidence. On the one hand, there are wide-ranging indications that the cults of Mary and James were popular throughout Scotland; on the other hand, their names are found comparatively rarely among the analysed samples of Scottish peasants and ships. It is not clear whether this was always the case or whether these trends reflect new developments and/or regional peculiarities in the non-Gaelic parts of Scotland. There are, of course, other methodological problems too with the use of the name evidence and fuller analysis of larger samples may perhaps iron out these disparities. Nevertheless, the contradictions and complications which the evidence seems to present are appealing – not least because they cast doubt upon the very simplicity of the McRoberts thesis and the rigidity of the chronological, geographical, political, and social certainties with which it is underpinned.

There are good grounds for accepting that, as McRoberts outlined, the fifteenth century witnessed new developments in the veneration of saints in Scotland. But we should not be surprised that changes occurred in patterns of saintly veneration. They occurred elsewhere too. Elsewhere, it was not unusual for old cults to be revived, for new cults to appear and even for the old lags of the saintly world to be quietly forgotten about. Perugia witnessed the emergence of no fewer than twenty-three new mendicant cults in the later middle ages while in parts of England there was a revival of interest in several female martyr-saints during the same era.[70] McRoberts explained change in Scotland by nationalism; and this should certainly not be ruled out as one catalyst for change. But nationalism (or local patriotism) was not the only explanation for changing patterns of veneration elsewhere. In Perugia at least religious considerations were also important and we cannot be certain that what provoked change elsewhere had no impact in Scotland. An analysis of mendicant cults in Scotland might, in this respect, prove illuminating.

If the changing patterns of veneration require broader and more flexible analysis, then the rigid dichotomy between 'national' and 'international' saints should also be loosened. Most obviously such a distinction ignores the highly important local and regional dimension to saintly veneration. But even if space is made for the inclusion of this within a modified McRoberts

---

[69] TNA, E122/99/26, fol.7r; Galbraith, 'Sources', 248.

[70] Dickson, 'The 115 cults', 11; Eamon Duffy, 'Holy maydens, holy wyfes: the cult of women saints in fifteenth- and sixteenth-century England', in *Women in the Church*, eds W. J. Sheils and Diana Wood, Studies in Church History (Oxford, 1990), 175–96.

model, to distinguish cults as 'local', 'national' or 'international' remains a rather blunt approach. Scotland was not the only place in which an amalgam of local, national and international saints was venerated. That was the case across the later medieval Latin West – in which case we perhaps ought to see 'local', 'national' and 'international' veneration as things which operated in parallel and not in opposition to each other, as McRoberts would have it, implicitly at least. Indeed, it seems significant that many of the new christocentric and Marian cults found popularity in Scotland at much the same time as the rediscovery of national saints was taking place. It was to Mary – and not Machar – that William Elphinstone, the driving force behind the 'devotional nationalism', turned when seeking to overcome the challenge of establishing a university from scratch; and even as a boy it was of Mary that the future bishop allegedly (and somewhat alarmingly) dreamt.[71] Similarly it was while *en route* for Jerusalem, and having left a bequest of £10 in his will to the Nithsdale chapel of St Mary of Garvald, that Robert Blackadder, the great patron of St Kentigern, died.[72] Men like William Elphinstone and Robert Blackadder seem to have felt no contradiction in fostering the local, the national and the international. Why, indeed, would they? Both were men grounded in their diocese, prominent on the national political stage but also experienced as students and then as diplomats on the wider European stage.

A third problem relates to the group of saints which McRoberts categorised as 'national'. By 'national' McRoberts meant Scottish, Irish, British. But to categorise national in this way is to ignore the national (and local) dimension to the veneration of international saints. How 'national' or 'international' were the pilgrims who gathered to venerate the Cross in fifteenth-century Montrose? There were, as we have seen, clearly also local idiosyncrasies and national variations in the popularity of the international saints. Dundee's ship names do not conform to the Scottish norm; and the Scottish norm does not quite match the North Sea/Baltic norm. Indeed, the ship name evidence suggests that ship owners did not quite conform to patterns of veneration evident in other sections of society. And herein lies a fourth, and final, problem with the McRoberts thesis. McRoberts categorised his rediscovered saints of the fifteenth century as 'national'. But how many people were actually involved in this exercise of national rediscovery? In many instances rediscovered cults were, so far as we can tell, promoted not by society as a whole, but rather by a clerical elite: Haldenstone, Bower, Blackadder, Schevez, Elphinstone, backed probably by their kings. But did their interests reflect those of the population as a whole? Social differences in attitudes towards saints and cults is suggested by the deep suspicion which educated humanists demonstrated towards the plebeian crowds which converged on the Lorettan shrine

---

[71] *Abdn. Fasti*, 31; *Hectoris Boetii Murthlacensium et Aberdonensium Episcoporum Vitae*, ed. James Moir, New Spalding Club (Aberdeen, 1894), 59–60.

[72] John Durkan, 'Archbishop Blackadder's will', *IR* 26 (1975), 121.

in Musselburgh during the early sixteenth century. By contrast, we know that, in naming peasants and ships, those responsible took little interest in the old 'Celtic' saints or in the new-fangled Marian cults fostered by leading clergymen – or even in the saintly namesake of Scottish kings. It seems strange too that despite their investigations Elphinstone's research team was unable to produce authoritative legends for many of those saints whom they were seeking to rehabilitate. As Colm Ó Baoill has demonstrated, they even had difficulty on their own doorstep, in identifying St Machar.[73] Were there no oral traditions regarding these saints to draw upon? We cannot be certain that the great mass of the population was all that interested in many of the saints in whom Elphinstone was seeking to revive interest. It is, then, time to rest the McRoberts thesis and to recognise that patterns of saintly veneration were considerably less rigid and more complex than has been traditionally acknowledged.

---

[73] Colm Ó Baoill, 'St Machar – some linguistic light?', *IR* 44 (1993), 1–13.

INDEX

STUDIES IN CELTIC HISTORY

Already published